James A. Erskine

Michiel R. Leenders

Louise A. Mauffette-Leenders

teaching
with
cases

Richard Ivey School of Business
The University of Western Ontario

IVEY

Teaching with Cases

ISBN   0-7714-2087-0

This book may be ordered from:

Ivey Publishing
Richard Ivey School of Business
The University of Western Ontario
London, Ontario, Canada, N6A 3K7

Phone: (+1) 519-661-3208
Fax: (+1) 519-661-3882
E-mail: cases@ivey.uwo.ca
Web Site: http://www.ivey.uwo.ca/cases

about the authors

James A. Erskine teaches Operations Management at the Richard Ivey School of Business where he has a special interest in the human in the system. He has Engineering and MBA degrees from The University of Western Ontario and a doctorate from Indiana University. Over the past 30 years Jim has conducted case method workshops and management development programs for thousands of participants in more than 20 countries. In 1988-89, he served as Dean at the Lahore University of Management Sciences in Pakistan and is a past chairperson of the Honors Undergraduate Business Program at Ivey. Jim is a 3-M teaching fellow recognizing him as one of Canada's best university professors.

Michiel R. Leenders is the Purchasing Management Association of Canada Professor at the Richard Ivey School of Business. He received a degree in Mining Engineering from the University of Alberta, an M.B.A. from The University of Western Ontario and his doctorate from the Harvard Business School. He is a former director of the School's Ph.D. program and has taught and consulted extensively both in Canada and internationally. Mike's texts have been translated into eight different languages. He has authored and co-authored nine books in the supply management field. In 1997, Mike received the Leaders in Management Education Award sponsored by the Financial Post and Bell Canada.

Louise A. Mauffette-Leenders holds a BA from Collège Jean-de-Brébeuf, a BBA and an MBA from l'École des Hautes Études Commerciales of Montréal, Québec. As case writer and research associate at the Richard Ivey School of Business at The University of Western Ontario for seven years, she wrote dozens of cases in all areas of management, including the non-profit sector. She and her husband Mike have taught case writing and teaching workshops in North and South America and Europe.

acknowledgements

The information contained in *Teaching With Cases* comes from a number of sources. We give special thanks to each of the more than 100 contributors who loaded us with information during the interviews and to the several authors quoted whose contributions to the literature continue to push the teaching effectiveness horizon.

Our own ideas have been nurtured and shaped by the several thousand experienced and aspiring teachers throughout the world who have participated in our case method workshops over the past 30 years. They provide proof that teaching with cases is indeed universal.

We are grateful to our colleagues at the Ivey Business School for their input, help and encouragement. They continue to raise the bar for effective case teaching.

We have been privileged with the opportunity to listen to and learn from a steady stream of highly motivated and competent students in our classes and courses at Ivey. Their genuine interest and high expectations in augmenting their skills and abilities through case discussion has given us a living laboratory to test the ideas in this book.

The Harvard Business School pioneered the case method for use in management education. We are most appreciative of our Harvard colleagues who freely shared their insights, experience and advice during the many interviews we conducted. In particular, we wish to thank Professors Roland Christensen and Andrew Towl for their enduring contributions to the field and to our personal learning.

We value highly the people at the European Case Clearing House for their work in disseminating cases and case literature and for providing opportunities for others to learn. They make it easier for teachers to access materials and augment their skills.

Finally, we are very thankful for the talents of a special person. Sue LeMoine prepared the several iterations of the text copy with great skill and patience. We are indebted to her high proficiency and continuous support.

foreword

The Richard Ivey School of Business is proud of its case method heritage which dates back to its inception in 1922. We gratefully acknowledge the ongoing assistance we have received from the Harvard Business School at our start and ever since. Over the past three decades the Leenders-Erskine team has carried the banner for more effective case writing, case learning and case teaching in their books and numerous workshops around the world.

This new edition of *Teaching With Cases* by Jim, Mike and Louise represents the very best that Ivey has to offer for those new to case teaching as well as to the veterans who may wish to reflect on their teaching effectiveness. This text and its companion books on case learning and case writing form a comprehensive overview of participatory teaching and learning with cases. In addition to Ivey's extensive development and distribution of new cases, these texts and our case method workshops are living proof of our ongoing commitment to the case method.

L. G. Tapp, Dean
Richard Ivey School of Business
The University of Western Ontario

London, Ontario
August, 1998

preface

We are delighted to offer this second edition of *Teaching With Cases*. Fully integrated with *Learning With Cases*, it forms a valuable two-volume set for anyone interested in the case teaching/learning process.

Our first edition of *Teaching With Cases* was largely descriptive, based on the literature and personal interviews with over 100 case teachers. This new version builds on the strengths of the first edition, augmented with additional interviews and our personal experiences in teaching regular classes, case teaching and case writing workshops around the world. We have added significantly to the core topics of preparation for class, teaching a class and after class evaluation. The new concept of the Case Teaching Plan joins our proven concepts of the Case Difficulty Cube, The Three Stage Learning Process and the Case Preparation Chart to improve the efficiency and effectiveness of case teaching.

Experienced case instructors can sharpen their teaching skills using the ideas presented in the case use variations and special considerations chapters. New case teachers can get started faster and more effectively using the ideas in the prerequisites, course planning and preparation for class chapters. Both the veterans and newcomers alike can counsel students better using the cause and effect analysis presented in the feedback and counselling chapter. Anyone seriously interested in case teaching can use the tips, tactics and techniques spread throughout this book to experience more fully the joy of teaching with cases.

contents

introduction

Almost a century ago the Harvard Business School chose the case method as an effective way of teaching business administration. The use of cases is now no longer the preserve of a few selected schools of business. Cases are taught around the world in a large variety of disciplines. Participatory learning, using descriptions of decisions faced in real life by real managers, has proven to be an exciting alternative to more traditional forms of education. Teaching with cases, however, presents unique challenges to instructors. That is why this book was written.

This book is part of the authors' trilogy covering case writing, case learning and case teaching. The first edition of *Teaching With Cases* was based largely on the literature available and interviews with over a hundred case teachers from around the world. This second edition builds on that heritage complemented by additional interviews, and our experience of instructing several thousand teachers in case teaching workshops over the past three decades. Lastly, the authors themselves count over a hundred years of case learning and teaching experience. They have class tested and proven the effectiveness of all the key ideas advanced in this text.

Learning With Cases, the companion book, is focused on the student or participant role in the case method. It explains why cases are used and what the case method is all about. The core of *Learning With Cases* contains detailed suggestions for students on how to prepare a case individually, discuss it in a small group and in a class. Also covered are case presentations, reports and exams, and effective management of the learning process.

The Case Difficulty Cube (see Exhibit 1-1), the Three Stage Learning Process (see Exhibit 1-2), and the Case Preparation Chart (see Exhibit 1-3), explained in *Learning With Cases*, provide conceptual ways of thinking about the

Exhibit 1–1
THE CASE DIFFICULTY CUBE

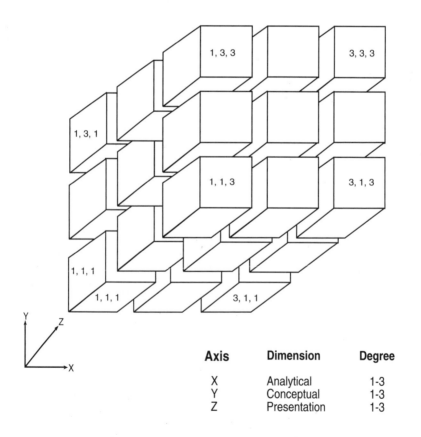

Axis	Dimension	Degree
X	Analytical	1-3
Y	Conceptual	1-3
Z	Presentation	1-3

case learning process and serve as useful basic tools. In short, *Learning With Cases* raises the bar on student preparation and participation. By applying the principles of re-engineering and focusing on the value-adding activities in the learning process, the authors have simplified the learning task, improved the output, and limited the time required for students to prepare and participate effectively. The net outcome is higher quality learning and more enjoyment during the learning process.

Exhibit 1–2
THE THREE STAGE LEARNING PROCESS

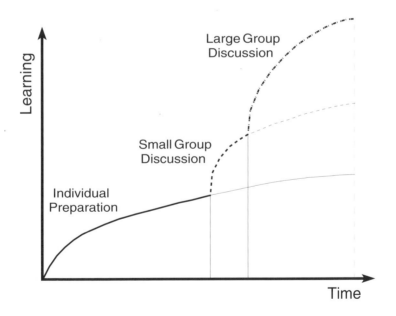

Exhibit 1–3
CASE PREPARATION CHART

Case Title: *Case Assignment:*

I. SHORT CYCLE PROCESS

        Name   Position

Who:

        Issue(s)

What:

Why:

When:

        Case Difficulty Cube

How: (_____, _____, _____)
        Analytical, Conceptual, Presentation

II. LONG CYCLE PROCESS

  A. Issue(s)

Immediate	Basic
1.	1.
2.	2.
3.	3.

IMPORTANCE URGENCY	LOW	HIGH
LOW	I	II
HIGH	III	IV

  B. Case Data Analysis

II. LONG CYCLE PROCESS (continued)

  C. Alternative Generation

      1.
      2.
      3.

  D. Decision Criteria

      1.
      2.
      3.

  E. Alternative Assessment

Quantitative	+		N		−	
Qualitative	+	N	−	+	N	−	+	N	−
Decision	go	go	?	?	no	no	?	no	no

  F. Preferred Alternative

      Predicted Outcome

  G. Action & Implementation Plan

                Timing
                Milestones

      Who
      What
      When
      Where
      How

Missing Information

Assumptions

The goals in *Teaching With Cases* are similar for teachers. Quality case teaching requires extensive preparation, careful thinking, intellectual intensity and a tremendous personal commitment. This text intends to give both new and experienced case teachers an organized perspective on the teaching task, as well as time saving and effectiveness improving suggestions. It ties in directly with the key concepts advanced in *Learning With Cases* and adds the Case Teaching Plan as a simple device to keep the instructor focused.

Our suggestion is that readers start with *Learning With Cases*. It is an easy and fast read and, since an instructor's class preparation starts at exactly the same point as a normal participant's, *Learning With Cases* is a prerequisite to *Teaching With Cases*. Moreover, thorough understanding of how students are supposed to learn with cases is fundamental to being able to teach with the case method. Rather than repeating everything in the "purple book" in this case teaching text, we decided to put the two together as a complementary set.

Some reinforcement of ideas advanced in *Learning With Cases* will be provided in this text. For the sake of brevity, however, this book will not discuss cases and the case method and all of the other topics covered in the purple book. Instead, it will focus on the exclusive domain of the instructor in the case method. Exhibit 1-4 provides a quick overview of how *Learning With Cases* and *Teaching With Cases* are integrated.

Exhibit 1-4
THE INTEGRATION OF *LEARNING WITH CASES*
AND *TEACHING WITH CASES*

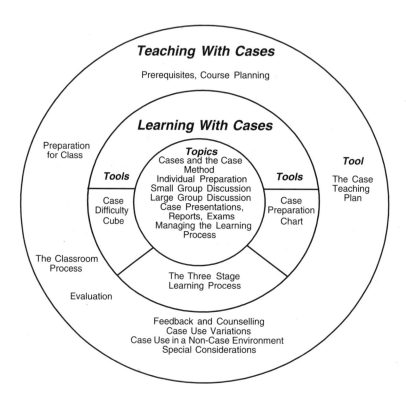

NEED FOR INFORMATION CONCERNING
TEACHING WITH CASES

"I don't know what I'm supposed to do." Almost every person new to teaching with cases says this to anyone who is willing to listen. Frequently, it is difficult to find sympathetic ears. Some people who know how to teach with cases have learned the hard way. "You sink or swim."

Many are convinced it is the only way to learn. As long as the use of cases was largely restricted to a few North American schools, "sink or swim" was acceptable. The use of cases is no longer an educational elitist process, but a practical answer to some of education's most basic challenges. It allows the student to: (1) participate in discussing the analysis and solution of relevant and practical problems; (2) apply theory to practice, instead of learning by memory; and (3) learn by doing and teaching others. Furthermore, it allows the faculty member to work with students as a guide and not as an oracle.

The use of cases continues to grow and has spread geographically to almost all parts of the world. Its applicability is being explored in areas beyond its management origins to other fields including engineering, theology, medicine, education, economics, mathematics, law, computer and actuarial science, hospitality and recreation, agriculture, nursing, the social sciences, and other educational areas which traditionally have not used cases. Part-time and in-house development programs increasingly use cases as well as degree and executive programs. This growing interest in the case method reinforces the need for information sharing and has increased the demand for competent educators.

Today's students, young or old, are leaning towards participatory education and are no longer satisfied to be passive recipients of knowledge. The educational process itself is becoming an important consideration and must be satisfying to its consumers. That is, the topic may draw students to a course, the process of learning will keep them. How to make the educational process interesting to an audience continually exposed to some of the world's most sophisticated entertainment on audio-visual media is not an easy challenge for today's teacher.

TERMINOLOGY

In this text a teacher, instructor, lecturer, professor, facilitator, faculty member, educator, case leader, trainer or moderator is someone who has program, course, class, seminar or workshop instruction responsibility. A student, participant or class member is someone who is part of a group taking a course, seminar, workshop or educational program. The terms have been used interchangeably to avoid monotony and will be clear in their context.

A case is a description of an actual situation, commonly involving a decision, a challenge, an opportunity, a problem or an issue faced by a person, or persons, in an organization. The normal assumption in this book is that a case will be based on actual field data, authenticated by a release and will not be of the armchair or fictional variety.

The Case Method

The term "case method" seems to mean different things to different people.

Walt: I don't like the expression "case method." It can mean many different things. Even here at Harvard, the range of case method teaching is enormous. I would prefer to call it "participatory education." The term "case method" comes from the fact that we use cases. But this is not the cornerstone of what we do. I think that the participatory approach is more the cornerstone.

We suggest that there are four potential sources of semantic difficulty. These may be revealed through the following questions: (1) What is included in the case method? (2) Does the case method require one specific teaching style? (3) Does the case method require a minimum number of cases? (4) Is the context of the case method course, program, or institution based?

1. What is included in the case method? A significant part of the ambiguity surrounding the case method seems to lie in the question whether the case method itself incorporates the use of other educational philosophies and techniques. For example, can someone be teaching by the case method and still use lectures, problems, exercises, experiential learning, simulations, games, films, field trips, reports or any other teaching/learning technique? Some interviewees seem to feel that the case method itself incorporates all of the above. Others feel it is more appropriate to separate the portion concerned about teaching with cases from the other educational techniques and call this portion the case method. Clearly, these differences can give rise to considerable confusion.

2. Does the case method require one specific teaching style? The myth of the nondirective instructor, passive or impassive, dominates the case method literature. Under this myth, the responsibility for learning rests solely on the student's shoulders. Any interference from the instructor is seen as a violation of the whole learning process.

In reality, we observed that the majority of interviewees found it difficult to identify with such an approach and preferred a more active role in the classroom. Thus, the reluctance to put all teaching styles under the same "case method" umbrella is quite understandable.

3. Does the case method require a minimum number of cases? Some interviewees claimed to be using the case method. Upon further questioning, it became clear that they used one or two cases per year in their course. Does this constitute using the case method? Generally speaking, there seems to be agreement that, if there is such a thing as "the case method," it would normally involve a higher rather than a lower percentage of cases taught.

4. Is the context of the case method course, program, or institution based? Thus far, the assumption has been that the context for the case method is a course. Some people hold that the case method can only be taught in a program context. Therefore, unless all the courses in a program are taught using a significant number of cases in each course, there can be no case method.

Advocates of the program context argue that there is a synergistic effect which must be shared by all teachers in the program for the case method to work effectively. Anything short of such a cooperative approach is not likely to result in "the case method." A program may include undergraduate, graduate or executive development. It could be a number of years in length, or be as short as a few days or a week.

A further extension leads to the institutional context. It might be possible to take all the institutions in the world teaching management, for example, and determine in which of those a significant number of courses or programs are taught using cases. In reality, such institutions exist and they are often called case method schools. One source of confusion for people not familiar with what transpires inside these schools is the assumption that 100% of class time is devoted to case discussion. Another source of confusion for the people within these same schools originates from the use of many educational techniques other than the case method. They argue that, "Because we are labelled a case method school, and I see us using every teaching method imaginable, the case method must include all of these."

Some believers in the case method hold that the only way the case method can possibly be taught is if the institution: (1) is involved in the writing of new cases; (2) has physical accommodation for effective class discussion and small group discussions; (3) schedules for adequate individual preparation and small group discussion; and (4) recognizes the teaching and development of cases as significant academic contributions.

Even for these people, the question remains as to what degree cases should be used to achieve the objectives of the institution, the program and the course.

TEACHING WITH CASES

Since the case method clearly means different things to different people, we have chosen the title "Teaching With Cases" for this book, as our way of reaching all users of cases. The purpose of this text is to assist anyone interested in teaching with cases. Our assumption will be that to be teaching with cases, someone has to use a minimum of one case in a course. Our assumption will also be that it is possible to use the case method on an individual course basis. We recognize that some of the benefits of the case method may not exist in an institution where only one course is taught with a minimum percentage of cases. We also recognize that it is possible to make a program or institutional commitment to the case method. We prefer to reserve the term teaching with cases for the total set of activities related to the use of cases in the classroom. We prefer to call a problem discussion, a film, a lecture, a simulation, a business game, a class discussion, a question and answer period, a field trip, a student presentation, a reading, and any other educational technique by its proper name.

Class Size

Should there be a minimum number of students in class before an instructor can reasonably use cases? Similarly, is there an upper limit to class size beyond which case discussion becomes inoperable? These two questions have elicited strong opinions from a number of contributors. Generally, the lower bound seems to lie close to a dozen and the upper near a hundred participants. An ideal case class varies from twenty to sixty, according to our respondents.

Andy believes his own behavior influences his optimal class size.

Andy: In a given class period, I don't work with as many people as some of my colleagues do. I think I stay with the student longer. So, if I'm working with 8-10 people who are well prepared, I would prefer a smaller class size of about 25-30. Some of my colleagues like a larger class size and will probably call on twice as many students as I will.

Barney bases his estimates of class size on the length of time he will be with the students.

Barney: For me, if it is only for one class and no more, it would have to be 15. But I wouldn't want to have 10 classes with just 15 participants. By the time we go to 10 classes, it has to be 20 or 25. And if it's a half year course, I would want to have 30 as a minimum. For a year long class, the question of size becomes, "What is the maximum size where you can deal with every individual student at a reasonably involved level?" Defining "reasonably involved" becomes difficult. Right now we have about 65 students in each of the first year classes. I have no difficulty getting to every one of my students.

The assumption in the remainder of this text will be that class size for case discussion purposes will be between 10 and 100 participants.

ORGANIZATION AND PRESENTATION
OF THE MATERIAL

This text is organized so that the central core covers the chronological sequence of preparation for class, in-class teaching and evaluation after class. Other topics, such as prerequisites, course planning, and feedback and counseling surround this core. The beginning instructor, faced with taking over an existing course which already uses some cases, may wish to concentrate on the prerequisites, preparation for class, in-class teaching and evaluation chapters. Those not so fortunate as to have the course pre-planned for them may wish to add course planning. For the more experienced case teacher, the classroom process, case use variations, special considerations and the conclusion will add some further insights to augment their experience.

Chapter 2 presents the prerequisites for case teaching.

Chapter 3 on course planning introduces the kinds of challenges involved in determining objectives and selecting case and conceptual/theoretical materials.

Chapter 4 covers instructor preparation for a case class. Experienced case teachers recognize the importance and necessity of thorough preparation for every class. However, new instructors are sometimes surprised to learn of the extensive time required for a case class preparation. The aim of this chapter is to complement the student Case Preparation Chart in *Learning With Cases*.

Chapter 5 focuses on the teaching of a case class. It is here that the results of planning and preparation will show. Starting from a reference base class description, a number of variations and practices are discussed. The normal chronological parts of a case class are identified, followed by sections on how instructors manage the participative process and what problems they commonly encounter.

Chapter 6 addresses evaluation after class. Evaluation includes measuring student performance, assessing the class itself, reviewing the effectiveness of the case in general, and, for some, the program in total. Exhibit 1-5 provides an overview of what teachers and participants are supposed to do in the standard case preparation, large group discussion and post class evaluation stages.

Chapter 7, on feedback and counseling, helps instructors deal with student performance issues. This chapter also discusses case exams and instructor evaluation.

Chapter 8 covers several aspects of the use of cases that, while not necessarily used on a daily basis, are, nonetheless, effective. Case use variations include: case presentations, case reports, role plays, case format variations, visitors to class, team teaching, field trips and interactive video conferencing.

Chapter 9 deals with the use of cases in non-case schools. Instructors in non-case environments face a special set of issues and challenges. Some instructors may offer the only case course in an institution. Others may be only using one or two cases as part of an otherwise lecture oriented course.

Chapter 10 is devoted to special considerations and covers subjects which did not neatly fall under any of the earlier headings, including teacher training, managing diversity, and shortcuts used by students.

Chapter 11 concludes with an operations overview of teaching with cases.

Exhibit 1-5
THE TEACHER AND STUDENT ROLES
IN A REGULAR CASE CLASS

When	Professor	Student or Participant
Before Class	Assigns a case and, often, readings for student preparation.	Receives case and reading assignments.
	Prepares for class. Completes Case Teaching Plan.	Reads and prepares individually. Starts the Case Preparation Chart.
	(May consult with colleagues about the case.)	Participates in a small group discussion of the case. Adds to the Case Preparation Chart.
During Class	Resolves questions arising out of the assigned readings.	Raises questions regarding assigned readings.
	Leads the case discussion by probing, recording and facilitating student comments, supplying data, theory or insight which may enhance the thinking and learning in the class. Executes the Case Teaching Plan	Participates in the class discussion by sharing insights on the case and listens carefully to what others have to say. Uses the Case Preparation Chart.
After Class	Evaluates the participation of students and records impressions.	Reviews class results in light of preparation and notes major concepts learned.
	Evaluates the Case Teaching Plan.	Reviews the Case Preparation Chart.
	Evaluates the case and other materials in light of the original teaching objectives and updates teaching notes.	

Material Presentation

In addition to quotes from written sources, this book contains many direct quotes from personal interviews. A number of contributors requested for reasons which may not have been clear to us, but which we wish to respect, that their names be anonymous. For this reason, as well as to avoid reference to titles and positions, disguised first names have been used for almost all contributors.

Direct quotes have been used wherever possible to preserve the liveliness, originality, and correctness of the remarks. Contributors are saying it the way they see it. Editing has only been done to clarify intent where it seemed necessary.

Throughout this text it will be apparent that various teachers have different and sometimes quite opposite opinions as to the best way to deal with the challenges inherent in the case method. Every teacher needs to find his or her own "comfort zone." The case method offers a large variety of options in executing the teaching task. The challenge is to find a way of teaching that is appropriate to the subject, the participants and the teacher as well. We are fully convinced that there are fundamentals to the case teaching process. These include paying attention to the prerequisites, proper course planning and preparation before class; being able to conduct the class according to a plan and congruent with one's own personality; consistent evaluation and feedback; and the right mix of rigor, humor and variety. These fundamentals will go a long way to ensuring teaching effectiveness. Hard work and willingness to experiment do have their payoffs. Few case teachers have such a scintillating charisma and outstanding intellect that they can short-cut the full set of tasks required to assure success. As Kim said, "Show me a good case teacher and I'll show you someone who has worked hard to get there."

CONCLUSION

Portions of this text have been used in a variety of case teaching training programs. These experiences have shown that many teachers find it useful to learn about teaching with cases from others. The "mystique" of teaching with cases is partially removed. It is reassuring for the new case teacher to know that others have faced similar problems. Some of the more elementary pitfalls may be avoided. The variety and richness inherent in the use of cases is amply documented. Also, it is a special privilege to share the deep concern for student excitement in the learning process shown by all contributors.

prerequisites for teaching with cases

In the first chapter of our book *Learning with* Cases, we provide an exhaustive rationale for the use of cases in the classroom and an inventory of the various skills developed by the case method. It is one step to make an intellectual commitment to this philosophy of learning. The participative nature of the case method actually requires a deeper understanding of what makes its effectiveness a reality. It all begins with a commitment to set-up time and effort. In the first place, physical facilities must be conducive to the use of cases. The layout of the classroom must encourage participation Secondly, means must be provided whereby the teacher can learn quickly the names of the participants and for the participants to become acquainted with one another. There is no room for anonymity in the case method! Lastly, materials must be available. Students must have the cases in order to prepare for the class. Failure to attend to these prerequisites or unwillingness to spend the time necessary to assure that they are fulfilled may well result in an unsatisfactory experience in teaching with cases. This chapter will present these three prerequisites individually: physical facilities, participant identification and material logistics.

PHYSICAL FACILITIES

Classroom Physical Layout

A proper physical layout for a classroom is extremely important in using cases. The basic principle behind a proper physical layout is simply that all participants, including the instructor, must be able to hear and see each other easily in class. If the instructor is unable to identify a student who is talking and if students are unable to identify and face other students who are contributing to the discussion, major blocks exist to effective participation. Since it is likely that educators will find themselves in classrooms not originally designed for using cases, a few comments are in order regarding physical layout.

The traditional classroom in most universities and educational institutions (or seminar room in hotels) is designed as follows: A rectangular room is set up with a podium or desk and board at the narrow end of the room and rows of seats and benches facing that end of the room. (See Exhibit 2-1.) For a one-way communication such as a lecture where the primary task of the student is to listen to the speaker, such an arrangement is functional. It may not be the best, because it is often difficult to see the speaker from the back. Nevertheless, it is normal.

From the point of view of teaching with cases, this layout has many difficulties. Since case discussion requires two-way communication, it is difficult for a student in the back row to talk to the backs of the heads of the people in the front rows. It is also difficult for those at the front to turn around and see the student contributing from the back of the room. As far as using cases is concerned, this layout places an undue emphasis on the teacher or instructor and not enough on the participants.

Exhibit 2-1
TRADITIONAL CLASSROOM LAYOUT

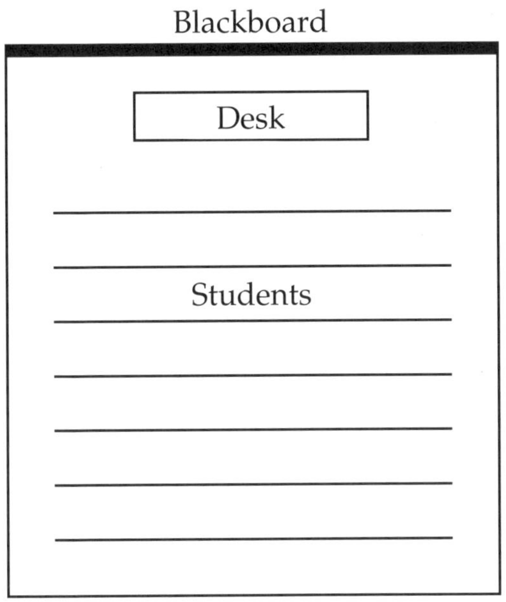

Blackboard

Desk

Students

The ideal layout for using cases with a small number of participants would be a perfectly round table and a circular seating arrangement. (See Exhibit 2-2.) The circle implies equality for all participants, provides perfect sight lines to everyone and allows face to face communication.

Other variations exist on the circle theme. For example, it is possible to use a square or a rectangular layout. Actually, a hexagon or octagon are preferable to either the square or the rectangle because both improve sight lines to participants. (See Exhibit 2-3.)

Exhibit 2-2
IDEAL ARRANGEMENT FOR
SMALL CLASS CASE DISCUSSIONS

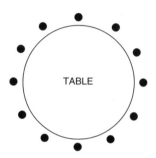

Exhibit 2-3
VARIATIONS ON THE CIRCLE OPTION

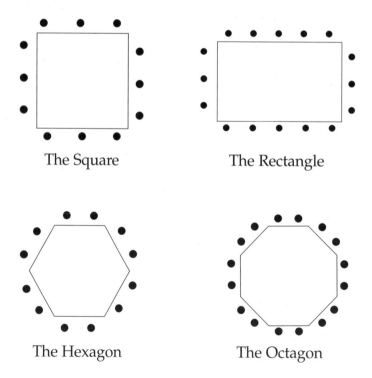

The Square   The Rectangle

The Hexagon   The Octagon

Unfortunately, as the number of participants increases, the circle and its variations start to have disadvantages. There is a limit to the size of the table. The distance between participants grows rapidly as their number increases. The amount of useless space in the middle of the table becomes a block to communication.

For larger groups, other options need to be examined. Various arrangements of row seating, preferably ramped, in amphitheater style are possible alternatives. (See Exhibits 2-4 and 2-5.) Chairs should be moveable or at least rotatable, so that participants in the front can easily turn around and see people behind them. Table or bench space in front of each participant is desirable both for comfort and as a place to put cases and reference materials, lap tops or to take notes. These should provide for slightly more depth than a normal written case. About 14 inches or 30 centimeters is adequate. Curved benches (see Exhibit 2-5) are preferable to long straight benches (see Exhibit 2-4). The curve helps make it easier to see others seated in the same row.

To preserve sight lines it is necessary to make each additional row at a substantially higher level than the previous ones (see Exhibit 2-5). For this reason, there is a practical limit to how many rows can be accommodated in one classroom. The maximum is normally four or five rows.

Sometimes it is possible to use small tables in a room and seat participants around these tables. Frequently, this is an effective setup in a hotel for short seminars. The group around the table can form a discussion group at the same time. (See Exhibits 2-6 and 2-7.)

Exhibit 2-4
BENCH AND CHAIR ARRANGEMENTS

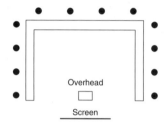

1. Simple Straight U

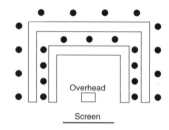

2. Double Straight U

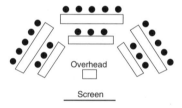

3. Double Angled U

Exhibit 2-5
CURVED BENCH AND CHAIR ARRANGEMENT

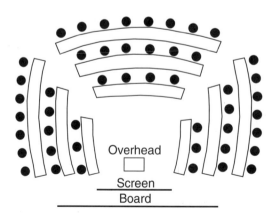

Sideview showing
increasing ramp
height with each
additional row of
seating

Exhibit 2-6
POSSIBLE LAYOUT USING ROUND TABLES

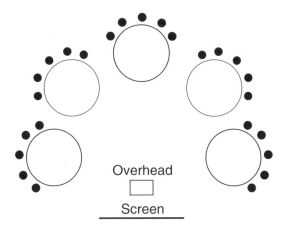

Exhibit 2-7
POSSIBLE LAYOUT USING RECTANGULAR TABLES

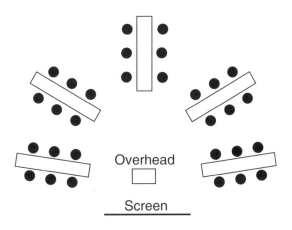

Most "case schools" have classrooms designed especially for the case method. Appendix 1, at the end of the book, contains some typical case classroom designs for rooms of 44 and 71 participants.

Adjusting to Non-Ideal Environments

A number of schools have experimented successfully with changing traditional classrooms (see Exhibit 2-1) to a more discussion oriented design (see Exhibit 2-8). One option is to move the (black, green or white) board from the short wall in a traditional lecture room to the long wall. Adding two more boards, including one in the corner, is a second option.

Exhibit 2-8
TRADITIONAL CLASSROOM
CONVERSION OPTIONS

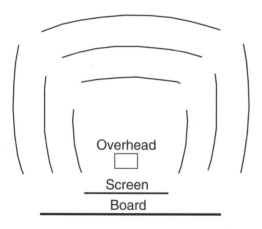

Option 1
Conversion from Exhibit 2-1 with Board on Long Wall

Exhibit 2-8 (continued)

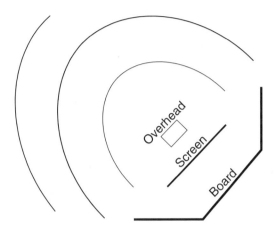

Option 2
Conversion from Exhibit 2-1 with Boards in Corner

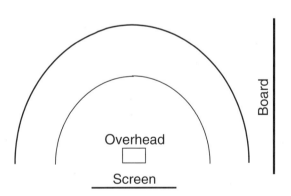

Option 3
Simple Temporary Conversion from
Exhibit 2-1 by Moving Chairs

It is even possible as a third option to take individual student chairs, provided they are not bolted to the floor, and move them in some broad semicircles. With a screen and overhead projector, this can be done even if no board is available on the long wall.

Sometimes the room available is too large for the number of class members. This in itself can create a communication obstacle.

Randy: Sometimes, I get a classroom too big for my needs. One of the things I try to do then is to pull everyone in close. Get them to feel a sense of unity as a group, close to each other, the physical proximity. Otherwise, the tendency is for people to sit at the back, as if they were in church. You've got to pull them to the front.

If the room is too small for the number of students and no larger room is available, breaking the class in two or more sections may be required.

Instructors who are used to the luxury of an "ideal" case environment find it difficult at times to adjust to new surroundings when they are teaching away from home.

Wilf: When you find yourself in an environment which has not been set up for case discussion, then **"you change it."** You do your best so that everybody gets to see each other. Overhead projectors can always be found if there is no board available.

Clint: The physical requirements are very important from my perspective. For private courses that I do, the hardest thing is to get them to set up a place in a "u-shape." You can tell them, draw them pictures, but they don't understand. So wherever you go, you always have to get there in time to redo the room and to adjust the overhead projector.

Dave: I try to minimize those things at the front of the room that would get between me and the class. I don't like a podium. All I want is something flat to put some materials on. I even like those arrangements where the overhead projector is built into the table so that it doesn't sit up to obstruct the view. You don't want things that physically separate you from the class. You should also make sure the lighting doesn't cause glare on the boards.

Many professors like to get the "feel" of a classroom before they teach their first class.

Stan: I think it is very important to get to know the classroom layout before you go in. You must get to know the landscape of the classroom. I like a classroom where there is a lot space to walk up and down, back and forth.

A director of continuing education talks about the reasons for concern with facilities and the difficulties with professors and staff when changes need to be made.

Rick: As to facilities, it's a question of, "Do you start with that 'I care' philosophy and then follow it up with good administration." I think you really have to start with, "I care about the students and the learning process." No question that you can fight for things. Flat floors are a real problem if you have too many people in there. I've fought and won the battle to buy risers. It's surprising how little it costs to get some lumber and bang some boards together; and now you've got two rows and you can really see the people in the second row.

No question, hotels are the toughest ones to deal with because they've got bars, because they've got lobbies, because they've got seven thousand symbols that say, "This is a hotel." And most managers spend so much time in hotels that they've got a hotel behavior. With that kind of reinforcement, they just keep behaving like they're in a hotel, which they are, rather than in a place to study and learn.

Chapter 9 on case use in non-case environment will provide further comments about the problems several instructors faced with physical facilities and, in some cases, how they overcame them.

Boards, Charts and Screens

The participatory nature of case class discussion also requires the availability of boards, charts or screens to facilitate the discussion. Traditionally, classrooms have been equipped with blackboards that instructors have used to document and keep track of the discussion. Over the years, these blackboards have turned green and become superimposed with sliding mechanisms. More recently, the messy chalk has disappeared to be replaced by colorful erasable markers used on white boards. Increasingly, these various types of recording boards or flip-charts, common in facilities not equipped with boards, are supplemented or simply replaced by overhead projectors which have the great advantage of allowing the instructor to face the participants instead of turning his or her back to them. With the advent of new technologies and the electronic classroom, the nature of recording mechanisms keeps evolving.

Chris offers some interesting projections on how future classrooms might change.

Chris: I can see the time coming pretty soon where we won't have white boards anymore. With video projection prices coming down and resolution quality going up, it is quite conceivable that you could have a classroom with two or three podiums and each podium having a notepad computer. Each computer could be projected onto a regular screen, allowing you to face your class. Having more than one podium would mean that students would be able to simultaneously see several images the equivalent of white boards. This would generate more energy as you would move from one podium to the next to process various parts of the case analysis.

While classrooms equipped with overhead projectors, screens and boards are normally adequate for teaching with traditional paper-based cases, special requirements are needed for multimedia or interactive types of cases produced in other formats such as CD ROM, video or for cases using software ancillaries. It is possible to have TV monitors, terminal hook-ups, video units that project onto big screens, microphones and other audiovisual equipment.

More on technological advances will be covered in Chapter 8 on variations to the standard case format and discussion process. At this point, it is sufficient to say that the facility where the large group discussion takes place must be equipped with adequate means to provide a visual record of the discussion.

Small Group Facilities

The last prerequisite for teaching with cases with respect to physical facilities concerns the availability of space for small group discussion. As described in *Learning with Cases*, small group discussion provides the vital link between individual preparation and large group discussion in the Three Stage Case Learning Process. Yet space and time for enabling this important stage of learning is often left for participants to arrange, especially in degree programs in non-case schools.

While some flexibility exists with respect to meeting space for such groups because of their small size, it remains important for institutions to provide small rooms, preferably equipped with boards, that may be booked ahead of time. The availability of these rooms, while reinforcing the importance of small group discussion, will prove especially convenient to participants enrolled in evening or part-time programs, who do not have regular contact with each other, or to participants of in-house programs.

While not ideal, the instructor can sometimes use the large classroom for the purpose of small group discussion, when separate rooms are not available. As we saw earlier, some classroom layouts are more conducive to such transformation than others. (See Exhibits 2-6 and 2-7.)

It is easy to underestimate the importance of suitable physical arrangements on the effectiveness of the case learning process. Anyone seriously contemplating using cases in class must first make sure that the physical facilities can be satisfactorily arranged. Considerable instructor ingenuity may have to be used to satisfy this first prerequisite to effective case use.

PARTICIPANT IDENTIFICATION

"Will the person with the glasses at the end of the row mind starting the class?"

"Will you, second in from the left in the third row, please tell me what you think?"

"Will the person with a beard wearing a yellow shirt comment on this?"

To dedicated case teachers these kinds of comments are totally unacceptable in a well-run case class. It is the responsibility of the instructor to get to know his or her students as quickly as possible. This means being able to identify the person by name in and out of class. It also means having background information, if possible, on each so that appropriate resource people can be called on at the appropriate time in the class to contribute. In case discussions a student is not a number. A student is not anonymous. A student cannot be allowed to hide in the classroom. It is the responsibility of both the instructor and the students to get to know everyone in the class. For this purpose a number of aids are normally available. The more common ones are listed below:

1. Personal data forms. Personal data forms on all participants, including the instructor, distributed to every class member, can be a very useful starting point for humanizing the class. This data can be obtained at time of registration or in the early stages of starting the course. A copy of a typical personal data form is shown in Exhibit 2-9.

2. Name cards. Name cards are a great identifying aid. Name tags, hanging around the neck or pinned to the lapel, can be used in degree programs during the first week or so, but tend to quickly fall into disuse. In executive and management programs, name tags are more likely to be worn for the total length of the program. Place cards in the classroom are most useful. These can be made of paper or plastic and can be of the "quick and dirty" variety or the very professional type. Legibility is crucial. The simplest ones are pieces of cardboard folded in two which can be collected by the instructor after class or left for the participants to bring back each class.

For executive programs, sometimes company affiliation is shown on the place card as well as the first and last name. It may also be useful to write the name on both sides of the name card so that people sitting behind know who is talking. (See Exhibit 2-10 for typical classroom place card options.)

Exhibit 2–9
PERSONAL DATA FORM

MBA STUDENT BIOGRAPHY

(Please do not attach extra sheets or write on the back of this form)

Mr. ☐ Ms. ☐

Name _____

Surname   First   Second

Name to be used by professors and classsmates _____

Marital status _____ Spouse's name _____ No. of children _____

Age as of September 15th this year _____

What field are you interested in pursuing upon graduation? _____

Please indicate your reasons for pursuing the MBA Program _____

Place of Birth _____   Student Status: Canadian ☐   Landed Immigrant ☐   Visa

First Language _____ Other languages fluently spoken _____

IINTERNATIONAL EXPERIENCE:

Education: Country _____   Duration: _____

Employment: Country _____   Duration: _____

Travel: Country _____   Duration: _____

EDUCATION

University	Location	From	To	Degree Awarded	Major

EMPLOYMENT

Estimate the total amount of full time work experience by the time you enter the MBA Program. Years _____ Months _____			
Employer	Location	Job Title	Dates of Employment (M/Yr. - M/Yr.)

EXTRA-CURRICULAR ACTIVITIES (include non-academic interests)

Activ'ties/Interests/Hobbies	Location	Position Held	Dates

Exhibit 2-10
TYPICAL CLASSROOM PLACE CARD OPTIONS

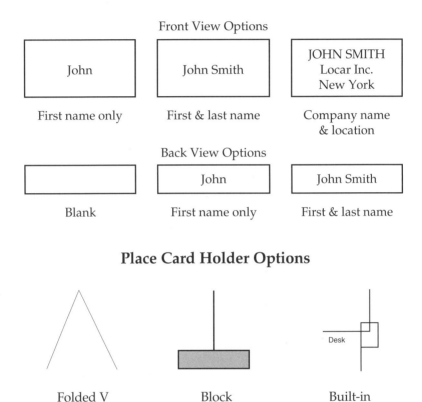

Front View Options

John	John Smith	JOHN SMITH Locar Inc. New York
First name only	First & last name	Company name & location

Back View Options

	John	John Smith
Blank	First name only	First & last name

Place Card Holder Options

Folded V	Block	Built-in

3. **Photos.** There are two types of photos which may be useful in identifying participants. Individual photos can be requested at time of registration. Sometimes, the quality of these can vary substantially as well as the age. Human rights laws also may make the obtaining of photos difficult. Classroom photos showing every participant in their place are of substantial assistance to get an up-to-date picture. They have the advantage of identifying for both

the instructor and the students a current picture and class layout in combination. It is a good idea to place a picture of this kind in the classroom so that students themselves can refer to it. Ideally, if every student can receive a copy, so much the better. When the services of a professional photographer cannot be retained, using one's own camera is always an option.

4. Layout sheets or seating charts. It is a simple matter for the instructor to pass a classroom layout sheet around the room and ask every student to fill in his or her name. This can subsequently be cleaned up, copied and passed around to everyone. (See Exhibit 2-11.)

All of the above means are clear and graphic indications to the student that individual identification is of high priority. The professor can take the following further steps to assist in participant identification.

5. Sitting in the back of the class. For certain programs it may be possible to sit in the back of the class when another instructor is teaching. It is possible then to observe every student and mark down individual characteristics on a layout sheet to help in participant identification. Experience has shown that it is possible to identify a group of 60 in approximately 80 minutes.

6. Participation in social activities. Further participant identification is possible during coffee breaks, lunch, social functions and other gatherings at which students and instructors can mingle.

7. Personal visits in the office. A student visiting a teacher in the office is a good way to get to know each other better.

Exhibit 2–11
TYPICAL CLASSROOM LAYOUT SHEET

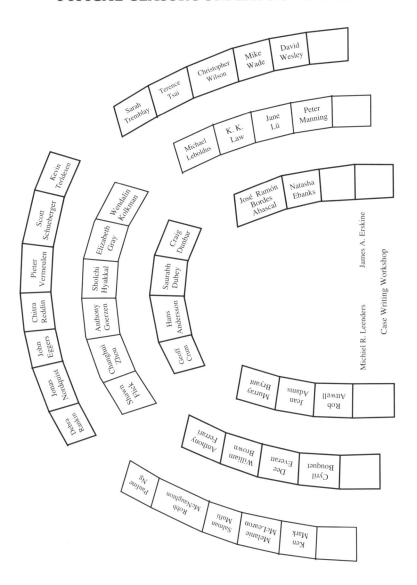

8. Small group visits. In programs that provide mechanisms to organize small groups formally, it is possible for the instructor to visit the groups and identify students. Such visits have the added advantage of reinforcing the value of small groups. (See Chapter 4 in *Learning with Cases*.)

It is normal to use a combination of the above means to assist in student identification.

A Typical Participant Identification Routine in Case Schools

In case schools a typical routine to acquaint professors with students is the following one:

Clint: Before our MBA students come in, we have a picnic or party and you get to know a few. We are also each assigned an advisee group so the first 2-3 days of school I usually take my group to my home. We also have the name cards in the class.

We also have our picture cards. We get these before school starts and 2-3 days before school begins, I go through them. I try to pick up something on everybody. This usually surprises them. I remember one year the first class I taught with a case set somewhere in Vermont. I called on a student and asked something about Vermont. He came up after to ask how in the world I had picked him.

Early in the course, I also try to pick out the experts. In every section, we've got to have a lawyer, a banker, an engineer. I use the cards to find these people and to help me determine whom I will select during particular sessions.

With executive programs, we also start with a cocktail party. I use this to find at least one person I can identify before walking into the first class.

Seating Arrangements and Data on Participants

Some programs have free seating arrangements. Other programs allow the participants to change place two to four times over the year. Many case programs have fixed seating arrangements with permanent place cards. For the professor who likes to think of the class as an orchestra, lack of seating continuity is a disaster. What would happen to the maestro if the violin section kept moving to a different location for every concert? Some professors are even used to an alphabetical class layout.

> **Kim**: One of my personal shortcomings in getting to know students has to do with their location in the class. For many years we used to sit the students in all of our degree and executive programs alphabetically, from left to right. I developed the habit of learning their names this way. Since our students' background cards or booklets are also alphabetically arranged, this system made sense. These days where individual freedom and creativity reign, I find classrooms without any alphabetical layout and it makes it substantially more difficult for me to get to know everyone quickly.

Place cards always are a big help, but not everyone uses them. Ross teaches at a non-case school:

> **Ross:** We don't use place cards at our school, but I ask my students to provide me with a seating chart. I ask them to sit at the same place for three weeks. Then with a picture book, the place cards are no longer necessary.

Most professors think, like Linda, that it is useful to know the backgrounds of the participants to conduct the discussion.

> **Linda**: I like to know each student individually. I use the cards showing their picture and their background. If you're skillful, you can use that information to structure the classes. For example, it is very important for me in my second year

course to get a student to start the first day who does not have an accounting background. I determine that from the cards. It is often very useful to pick people with particular backgrounds which may relate to the case. There are times when you want to speed up the discussion, so you call on one type of person. Or if you want a thoughtful kind of response, you call on another type of person. Who you call on and in what order can be very important. So you've got to get to know your students very quickly in order to make that process work early.

Even on very short courses, workshops or seminars, some professors make a serious attempt to become acquainted with participants.

Kim: Even in one day seminars with groups of executives I make a point of having every participant introduce him or herself. I often make out the name cards myself and make a rough seating chart. While they are busy in individual preparation or small group discussion, I make it my task to get to know all of their names quickly. As long as the group size is not too much over forty, I find I can usually do this in ten to twenty minutes and it certainly pays off for the rest of the seminar.

The process of getting to know the group may be difficult for some but is worth the effort.

Rick: Everybody has their own way of doing this, but the thing is to recognize that it is important and that you've got to work at it in a way that makes sense for you. You know, pictures, seating plans, class cards, they're all devices. There are some people in any group that I just don't get to know unless I get them into a one on one conversation and something they say finally makes their name fall into place. It's hard for me. It's not my particular strength, but I get there. It's part of the "I care" philosophy and absolutely critical. I mean, "How can I care if I don't remember your name?"

The principle behind all of these remarks is that without identification it is impossible in a case context to run a suitable course. It is important that the student senses that he or she belongs. The student must feel a responsibility to self and the group. The student must also know that the professor cares.

Knowing the students is also necessary for evaluative purposes. Moreover, a professor seriously interested in proper student identification can gain valuable student support. Students are visibly surprised when they're called by their own name during their early days around the school. "How come you know my name?" is a frequent comment on their part.

Professor Donald C. Hambrick of the Graduate School of Business, Columbia University, says, "Students will attend to you if you attend to them. I try to learn all the students' names, even in a class as large as 60, in the first three weeks, becoming able to address them by name without their name cards in the classroom and in the halls. This task is particularly essential because I grade class participation and can only do so credibly if it's clear I know who's who"(247).

In Brazil, Professor Jorge Gomez diligently studied the personal data sheets on his students before his first class. When his first class came, he bet his students that he would be able to call them by name and identify the institution where they received their earlier degree. The students quickly came to the conclusion that here was one professor from whom it might be difficult to hide. A year later, at an introductory session for his course, Professor Gomez explained that he counted classroom participation as a significant portion of his course evaluation. A newcomer argued that this was unfair and that the professor would be unable to do a reasonable job of this.

One of the second year students commented, "I can assure you that here is one professor who probably already knows more about you than you know about him and who will have no difficulty identifying your participation in every class you have with him."

Professor Chris Christenson of the Harvard Business School was addressing a group of 36 participants at an International Teachers Programme held at the London Business School. It was reported in ECCHO, the newsletter of the European Case Clearing House, that, "He (Christenson) led by example, arriving already knowing thoroughly the identity and background of every participant and being able to converse with them instantly from this base. This proved to be an enormous highlight of the course" (No. 17, 21).

Our late Dean Jack Wetlauffer was well known for his great ability to identify students, current and past, by name.

> It is just hard work. I have always believed that it is very important to know the students in my course. And it is much more important when I teach with cases, because what I try to do as a case teacher is work with all the experiences that the people in the room bring to that class. So, before I go into a classroom and well before the course starts I get the class cards. I sort them out, first of all, in terms of my particular area, industrial relations. I check through to see what people in that class have had some experience with industrial relations. That's my first priority group. The second is to go through in terms of work experience with specific companies or institutions. Many organizations are steady customers of the school. For instance, G.M., Ford, I.B.M., or whatever company it is, will have sent people before that I remember. I can use the names of some of the people who were sent before as a way of establishing a bridge with that particular student. My third bridge is their

geographical background. Are they from another country, and if so, they will receive high priority. Finally, where are they from in North America?

As soon as I get the class cards, I take them to bed with me at night. Every night, before I go to sleep, I go through the cards which are now arranged in terms of priorities which I have set. I just keep repeating through them and try to hang a face on a function, on an organization, or on an area, and try to find some way so that when I see a student I'll think: engineer, 3M, West Coast, Alice Jones. With the help of these references, I can get to know at least 130 people. The pictures are not always good, that is difficult. But, I keep reviewing them in my mind, so I've catalogued all participants, even though I don't know them yet. Then when I go down for coffee I talk with some and immediately afterwards go through the book and circle everyone I've talked to over coffee. Then, that night, I go through the book and those I make certain of now. I have met them in the flesh as well as in the picture. And I do that at lunch and in the classroom. After the course is over and when I meet a participant later on at an airport, hotel, or some function, something flashes to give me a clue. It is not necessarily the face and the name, but I may recall at least the company or something else, sufficient to start me on and away I go...

This example illustrates that it is certainly possible to do an excellent job of student identification when one cares. With cases, the professor faces this as a basic prerequisite. Just like a suitable physical layout, proper student identification is key to effective communication.

MATERIAL LOGISTICS

The assumption behind using cases is that cases will be available for use. In the so-called "case schools," reproduction facilities and ordering procedures are usually geared to create a minimum of fuss and bother to assure case access to students.

The European Case Clearing House (ECCH) provides through its Case On Line Information System (COLIS) the most comprehensive electronic bibliography of business cases in the world. COLIS contains abstracts of cases and supplementary materials from the major case producing management schools of the world (see Appendix 2) in addition to information on cases submitted by individuals.

In North America, the best known source of cases remains the Harvard Business School Publishing Division. It publishes a number of bibliographies which comprise several thousand case studies, including teaching notes, case videos and a selection of software ancillaries. The Richard Ivey School of Business at The University of Western Ontario is the second largest producer of cases in the world and is the main source of cases in Canada. Harvard and Ivey have introduced an update system designed to inform faculty by e-mail about new cases on a subject specific basis. Harvard and Ivey also have watermarked copies of selected cases on their websites which can be inspected and printed free of charge to registered academics. Appendix 2, at the end of the book, presents a list of the major case distribution centres of the world.

Lead time for ordering cases will vary depending on size of the order, location of user, location of source, and time of year. How students are to pay for case materials can apparently be tricky in some institutions and may well be a nuisance barrier to the use of cases.

Arthur: The book center at our place is just not set up to handle cases. They have to order them from Harvard. Their control system requires them to charge students only for material which they give them. Therefore, if I want to use series cases, it's very difficult to hand out material in class. We've now ended up with two separate accounting systems to be able to get around that and we literally end up with administrative assistants collecting part of the student charges from the students in class. All of this creates a strong incentive to buy a case book and stick with it — it's much simpler from a price and logistics point of view. However, this makes it difficult to make adjustments to your course.

Clint: Since the publications office falls under my office, it must be supportive. In other words, it has to be flexible and get the material out on time. One of the biggest problems is getting the faculty to get their orders and materials in on time.

While access to cases has been simplified greatly with the advent of new communication technologies, it is still not always easy to acquire relevant case material for student use. Instructors should never consider modifying existing cases to suit their needs. They should keep in mind as well as remind students of copyright regulations.

Nowadays the Internet facilitates access not only to cases but also to teaching notes, peer support and other curriculum resources. For example, eligible instructors can subscribe to services that will give them access to full-text files of cases and teaching notes to view on-screen or to download and print. Instructors can also join various case discussion groups; or associations such as the North American Case Research Association (NACRA) and the World Association for Case Research and Application (WACRA) to participate in professional activities, to share expertise and experiences, and to learn with colleagues from around the world.

Instructors can also receive training and assistance in case writing because the best source of cases remains undoubtedly cases that they have written themselves. Our book *Writing Cases* provides a proven approach to quick and effective case writing and has been used by thousands of instructors in workshops throughout the world.

Chapter 3 on course planning will offer further insights on case selection and the difficulties of finding good case materials.

CONCLUSION

Teaching with cases requires a commitment to set-up which may be significant in terms of time and effort. Making sure the physical facilities are conducive to small and large group discussion is the first major step. The second is the commitment to get to know the class participants quickly. Lastly, materials must be available in time. Simple as these prerequisites may seem, they could create serious stumbling blocks without adequate attention.

course planning

Selecting a topic area, deciding where to start, how far to go and how to get there are the essential decisions in course planning. Course planning using cases is not all that different in the broadest sense from non-case course planning. The four common parts to the course planning process are: (1) setting the learning objectives; (2) the general course design; (3) detailed planning - sequencing of the sessions and materials; and (4) defining the performance evaluation measures. The special aspect of using cases raises parallel questions such as: (1) Which of the learning objectives require cases? (2) How many cases will be used as a percentage of all class sessions? (3) What specific cases are to be used and where in the course? Will they be used to introduce the need for theory, concepts, tools and techniques or will they be used later to give practice in application? (4) What percentage of the course grade will be credited to case work and how will case work be assessed? Learning by doing and learning by teaching others are the two fundamentals of teaching with cases that permeate the learning objectives in case course planning.

SETTING THE LEARNING OBJECTIVES

Courses that do not use cases typically have learning objectives tied to the conceptual dimensions of the Case Difficulty Cube. For example: "Students must be able to identify the major theoretical constructs in the field and explain the key differences between them."

The use of cases and the analytical and presentation dimensions of the Case Difficulty Cube add a list of additional learning objectives. Analytical, decision making, communication, information handling and time management skills can be perceived more as life versus academic skills. They tend to be non-course specific and thus tie in to school or program philosophy and intent. Instructors keen on using cases must face up to the reality that trade-offs are unavoidable, if student preparation time is viewed as fixed. It is not possible to assign the same amount of theoretical reading in a case course as is possible in a non-case course. A serious cost-benefit analysis is inherent in any case course design. The course designer has to be fully aware of the trade-off decisions made and the reasons for them. Given the scarce resources of student preparation time and class time, the subject to be taught and the end results desired, what is the best way to proceed?

The following sections identify the potential learning objectives inherent in the use of cases. First, objectives will be identified as they might relate to Bloom's Taxonomy. Then the objectives will be tied to the Case Difficulty Cube as discussed in Chapter 2 of *Learning With Cases*. Learning objectives will also be addressed as part of the Three Stage Learning Process also discussed in Chapter 2 of *Learning With Cases*. Next, learning objectives will be related to the Case Preparation Chart discussed in Chapter 3 of *Learning With Cases*. Learning objectives are also connected to the eight participant skills developed through case use reviewed in Chapter 1 in *Learning With Cases*.

Bloom's Taxonomy

J. S. Bloom has described a taxonomy of cognitive learning that is commonly known as Bloom's Taxonomy. His model classifies a broad range of learning outcomes into six major learning objective categories.

- Evaluation: Form criteria, make judgments, detect fallacies, evaluate, decide.

- Synthesis: Produce a new combination not clearly evident before (requires originality or creativity).

- Analysis: Identify components, how they are related and arranged; distinguish fact from fiction.

- Application: Apply understandings to solve new problems in new situations when no directions or methods of solution are specified.

- Comprehension: Change the information to a more meaningful parallel form, paraphrase, interpret, infer, imply, extrapolate when told to do so (lowest level of understanding).

- Knowledge: State terms, specific facts, definitions, categories, ways of doing things..... (No evidence of understanding is required. The learner needs only to "boomerang" back information given) (*The Process of Learning*).

Cases afford the opportunity to address all seven levels of Bloom's Taxonomy, provided that is the instructor's intent.

Learning Objectives and the Case Difficulty Cube

Learning objectives for cases can be connected to the Case Difficulty Cube by focusing on the three dimensions of difficulty and the degrees within each dimension as summarized in Exhibit 3-1.

Exhibit 3-1
LEARNING OBJECTIVES
AND THE CASE DIFFICULTY CUBE

ANALYTICAL DIMENSION
Difficulty 1 The student must be able to evaluate a decision taken by others; assess the appropriateness of the decision to the problem or issue identified, whether the appropriate alternatives have been considered and the appropriate decision criteria applied; suggest other alternatives, should the one offered in the case be deemed inadequate; and develop an appropriate action and implementation plan.
Difficulty 2 The student must be able to assess the issue, decision or opportunity identified on an importance and urgency matrix; assess causes and effects where appropriate; develop alternatives and decision criteria and select the alternative that best fits the quantitative and qualitative assessment of them; develop an action and implementation plan; and specify missing information.
Difficulty 3 The participant must be able to assess the situation and identify problems, issues and challenges. From here the learning objectives are the same as under Difficulty 2.

Exhibit 3–1 (continued)

CONCEPTUAL DIMENSION

Difficulty 1
A participant should be able to apply a single, simple theory or concept assigned in readings to a specific case problem or issue without requiring extra explanation of the theory or concept in class.

Difficulty 2
The participant should be able to identify the appropriate theory or concepts or a single complex concept with some assistance or further discussion and explanation in class.

Difficulty 3
The participant should be able to identify a variety of those theories and concepts which might be relevant to the case issues. The participant may require a substantial amount of assistance and explanation in class to understand the integration of these theories or the explanation of the complex theories which are part of the total set.

PRESENTATION DIMENSION

Difficulty 1
The participant should be able to analyze correctly a short, well-organized case, containing no extraneous information, little missing relevant information and presented in a single format.

Difficulty 2
The participant should be able to analyze correctly a medium length case with some disorganization, containing a medium amount of extraneous information, with some missing information and presented in a single or double format.

Difficulty 3
The participant should be able to analyze within a reasonable length of time a long case which may be disorganized, containing lots of extraneous information, a substantial amount of missing information and presented in a variety of formats.

In summary, it can be seen that the primary challenge in the analytical dimension is the participant's ability to apply the typical decision making process steps to a situation. Under the conceptual dimension, it is the participant's ability to apply theory and concepts, tools and techniques, in an appropriate way to a specific decision. In the presentation dimension, it is the ability to deal with complexity, ambiguity, incompleteness of data; information sorting, specification and organizing; time management; as well as the ability to access a variety of data sources and integrate the appropriate data into a complete analysis.

Learning Objectives and the Three Stage Learning Process

Learning objectives can also be connected to the Three Stage Learning Process.

Stage 1 - Individual Preparation

The participant has to learn how to read and prepare a case on his or her own using the information provided, apply the Short and Long Cycle Processes of analysis and prepare a Case Preparation Chart in a period of less than two hours. The participant has to learn to work independently, and develop self-confidence, time management and critical thinking skills. The participant has to learn to recognize what constitutes satisfactory preparation for the next stage: small group discussion.

Stage 2 - Small Group Discussion

The participant must be able to contribute his or her ideas to the small group discussion dealing with any topic on the Case Preparation Chart; be able to understand and evaluate the contribution of others in the small group and incorporate worthwhile ideas on one's own Case Preparation Chart; be able to contribute to group effectiveness and cohesion by concentrating on value adding ideas; manage group time effectively and maintain the morale of the group and its members. In this stage, each participant learns to work effectively in a small group or team and has to be able to provide valuable inputs and incorporate useful ideas from others in his or her own perspective. The participant also has to learn to recognize what constitutes satisfactory group preparation for the next stage: large group discussion.

Stage 3 - Large Group Discussion

There are a number of learning objectives specific to the large group discussion. Clearly, many of the learning objectives for the Case Difficulty Cube and individual and small group work become reinforced in the large group. The participant must be able to contribute his or her ideas when called upon or volunteer at the appropriate time. The participant must be able to listen actively and assess the class discussion against his or her own Case Preparation Chart. The participant must be able to identify where other contributors present ideas that coincide or disagree with his or her own. The participant must be able to update his or her Case Preparation Chart. In the large group, the participant learns to work effectively with others and test his or her own individual and small group work against the large group result. Communication skills such as critical listening, effective speaking, evaluating others and learning to build on the ideas of others are an integral part of large group discussion.

Learning Objectives and the Case Preparation Chart

The Case Preparation Chart gives an organizational context to a different set of learning objectives. During both the Short and Long Cycle Processes the participant is exposed to a successive set of steps which encourage learning as summarized in Exhibits 3-2 and 3-3.

The Long Cycle Process is the intellectual heart of the case method, focusing on analytical and conceptual skills as well as the data management skills of the presentation dimension. The content of the Long Cycle Process is what most of the small group and large group case discussion time should be focused on.

Exhibit 3-2
LEARNING OBJECTIVES AND
THE SHORT CYCLE PROCESS

Step 2	Learning Objectives
Who/Position	Learn to identify with a specific position in an organization and to put oneself into another person's position.
What	Learn to identify with the types of decisions connected with a particular position in an organization and become acquainted with the range of responsibilities attached. Learn to become skilled with issue and problem identification.
Why	Learn to define causes and effects and the chronological sequence of events in a specific context.
When	Learn to develop a time plan, recognizing the time required to do certain tasks and specific time constraints.
How	Learn to assess a case on the analytical and conceptual dimensions of the Case Difficulty Cube.

Exhibit 3-3
LEARNING OBJECTIVES AND
THE LONG CYCLE PROCESS

Part 2	Learning Objectives
Immediate Issue(s)	Learn to recognize and focus on the immediate task(s) to be resolved. Learn to prioritize if more than one task needs to be addressed in a specific organizational context.
Basic Issue(s)	Be able to put the immediate issue into a larger context. Develop the ability to generalize. Take a particular decision beyond the case specifics into the course context and into the real-life large picture. See the connection between a variety of basic issues and their interplay in a specific real-life situation.
Importance/ Urgency Matrix	Be able to assess both the importance and the urgency of an issue in an organizational context. Be able to prioritize and provide a context for an eventual alternative selection and action and implementation plan.
Cause and Effect Diagram	Learn to identify and categorize the variety of causes contributing to a specific effect or outcome. This diagram is a key analytical tool for a host of management situations where improvement is sought.
Other Analytical Tools, Theories, Techniques	Learn additional tools, theories and techniques which may be course specific or related to the decision making model in general. Learn how to distinguish the appropriateness of various theoretical perspectives to the decision or issue under consideration and how to apply concepts correctly. Learn both the usefulness and limitations of various theories, concepts and tools.
Alternative Generation	Develop creative skills to generate a list of potential alternatives.

Exhibit 3–3 (continued)

Part 2	Learning Objectives
Decision Criteria	Be able to identify qualitative and quantitative criteria tied to the context provided in the case and appropriate in view of the importance/urgency matrix assessment. Be able to prioritize both qualitative and quantitative decision criteria.
Assessment of Alternatives	Be able to assess quantitative versus qualitative tradeoffs and connect alternatives to the importance/urgency matrix.
Selection of Preferred Alternative	Be able to make a decision. Be able to move from an analytical mode into a decision mode.
Prediction of Outcomes	Be able to look ahead to consequences flowing from decisions, forecasting and predicting quantitative and qualitative outcomes. Learn how to develop and evaluate best and worst outcome scenarios.
Action/ Implement- ation Plan	Be able to plan a series of actions which lead to a desired result. Be able to tie the financial, physical, human, and technological resources to a chronology with a specific deadline.
Missing Information	Learn to identify missing relevant information, assessing its potential availability, location, time and cost of collection, and impact of the missing information on the decision and plans at hand.
Assumptions	Learn to distinguish between facts and assumptions and develop a reasonable assumption. Learn to live in a world with incomplete information. Be able to assess the impact of assumptions made on decisions, actions and implementation plans and be able to develop alternative scenarios if an assumption is found to be incorrect.

Learning Objectives and Skill Development Overview

In the introduction to *Learning With Cases* eight participant skills are listed as reasons for the use of the case method. These are analytical, decision making, application, oral communication, time management, interpersonal/ social, creative and written communication skills.

It is possible to connect these skills to the Case Difficulty Cube, the Three Stage Learning Process and the Short and Long Cycle Processes culminating in the Case Preparation Chart. Exhibit 3-4 provides an overview where the maximum impact of skill development is likely to occur when viewed from these three different perspectives.

The Participant as a Starting Point

It is useful to identify the profile of the class and the education and experiential background of those who will be participating. It is quite different if none of the class participants have ever used cases before, than if all participants have extensive case experience. Similarly, if the participant group has a single company affiliation, such as for an in-house program, it is quite different from a group with a varied organizational background, such as a public program. Maturity and work experience of the participants is always relevant and, particularly, with respect to the subject matter taught. Teaching a marketing course using cases to non-marketing people is quite different from teaching it to marketing professionals.

The educational background of participants is also relevant. What conceptual and theoretical building blocks are already in place at the start of the course? For case teaching, the participants' level of qualitative and quantitative skills will also be a factor in course design.

Exhibit 3-4

SKILL DEVELOPMENT, THE CASE DIFFICULTY CUBE, THE THREE STAGE LEARNING PROCESS AND THE CASE PREPARATION CHART

Skill	Case Difficulty Cube			Three Stage Learning Process			Case Preparation Chart	
	X Axis	Y Axis	Z Axis	Individual	Small Group	Large Group	Short Cycle	Long Cycle
Analytical	✓			✓	✓	✓	✓	✓
Decision Making	✓	✓		✓	✓	✓		✓
Application		✓		✓	✓	✓		✓
Oral Communication			✓		✓	✓		
Time Management	✓	✓	✓	✓	✓		✓	✓
Interpersonal/Social					✓	✓		
Creative	✓	✓	✓	✓			✓	✓
Written Communication			✓	✓	✓		✓	✓

Constraints

Instructors have to design courses within the constraints of their teaching environment. For example, the length of class, the amount of student preparation, the facilities, the budget and the attitudes towards case teaching within the institution will affect the options available.

The essential point in setting the learning objectives for a course revolves around the old adage, "If you don't know where you are going, any road will do." Certain roads will be cut-off by time constraints, administrative policies, student level, student mix and other factors beyond the control of the instructor. Nonetheless, many roads will remain open and it is up to the instructor to specify the learning priorities and goals. The better this activity in course planning is executed, the more valuable it becomes for both instructors and students.

THE GENERAL COURSE DESIGN

Once the learning objectives have been established, it is possible to proceed with the general course design. The assumption that these two are sequential is probably naive. Most people seem to proceed with both simultaneously, adjusting each with every iteration. The end product of general course design is a topic sequence outline by major modules, along with the number of class and case sessions within each module. For example, Exhibit 3-5 gives a generalized course outline by headings.

New Course Design

New course design normally starts with an overview of the literature from which the instructor selects the topic areas most relevant for the course. If an instructor wishes

Exhibit 3-5
GENERALIZED COURSE OUTLINE

Course Title:

Target Student Group:

Educational Objectives:

Topic Outline	# of Sessions/ Classes	# of Cases
A. Introduction	3	1
B. Major Topic X – Subtopic 1 – Subtopic 2	7	4
C. Major Topic Y – Subtopic 1 – Subtopic 2 – Subtopic 3	7	3
D. Major Topic Z – Subtopic 1 – Subtopic 2	8	5
E. Conclusion/ Overview	2	1

to use cases in the course, discussion with practitioners in the field can provide valuable guidance, both to major topic areas and to cases which could be useful. Sam and Jack discussed their experiences in this regard.

Sam: I very quickly decided the investment textbooks didn't have much to do with the management of investments. I decided to go talk to people in the investment business. I quickly got an accurate picture of what problems leading practitioners — I mean high ranking practitioners who were thought to be at the leading edge — wrestled with, specific examples, possible cases, as well as recommendations of who else I ought to talk to about the business in general. Then I thought about the field itself and decided where I would put my emphasis in the course.

Jack: In designing a new course I must get excited, concerned, worried, enthusiastic, and very much involved with problems that I see in business, in the economy, and with managers who are struggling and attempting to cope.

For example, my sense is that the conceptual knowledge and the theoretical frameworks for better management of human resources are all up there in those books on the third shelf and a couple of thousand more in the library. So why doesn't it work? This is what I want to get at in a new course. What are some companies doing about it? What are some managers of human resources doing about it? What is their role, their opportunity? Many companies have set up V.P.'s of human resources. I know of one company in Chicago that has a very aggressive president. He said to me, "Look, we're a tough, rough, demanding company and it's working pretty well, but we're only getting about 30-40% commitment out of our people. I'm going out to hire a guy who I think could help us."

As it turned out, the new guy was a professor. My question is, how is this one man going to influence the lives of 55,000 employees in that company? So I start with those kinds of problems. I can't get excited, get involved in a course, and in a case, unless I feel that it is a truly vexing, difficult, challenging problem of real substance, real relevance. If I were in that case, it would be a very serious and important thing for me in my career, or typical at least of the things I must do well in my career.

Course Redesign

For most instructors, new course design is something which occurs relatively infrequently. The normal task is one of course redesign.

With much the same view as Jack implied, several people stressed the idea of trying to have an overall framework or model of what the course was about. Dave and Chris are representative of this view.

Dave: If you are putting together a course, you have to be very careful about what exactly you are trying to achieve. For example, in operations courses, the risk is that you're going to have 1001 topics, all of which are deadly important at one stage or another in a manager's day, week, or life. If you have no way of getting rid of those topics, you end up trying to teach a smorgasbord all the time, because nothing is unimportant enough to drop.

I've always hoped that you could have an overall framework about what a manager who has to deal with this particular topic has to think about, has to worry about, and how those things relate to each other and to other areas in the business. Ideally, I like to think that you can bring that framework in right at the beginning and teach it over and over again.

Chris: For a course that I teach, I have to have some sort of framework, concepts and tools that I'm trying to transmit to the students. I want to know what those are beforehand. I've got to have some way to hinge the cases together. This is important as I start thinking about the course. The more they fit and the more they build on each other, the more fun it is for me to teach. Taking twelve pieces of unrelated material is not a lot of fun. Taking twelve that fit, that add to each other and that constitute a whole, is important in order to do a good job.

Eric draws a useful distinction between major redesign and a tune-up or minor adjustment as an existing course changes over time.

> **Eric:** If you take course development activity and divide it between what I would call course maintenance and development, a mature course is probably 90% maintenance: a better case, a little better teaching note. But basically the structure, the big pieces are there and ready to go. For example, over the five years we've been working on our course, in year one we were 100% development. This fifth year, we're probably at 60% maintenance, 40% development. Next year, we'll probably be at maybe 70/30 or 80/20. In a couple of years, we'll be at steady state for a while.

The course design task may be a group process as underlined by Bill's experience. He discusses a first year marketing course design involving a number of instructors responsible for teaching the same course to different groups of students.

> **Bill:** With a group putting together a course, it means there is some negotiation because people come from different backgrounds or are at different stages of their teaching life. For instance, this last year I was in a group with Graham and Mel. Graham has lots of teaching experience. Mel has some, but is new to this school and our system. Graham was the coordinator and he put together the first half of the course by e-mail. I guess the key decision involved where to start in terms of content. Traditionally, marketing has tended to have an opening sequence about the scope of marketing followed by product policy. For a number of years I've started with the scope of marketing and then moved to advertising because I think it is simpler to cover at that stage in the year.

> I worry early in the year about students having a feeling of gestalt, or a feeling of completeness at the end of the class. I think it's important for them to have successes in terms of

getting through the material. We also talked about issues with respect to the commonality of content, commonality of grading, the kinds of things that are housekeeping, but that are important in terms of students perceiving that courses are roughly equivalent across sections.

In our course planning, the initial decisions were an interplay of sequence and finding common agreement about how many sessions in each of those sections. We also had some concern in terms of a natural break at Christmas.

In addition to the positioning of segments within a course, the process of rationalization and sequencing between courses is often an issue in course design, especially in required courses. For example, some concepts and tools, such as relevant costs and discounted cash flows, normally should be presented before applications and analysis are introduced in other courses. However, what does happen is sometimes different from what should happen.

Clint: We vary the sequence in the course to fit our needs as well as other course needs in the first year program. We accommodate as much as possible the program demands for material sequencing but we'll object violently if we think it destroys our course integrity.

Doug: We found that the integrity of our presentations was altered in the wrong direction when we tried to organize our stuff to dovetail with marketing and operations. So we virtually march to our own drummer.

Even with the topic outline in place and the number of classes assigned per topic, it is not safe to assume the final course outline will adhere to the general design. Once detailed planning has started, new information may become available resulting in further modifications. As is obvious, there is no easy answer to the selection of topics and the number of class sessions per topic. It appears to be a trial and error process which may well extend over a number of years. Continued questioning and vigilance is necessary to avoid the trap of complacency.

In the sequencing of major modules, prerequisite knowledge and skills form a theoretically logical basis. Where and when to use cases may be built on the same logic, but may also depend on what other instructors are doing in the program, the availability of suitable case material, the type of participant group and the instructor's personal preferences.

DETAILED PLANNING — SEQUENCING SESSIONS AND SELECTING MATERIALS

Detailed planning concerns itself with the sequence of individual sessions and the selection of materials. In teaching with cases, the instructor must be concerned about how to integrate theory and practice in making the appropriate sequencing decisions.

Integrating Theory and Practice in Course Design

One of the enduring academic questions in business education has been whether to integrate theory with practice. The strategy to remain totally at the theoretical, conceptual content end or totally at the application, process, case end has been debated by the respective adherents. However, the debate in many ways is sterile and non productive. Kim's concern is how to integrate, not whether to integrate.

Kim: Frankly, I think enough has been written about this idea that the issue should no longer be one of whether to integrate theory with practice but rather of how. Some interesting issues are around the question as to which comes first. Should students first get exposure through some cases to some practical problems so that they can identify a need for a theory or derive a theory? Or should the theory be given first and then the practical problems for application? Both have their inherent advantages and disadvantages attached. It's probably judicious to say that both approaches may have to be used in a successful course design.

Gordon and Gary talk about how they integrate content and process.

Gordon: I teach a relatively more theoretical, text-bookish course. I try to get across some facts, some history of what's happened in financial markets plus a modest amount of theory about why corporations or governments demand the financing they require and how the securities issued might get priced. There is a great temptation to give students all the theory and all the institutional facts before they ever do anything. Then, in every one of the cases they could do better later in the course. On the other hand, they develop some very bad behavior patterns and they get bored because they want to do something concrete like they do in other classes. The bad behavior is that when they've got to prepare for every other class because they're going to get called on, and asked to participate, and they're not going to get called on in my course as often, then they don't prepare for my classes. Students think it's safe not to prepare.

So partly to induce behavior and partly to get the course to be a priority for them, I schedule cases in early on so they can begin to learn from both cases and notes. We have maybe three days worth of theory, then do three or four cases that are related to the theory. Then we back off to introduce some more players and mix in more cases.

Gary: My students don't get the fun cases, that real learning, until they have gone through the methodology part. I structure the course this way. It's a two term course. The first term is all methodology with only one case at the end of each module, just to make sure they see the potential applications rather than think those are "Mickey Mouse" problems. Now during the second term, we have strictly cases. They come in an order that students don't recognize as a pedagogical sequence, although I have some underlying themes. I think this is one of the courses in the school that comes closest to real life. You have to take the dirty problems one at a time and to recognize what they are. And that's what I want to develop and that is my philosophy to course design.

For Al, the issue appears to depend upon the audience.

Al: In my experience the use of cases is quite different with degree versus non-degree students. With experienced people my best efforts are where I use the case as a problem, "Here is an issue, what are you going to do about it?" Executives have the experience to recognize that there is something worth discussing. They immediately consider that their time is going to be well spent because this is an issue relevant to their working life or at least having high potential to become relevant to their working life. So, initially, there is no problem getting them to discuss alternatives and what the best alternative is. I am also able to point to any relevant research studies which have been done to help them understand the problems. The sequence here for me as a teacher seems to be: a definite problem, analysis of problem, review of alternatives, and review of the literature which might illustrate the alternatives.

The sequence with the undergraduates very often is reversed. They may not see the problem or they may trivialize the alternatives that might be applicable. Then it's sometimes hard work to get them to work through the case. So often I anticipate this and start at the end and say, "The topic we need to talk about is measurement of divisional performance. The main contributions to the literature are these and the main points of the authors are these." I will then use a case to illustrate the publications and will tend to use the case in a descriptive form rather than in a decision form. More often than not I would precede cases with a review and discussion of theory. Then I'll take 2-3 cases to illustrate and discuss applications and problems using the theory.

Don and Brian talk about sequencing in their courses.

Don: Let me use regression as an illustration. For the first session, students basically read some textual material and I essentially lecture. The second class, they work through exercises not cases. The exercises are to reinforce the mechanical aspects of what goes on, to start pushing their understanding of the basic idea of regression a little bit further, and literally to make sure that everybody knows what is going on. The third class is a relatively easy case. When we get up to the 4th and 5th class, we move into really complex cases using the ideas.

Brian: When I go into a new module in organizational behavior, I like to start with one case that is highly frustrating to make students realize the need for tools. I like the next case to start providing some tools and if students don't do it themselves, I will push towards it. The third case should provide a really nice fit of accepted conceptual frameworks with the case. The fourth case should be an application case. The fifth case should then be a case that shows the conceptual framework which we developed does not handle all the circumstances.

Material Selection

Material selection and sequencing are interdependent decisions as the quotes show. In material selection the emphasis will be on the selection of cases, even though the existence of many other options is recognized. For example, lectures, reading discussions, business games, field trips, student presentations, videos, visitors to class, simulations, exercises, role plays, programmed instruction and projects are just some of the options which may be used with or without cases.

Case options include a wide variety across the Case Difficulty Cube spectrum as well as sequential or series cases, illustrative cases, historical cases and incident cases. Not all of these options are appropriate for all courses nor should one attempt to include them all in any one course design. However, based on the learning objectives and the major conceptual modules as laid out earlier, some combination of these various methods is entirely appropriate and, probably, desirable. A selected short list of these methods will be discussed in Chapter 8 under Case Use Variations. Only the two basic materials, cases and reading, will be covered here.

Case Selection

The selection of a case for a particular slot in a course module is a process which has been carefully considered by a variety of people. Phil starts off.

Phil: If the objectives are to get students to understand and be able to use some conceptual framework, then the professor's rule from day to day is to be sure he/she uses that framework. I am really concerned about the relatively small proportion of people who profess to be professors of management who are very explicit in the framework they use.

The beauty of cases is that they allow the professor to build up a sequence of experiences in which students can get involved. Then, as the professor, he/she can be using his/her knowledge of the conceptual framework in asking questions, using the board, and calling upon students for reactions. So the students gradually begin to get a working capacity to deal with the fundamentals. It sounds very simple but if an instructor hasn't had in his/her education any experiences that build confidence, then there is a tremendous act of faith required to jump into the case way of doing things, instead of hanging onto the security blanket of a textbook outline and hoping that the students will somehow get a working understanding of what the instructor is talking about. In addition to the act of faith, there's a tremendous investment of time and effort required to make this switch.

Earl and Rick discuss case selection and their personal decision rules.

Earl: My cases have to meet a number of criteria. One, I pick nothing but decision cases. The appraisal cases or the "ho-hum" cases are acceptable in the first year, but not in the second year. Two, cases have to be relatively short. Three, I believe every good case has got some simple numbers in it. Calculations tend to drag the students into the issues. Four, I like a mixture of straight decision cases and what I call "Easter egg" cases or "the rabbit jumps out of the hat" kind of cases. About 5 out of the 30 cases are these "Easter egg" cases where you pop the rabbit out of the hat near the end and you hammer the students really hard. This mixture adds a great deal of interest to the course. Five, I try to pick about 5 new cases a year. I try to schedule the new case next to an old case that I'm sure about its classroom outcome. I don't want students to walk away from any week saying it was a bummer. So, if I have a bummer on Monday, I try to counter with a strong one on Tuesday.

Rick: I have three categories when I select cases. Category one is your "chestnuts," and I think it's fair that everybody has some of their personal chestnuts in every package. Then there's obviously the cases that are the standard, "Hey, I know it'll always go kind of thing. It may not be my personal favorite case but it's a good safe case." Then thirdly, there are the risk cases. "I tried it and it didn't go well, shall I try it again?" This is one kind of risk case. Another kind of risk case is, "It's new, should I use it?" And

I think that in any package that people put forward, there should be some balance between the chestnuts and the risks.

Participants' Favorite Cases

The selection of cases suitable for a particular course goes well beyond the standard issue, industry, company criteria. Participants are aware that some cases are "good" and others "bad." Given that participant motivation and excitement are important components in the overall learning process, paying attention to factors which participants consider in assessing cases may help the overall acceptance of a course.

Qualities of cases which participants consider highly attractive can be tied into the Case Preparation Chart. A student's first reaction after the Short Cycle Process will significantly influence his or her energy level and excitement in preparing the case carefully.

Who. Participants are more interested if they can see themselves in the position of the decision maker shortly after they leave school or a reasonable time into the future. Likewise, if the organization itself is well known and respected and not disguised, it is also very positive. Cases that are located in a geographical area of the world where the students expect to be working are also preferred.

What. If the immediate issue and basic issues are seen as relevant to the course and to the participants' future experiences, then student reaction is positive. A second dimension here deals with the size and excitement over the issue. A failure to balance the books by $100 is not nearly as interesting as a failure to balance the books by several million dollars. A third dimension deals with the product or service involved. A case about marketing a new computer game is more exciting than marketing a liver pill for 90-year-olds. Cases that tell a story, have an interesting plot and fleshed-out characters are also appealing.

Why. Cases that have clear causes or trigger points for creating the issue or concerns are more interesting to students than those that have no apparent reason. A significant competitive move, an organizational crisis or a request from one's boss more readily capture participant involvement.

When. There are a number of issues surrounding the time and timing of the case. Generally speaking, the more recent the case the better. Cases set in time periods before participants were born may well fit the educational purpose beautifully, but they fail at the appreciation polls. Similarly, cases where there is a significant time pressure tend to be more exciting than those that require eventual resolution.

How. The Case Difficulty Cube position also impacts receptivity by students. Short cases tend to be preferred over longer cases and well organized cases tend to be preferred over cases poorly presented. A lot of extraneous information is disgusting. A lot of missing information makes it easy to give up. A lot of different formats may take too much time. Clearly, the (3, 3, 3) type of cases tend to be unpopular, unless enough time is provided to allow for proper preparation before class. On the other extreme, (1, 1, 1) types of cases can be perceived as trivial.

Each step in the Long Cycle Process will condition the continuing intensity of student involvement in case preparation.

The Importance/Urgency Matrix. Cases of importance to the organization are preferred. Urgency is somewhat less significant, particularly for important issues. Having appropriate time available in the case context to resolve an important issue properly is preferable over having to make shortcuts.

The Cause and Effect Diagram. Playing the commercial detective can be lots of fun provided sufficient clues are available in the case. Diagnosing what did not go according to plan and why is a fundamental role in management that students easily appreciate.

Alternative Generation. Better cases have significantly different and opposed alternatives. Innovative alternatives are preferable over standard suggestions.

Decision Criteria. Cases with both quantitative and qualitative criteria requiring careful prioritization sure beat those that just need to meet a financial target.

Alternative Assessment. Cases that require a decision, scary as it may be for some students, tend to be better than "talk about, don't decide" types of cases. Cases containing alternatives which can make a significant difference in the future tend to be preferable.

Action/Implementation Plan. Cases which contain sufficient information to put a realistic plan forward tend to be better.

Missing Information. Cases where not too much critical information is missing tend to be preferable.

Assumptions. Cases which permit participants to make realistic assumptions are preferable as are those which require little guessing as to what might be reasonable.

Samples, videos, and visitors to class add reality and importance and relevance. It should also be noted that an exciting instructor can make a big difference in the reception of a case.

A caution needs to be sounded. Not every class will react the same way to every case. Timing in the course or program, factors in the environment that affect preparation or the mood of the class may quickly alter perceptions. Changes in assignment questions and the way the class is taught can have a huge impact. Many participants who have experienced cases in their educational background can recall years later some of the outstanding case experiences they have had, quoting case and, occasionally, the instructor by name.

That certain cases are more memorable than others is no secret. Putting a course together with only memorable cases is probably not possible. Trying to include cases which fit educational objectives as well as impress participants is an integral part of effective material selection.

Case Selection and The Case Difficulty Cube

The Case Difficulty Cube may provide a rationale for case sequencing and selection within a course. For instructors who wish to bowl their students over at the beginning of the course, a (3, 3, 3) type of case, well beyond the capability of the class, may give an introduction to the course which says, "Right now you cannot handle this, but by the end of the course you will be able to." Thus, the same case can serve as an introduction and conclusion to the course and participants can assess their own progress. Other instructors believe that the case challenge and difficulty has to match the capability of the participants. They might start a course with a (2, 1, 1) case and gradually increase the difficulty level across the three dimensions, if that is part of the course objectives. Thus, for the cases chosen a potential sequence might be as shown in Exhibit 3-6.

Exhibit 3-6
A COURSE OUTLINE RANKING CASES BY
THEIR CASE DIFFICULTY CUBE POSITION

Class	Case	Class	Case
1	2, 1, 1	8	2, 3, 2
2	2, 2, 1	9	3, 1, 1
3	2, 1, 2	10	3, 2, 1
4	1, 2, 2	11	3, 3, 1
5	2, 2, 2	12	3, 3, 2
6	1, 3, 1	13	3, 3, 3
7	2, 3, 1		

Depending on the instructor's objectives, there are many potential combinations. Certain patterns may be repeated at various times of the course for review and reinforcement. A total measure of difficulty may be established by using the arithmetic sum of the three dimensions. A total of 3 to 6, for example, ranges from easy at 3 to medium at 6. From 7 to 9, the case would be on the upper end of the scale with a (3, 3, 3) case being clearly very difficult.

Additional Reading/Data Gathering

Additional reading and data gathering in a course which uses cases need to be selected and planned with the same care as the cases and other materials. Since most instructors are familiar with the selection and specification of reading materials, the few comments here are directly related to the connection with cases.

Course readings are often specifically relevant in terms of the theoretical objectives of the course. Sometimes it is possible to assign specific readings which fit perfectly with the immediate and/or basic issues in the case. A good example would be a case where the key issue deals with the application of the learning curve to a pricing or scheduling issue and the reading covers the theoretical aspects of the learning curve or manufacturing progress function. Such a perfect fit is not always possible, however, and additional readings may be useful from a course, but not a specific case perspective. Whenever readings are assigned along with cases, the amount of reading time needs to be added to the expected case preparation time. There is always a concern that if the total time required exceeds the participants' willingness or ability to devote to it, then the trade-offs — skip the reading or skip the case preparation — become counterproductive. Separating readings into required and optional may be one way of distinguishing the relevance and importance of readings from the instructor's perspective.

Cases which require additional data gathering from the Internet or other sources permit a learning dimension generally not available with most standard cases. To be able to do original research or data gathering is in itself a worthwhile educational objective. The same caution regarding participant time applies, however.

DEFINING THE PERFORMANCE
EVALUATION MEASURES

The fourth common element in course planning deals with defining the performance evaluation measures. If cases are used in the course, what weight will case work carry as part of the overall course grade and how will case performance be measured? In this chapter we will discuss the definition of performance measures related to the use of cases. In Chapters 6 and 7 the way instructors go about evaluating case performance and how they provide feedback will be the key topics. In Chapter 5 of *Learning With Cases* effective and ineffective participation are discussed and a number of examples for participants to consider are provided.

Every course plan and syllabus needs to indicate how participants will be graded, whether cases are used or not. On the assumption that at least some recognition will be given to case work, the first question deals with the percentage of total course grade devoted to cases. The most common case activities which are assigned grades are class participation, case presentation, case reports and case exams.

Weighting Schemes

It is not surprising that considerable variation exists on the course weights assigned to case related work. Generally, the fewer cases used in the course, the lower the weighting of case related work is to other aspects of course evaluation. Some instructors feel strongly that every course component needs to have a grade attached to it to motivate participants to do the work. Other instructors are of the opinion that such a strong grading focus stands in the way of effective learning. They argue that, provided the instructor can explain the educational value of various course components, grading should be downplayed. Both camps have ardent followers who can prove their point with personal experiences. Thus, it appears that strength of conviction as to which path is right is a greater factor in successful application than either path itself.

It does seem reasonable that in a course composed a hundred percent of cases, the course grade should be solely based on case work. Even here, how much of the course grade should be based on class participation as opposed to the final case exam still needs to be resolved. Given that most case courses have a case use ratio between 1 and 99%, it is not unreasonable to have a variety of weightings, partially based on the course objectives, case frequency in the course, and the role cases play in the course.

The second aspect of case grade weighting concerns the division between class participation and written work. Class participation includes the normal large group or class discussion role as well as presentations. Written work includes hand-ins, case reports and case exams. The following comments from five instructors show that each has his or her own rationale for assigning weight to participation compared to written work.

Leanna: I only use participation at the margin. I will use participation to help move my performance assessment of written work to the next level; i.e., from a C+ to a B- or even from a B- to a B+. But I do not use participation to down-grade my assessment of written work.

Others say the weights are 50-50 and in Kim's case, 60% is on participation and 40% on written work.

Brad: Fifty percent of the evaluation in my course is on an examination or paper. The other 50% is a subjective evaluation of the student's participation in class.

Bert: I tell my students they are dumb if they rely upon their examination grade to pull up a class grade because they have 30 times to impress me in class and only one time in an exam. So if you're ready to go 100% on 6-7 classes, you don't have the pressure upon you in an exam. Because if they have a C in participation and a B- on the exam, they get a C. That's the way I have it: 50-50 on class grade and exam grade and if the class grade is next to but lower or higher than the exam grade they get the class grade for the course. It goes both ways. I favor the class.

THE FIRST FEW CLASSES

In any course using a reasonable number of cases with participants who have little or no case experience, it is important to design the first few classes to introduce both the course and the case method. One effective way is to use a small, one-page case in the very first class, hand it out at the beginning of the class and go through the Three Stage Learning Process right in class. It is useful for the instructor to explain some of the key points regarding each stage before having the participants do each stage. For example, the instructor can reinforce the importance of taking ownership of the position of the decision maker in the case before the participants do individual preparation. Small group guidelines can be explained before the small group discussions start. Common understandings on large group discussion can be reviewed before the third stage. Further concerns for the first class may deal with: (1) introductions, seating arrangements, name cards, personal background sheets, the class photo; (2) the course plan, the number of cases and why they will be used, when and how; and (3) the assignments for the next few classes in detail.

Some instructors prefer to leave the course syllabus to the second or a later class, focusing primarily on establishing class norms regarding case use and discussion in the first few classes. The key course planning decision for the first few classes is how much course and class time to devote to the case learning process versus the course content. Some instructors make comments like, "For as far as course content goes, I see the first few classes as throw-aways." Others still manage to hold on to some course content by using the early classes to teach some basic simple building blocks, while simultaneously covering the participative aspects of the learning process.

Given the importance of starting off on the right foot, it is certainly appropriate to plan opening classes carefully. Class participants will very quickly perceive norms like: Is the instructor fair? Does the instructor appear to know what he or she is doing? Is everyone expected to participate? What kind of comment is acceptable or unacceptable?

In our experience, the text *Learning With Cases* can be a valuable aid for participants to get up to speed quickly on the use of cases. In a three class module it is possible to introduce the Three Stage Learning Process and Case Difficulty Cube in the first class, the Short and Long Cycle Processes and Case Preparation Chart in the second class and class participation in the third class, along with a one-page case in the first class, a three-page case in the second, and a five to six-page case in the third class.

COMMUNICATING THE COURSE PLAN

Some instructors believe that a detailed course outline is necessary to help students understand the particular area of study and its scope. A syllabus can provide a reference point by showing relationships within the course as a whole. On the other hand, some instructors feel that a course outline is too much of a crutch. They fear students are guided so much that their views may become too narrow and not seek to develop their own frameworks and understanding.

Barney: For second year courses, I am a little more explicit about laying out what we are doing. I'm thinking in particular of my marketing planning course and I've gone to the point in that course of setting out daily statements of objectives for the class, stating them in terms of behavioral objectives. It says the objective of this class is that students will be able to do the following things: make this analysis, make those relationships, be able to develop a marketing plan. I've stated the case, the reading, the assignment, maybe some linkage statements, such as: this is connected to that; or this is a follow-up on the last three classes; or this summarizes or this is the beginning of a new section.

I'm not sure if this is right or not. I think it becomes a crutch that allows the sore leg to remain sore, rather than forcing people to walk on it and get it stronger. I suppose when I did it, it was as much for my own purposes, for my own sake, to keep my own thinking straight. Having done it for my own purposes, I might as well pass it around, because students are clamoring for more structure, as a rule. They want an easier way to learn. As soon as we succumb to that clamoring, we give them an easier way through the course but not an easier way to learn. I suppose it's OK to hand out a one page course description; I'm not really sure how detailed it should be. I lean on the side that we shouldn't do it, although I have done it in great depth at times myself.

Les: I use my course syllabus for a very explicit purpose. For me, it forms the basis upon which the students and I develop our contract for the course: "Here's what you can expect of me and here's what I expect of you."

In my required introductory operations course I assign the syllabus for the second or third class of the term. This outline contains sections regarding:

- What the course is trying to achieve
- How it will be taught
- How performance will be measured
- Standards for satisfactory development
- How final grades will be determined
- The course plan by major modules and session sequence

I ask my students to read it carefully and jot down any concerns or queries they may have. In class I literally read parts of the syllabus to underscore important elements such as performance requirements, evaluation, major dates such as exams and reports, and major milestones within the course plan.

In my second year elective courses, I use the syllabus a little differently. The objective here is to provide the students who may be shopping with as much information and understanding about the course requirements and scope as possible. I want their decision as to whether or not to take the course to be based on informed judgement rather than hopes and wishes.

So on the first day of class, the first thing I do after writing my name and the course name on the board is to pass out the syllabus. This syllabus typically contains statements regarding:

- my name, office and phone number, and assistant's name
- target students
- educational objectives
- course content and organization
- textbook(s)
- report/project assignment and due date
- performance evaluation
- class schedule session by session including assignments for readings and cases

I spend the rest of the session emphasizing specific aspects of the syllabus; asking students to make notes in the margins, having them write key dates in their personal calendars and trying to clearly establish what the expectations are. I finish this first session by handing out the first case for them to sample and asking them to re-read the syllabus to be sure they understand the rules and parameters for the course. If they decide to take the course, I want them to be in with both feet. I don't want any fringe players.

CONCLUSION

The course planning process is a difficult one for many. Most instructors would like to be able to accomplish more than they realize they can, so that what not to include is as much a decision as what to include. There are no easy solutions available and the course design task appears to be iterative through objectives, general and detailed planning, to material selection and back again. Teachers have been able to develop their own approaches and decision rules for these tasks, many of which appear to have merit. Trade-offs are inevitable in this kind of process and once teaching groups get involved, negotiation may have to be used to reach a common agreement. For many, a written document, the course plan or syllabus, is the final product of this process which normally, but not always, is distributed to students.

Having completed the design task, the instructor can now turn to the preparation for class.

CHAPTER FOUR

preparation for class

Proper preparation, both by instructors and participants, is required to make case teaching and learning effective.

In terms of certain basic minimum requirements, such as becoming thoroughly familiar with the case content, analyzing and making judgements regarding case information, participants and instructors have a common individual preparation task. Beyond this common level their respective tasks change. Students in some schools often have two or three such preparations per day, four or five days per week. Teachers seldom face such a large number of preparations. However, instructors must go well beyond the student level of preparation for the case and must prepare strategies and plans for conducting the class.

The student preparation task has been well covered in Chapter 3 of *Learning with Cases*. Instructors will find this information not only applicable as a key part of their own preparation, but also helpful in counseling students, since students generally need some coaching in order to develop case analysis skills.

After addressing purpose and time considerations, this chapter will focus on the additional aspects of instructor preparation as it relates to case content. It will then shift to the priority and execution aspects of preparation, including teaching notes, student assignments, time plan, board plan, call lists, teaching aids and teaching meetings.

It will conclude with the Case Teaching Plan , a comprehensive tool to guide instructors in the classroom.

WHY PREPARE

It should be obvious to all that preparation is a prerequisite to conducting an effective class and that no further reasons are necessary. Afsaneh Nahavandi, of the Arizona State University West School of Management, brings another dimension, however, as she refers to her students.

> My preparation also sends a very strong and clear message to my students. If I do it, they have to do it. I can only expect them to do what I do. Being prepared means that I am fulfilling a big part of my responsibility to my class; expecting them to do the same is, therefore, reasonable and appropriate (202).

WHEN TO PREPARE

The instructor's preparation is a continuation of a process that started with course planning wherein case selection and sequence were established. The time span has now shortened and the instructor must prepare for the class scheduled in the course plan.

Some instructors prefer to leave this preparation to the day before the actual class is taught or even the same day; others think more lead time is necessary.

> **Don:** I usually prepare for class the day before I teach. This has become a personal routine and I plan my schedule accordingly. After some experimentation, I found that I can keep the case facts clearer in my head if I don't prepare too far ahead. Otherwise, I have to prepare twice.

> **Chris:** In our area we all teach the same case on the same day to different groups. We found that an instructor group

planning meeting at 7:30 a.m. on that day is the way to make sure everybody is fully prepared and keenly interested in what everyone else has to say.

Dave: I would be too nervous leaving preparation to the last minute. Emergencies may arise, and then I would be caught. Therefore, I start my preparation at least two or three days before class and use a 15 minute refresher just before class to concentrate on the vitals. My assistant knows to keep that time just before class absolutely clear. I will not see anybody and take no calls, so that I can really concentrate on that last review.

HOW LONG DOES IT TAKE TO PREPARE

The instructor new to case teaching is sometimes surprised to learn of the extensive time required for a case class preparation. A simple rule of thumb for the experienced instructor is that it takes four times as long to prepare as the class length. For example, an hour long class would take four hours for the instructor to prepare. A new instructor may significantly exceed this preparation time. Of course, time required to prepare will also depend on the length and complexity of the case; whether a teaching note exists already or needs to be developed; or whether the instructor has taught the case before or not.

HOW TO PREPARE

Instructors engage in a variety of activities associated with their preparation.

Don: Ideally, in my preparation of a case, I read it through rather carefully, underlining, going over it, looking for the salient issues. I don't necessarily do much analysis the first time.

Then I read it through a second time, this time doing the individual pieces of analysis.

Thirdly, I like to pick out what is vital or unique in the case and what is in the case that, if I don't get to it, I can adequately emphasize in other materials.

Fourthly, I try to think through what, in the ideal world, would be the order in which I would like those components of analysis to arise and be discussed in the class.

Fifthly, I think I arrive at a judgment about whether any one sequence is vital or whether I can tolerate a variety of sequences. If any one sequence is vital because of immense interdependency among the case analysis sections, then I'm likely to structure the class. Otherwise, I'm likely to start by saying, "What do you think of this situation?"

Sixthly, if the case is of the second nature, the question I have is how can I help develop logical sequences of analysis regardless of where students choose to start.

I also like to make an assessment as to whether the discussion will be one-sided or whether there will be real controversy. If it's one-sided, I may look for ways to play the devil's advocate. Or I may look for aspects of the case that can get greater ventilation in view of the absence of controversy on some of the main issues.

Finally, I would think about what students are likely to be able to contribute to this particular case because of skills or backgrounds. For this, I have to use my class cards and my personal knowledge of the students. I may or may not want to emphasize or call on those students given my perception of the complexity of the case. If the case is exceptionally complex, I better get my guns out early or else we'll never get to the heart of the case. If it's not exceptionally complex, I can tolerate a greater variety of participation.

After all of this preparation is complete, I put it in the context of, "Do I have some wall flowers who need to be brought out or some loud mouths who need to be ignored?"

I've paraphrased all of these remarks with the word "ideally" because I'm not sure I have the time to do this for every case discussion.

Don's statement provides an excellent overview as well as a way to structure the instructor's preparation task. Analysis shows that these preparatory steps may be divided into three major categories: content, priority, and execution focused. Don's first two steps are content focused. These steps parallel the normal student analysis, concentrating on case content and the assigned readings. Don's third step starts to establish a priority focus. His remaining steps relate closely to what we label the execution focus. The experiences of others will be presented to reinforce and amplify Don's basic preparation strategy.

The Content Focus

Instructor preparation starts at the same point as student preparation and continues with more rigor through exactly the same steps outlined in the approaches for student individual analysis in Chapter 3 of *Learning with Cases.* Just like students, instructors need to go through the Short and Long Cycle Processes of case preparation. For this reason, only a few additional comments will be presented here. Different from students who need to know where the information can be found in the case, instructors must be more familiar with the key facts. Knowing the case facts and doing a thorough analysis of the information is basic for content focused preparation.

Dave: The first aspect about case preparation is a thorough and intimate knowledge of the case itself. You really shouldn't have to paw around looking up key statistics during the class. You should have those as close to your fingertips as you can. I would suggest that you have some competence in looking through exhibits to find a number or whatever so that you don't disturb the pace of the class. And if you like to show off a bit, it doesn't hurt to know what page they are on! It's this kind of preparation that helps a lot. The professor needs so much flexibility in the classroom that the more familiarity he or she has with case facts, the better off he or she is.

Chris: Each day I make sure that I know the case backwards and forwards. I don't assume just because I've taught it before that those facts are in my grasp because this is when I usually make mistakes. I mean, you really have to prepare that case each time! There are maybe four or five cases that I could teach now without much preparation. But this is after teaching them ten times. I always have to go back and understand, know the names of the characters and their positions. I've got to know the numbers and what exhibits those numbers are in.

Sam: I always expect that I know more about the case than the students do, either because I've written it or I've studied it. This is the first thing.

Secondly, I try to know a lot more than what is in the case about that situation. I try to know a lot about the company, about the industry. I like to know why the case was written and why it was written the way it was. Almost with every case, material is editorially selected. It's a piece of theater that has been focused in a particular way. Sometimes I'll introduce it in class with why it's focused the way it is.

Newspapers, magazine articles and peer conversations are some of the obvious sources of additional information. A growing number of discussion groups exists on the Internet about case teaching in the area of business administration as well as in other disciplines where the use of cases is gaining popularity. For example, Harvard's Case Teaching Network discussion group provides a forum for sharing ideas, suggestions and comments about case teaching in management and CaseNet is a World Wide

Web site for teachers interested in the use of the case method in International Affairs. The Internet also provides information about various national networks or associations such as WACRA, the World Association for Case Method Research & Application, or NACRA, the North American Case Research Association.

Teaching Notes. Other sources of information of great interest to many instructors are teaching notes. These notes may contain material which may aid in all three areas of instructor preparation.

Teaching or instructor's notes are often available from different sources. Teaching notes normally accompany published case textbooks. Publishers would have difficulty selling case texts without them! Other sources include case clearing centers, colleagues and one's own files. The intent behind the teaching note is to help an instructor in preparing for class. Normal topics include identification of the case issues, an identification of the educational objectives, a suggested student assignment, suggested questions which could be asked during the class discussion, and comments regarding the analysis and solution. (See Exhibit 4-1.) The quality of teaching notes will vary considerably from author to author. Particularly useful comments may relate to what actually happened in class with this material. Since a teaching note has been written within the context of a particular course, each instructor has to ask whether these same conditions pertain to the course under consideration. A straight transplant of a case from one environment and one course to another environment and another course may not produce the desired results. The instructor must ask , "Will this case work for me?" A teaching note may provide some valuable clues to help answer this question. In the end, every instructor must develop his or her own teaching note.

Exhibit 4-1
POTENTIAL TEACHING NOTE HEADINGS

1. Case Title

2. Brief Synopsis of the Case

3. Immediate Issue(s) *(the case decision maker's key concerns)*

4. Basic Issues(s) *(the instructor's reasons for using the case in the course)*

5. Teaching Objectives

6. Suggested Student Assignment

7. Suggested Additional Reading/Data Gathering

8. Possible Teaching Aids *(such as samples, advertising material, photos, articles, videos, computer programs, CD ROMs, visitors to class)*

9. Discussion Questions for Use in Class *(to use if the discussion dies or a change of direction is desirable.)*

10. Case Analysis *(the answers to the suggested student assignment questions)*

11. Additional Points to Raise *(beyond the student assignment questions; may include what actually happened)*

12. Suggested Time Plan *(how total class time might be divided)*

13. Teaching Suggestions

14. Suggested Board Plan

15. Case Teaching Plan *(the instructor's supplement to the Case Preparation Chart)*

Some instructors have misgivings about teaching notes.

Clint: I find most teaching notes worthless most of the time. Most people who write teaching notes do a pretty good job of not putting in the necessary details. This is probably the right thing to do since a lazy instructor will try to teach the case without preparing it. Consequently, he or she really won't understand it.

Rick: I think there's a tendency, certainly with your "old chestnuts," to over-rely on your teaching notes. The first three years I taught, I maintained zero teaching notes. I guess it was because of being afraid of falling into bad habits. I developed teaching notes for every class and then tore them up at the end of the class. If I ever used that case again, I would have to start at base one. I sure don't do that today! But I'm not so sure that it isn't a good process to force yourself to go through in the early stages. I think it's important that everybody get stuck in a class once, through poor preparation or using somebody else's teaching notes, to find out that their numbers won't stand up under a junior high school student's examination. From then on you'll never accept anybody else's numbers. I guess you have got to go through that once and get egg on your face.

On the other hand, others believe teaching notes are indispensable.

Mark: If you're dealing with a required course where there may be multiple sections and several teachers, formal teaching notes are very useful to aid instructors to prepare for class. It is much easier to prepare for class if you're part of a teaching group where big teaching files exist.

The Priority Focus

Most instructors also engage in preparatory activities which have a priority focus. These activities include a review of course objectives, case objectives, and plans for this particular class within the sequence of all classes. Why is it so important to have this class and this case within this class? The implication of priority planning is that, given time in class as a scarce resource, priority topics will receive preference over others. In teaching with cases, priorities may lie with making sure that certain concepts are fully understood, an objective that parallels many other forms of teaching. Peculiar to cases may be the priorities dealing with problem identification and analysis, alternative generation, decision making, implementation planning, sorting or specification of information and proper application of relevant theory to practice. In the first few classes in a case course, priority may well lie with getting the class familiar with the discussion process and the instructor's expectations regarding proper student preparation and participation in class. Priorities in case teaching are, therefore, multidimensional, and are both process and content based.

> **Steve:** I think in the first year of our program, we are really trying to teach process learning more than anything else. We teach a certain amount of content but the key is really that mental process to get students to think, "What is the problem? Start with defining the problem, because if you do not define the problem, you cannot analyze it." I often get the impression and I noticed this year, even in March, that students want to jump in to the middle of the solution without ever really stating what the problem is. It's like being a plumber. If you take the wrong tool, you can't fix the pipes. So you have to know what the problem is in order to select the tool. A lot of students don't see it. We instructors like to get in there and show how smart we are. What we should be trying to do is help them develop a disciplined mental approach to an unstructured problem.

> **Jack:** I want every class to be like a great short story. The great short story writer is able to condense in a few thousand words a whole lot of vague things and a variety of feelings in a compressed, compact way. It's also theater like

a great production. I don't mean   dramatics, but I mean when students come to class at an operating level of 10 and go out at 100, something has happened. They go out saying, "Wow, that was something." So every class becomes an experience with a capital "E." I say that I want that to happen. I don't mean to imply that it always does. The first thing is simply wanting it to happen. But then in my selection of cases, my analysis of the cases, and putting myself in the shoes of the students trying to get a sense of what they're thinking, there need to be several levels of breakthroughs.

1. Level one breakthrough involves the very routine, but very important calculations, issues and so forth.

2. Level two breakthrough is when the implications of the data at first seem to be coming to the same conclusions. But when you stop to think about it, they lead you to quite opposite conclusions. Pow! When you see that you say, "Something is fishy here." That can lead to the question of, "What is going on here anyway?"

3. You move then to level three breakthrough. Where did the data in the case come from? In the case I'm thinking of, the data ends up almost totally useless. Then you suddenly realize that the manager in the case, although it looks beautifully controlled and planned, really has nothing to work with.

4. At level four breakthrough, you begin to introduce a very human element. How did this happen to this guy? What's he going to do?

5. Finally, you get a major breakthrough when it leads students to think about something they've never thought about before.

In any event, the students usually come in with a level one breakthrough. A few of the brighter ones have got some hunches about level two and maybe level three. But they realize when they leave that classroom that if they'd been in that case, they would have blown it. They would have failed utterly and completely. And that's how this manager failed. When they see that, they go out of class shaking their heads and saying, "Oh, brother, managing is hard."

Now, too many courses and too many schools and too many people teach management as easy. "If you just use this technique or that one; just do it by the book, it will work." The fact is it won't. So I want students going out of a classroom feeling very differently than when they came in, a little ashamed of themselves in a way, or thinking, "I'm not going to get caught on that one again." They go out with enormous respect for the course, for the school, and for managers and with the sense that, "I want to be good at that."

So there's the theater, the short story, the experience. The way you go out of a great movie stumbling up the aisle back in your own world saying, "Fantastic!" That's what a great class should be. That's what a great course should be. That's the goal.

Dave: Just as important and maybe more important than case content preparation is that you should know, in terms of the behavioral, conceptual, and analytical teaching objectives, what it is you're going after in the class. I think a young instructor's problem is that he or she has worked out an analysis of the case from a scientific point of view that is totally exhaustive, mutually exclusive, and gives a clear and penetrating breakdown; and that he or she wants to make sure the class gets there. If you start trying to force students into your assumptions and your framework, you end up with a "dog and pony show" sooner or later.

Personally, I don't think it is so important that you get to that level of penetration because if you force that level of analysis, then you're trying to teach analysis of numbers specifically. You end up being perceived by the class as an operations research specialist and the name of the game is achieving the right numerical answer.

The name of the game in my class is having an identification with the manager or decision maker in the situation, and finding what the problem is and what the options are. In terms of that decision, what approach or set of attitudes towards the problem in the case will lead him or her to the solution so that the activities with the highest pay-off can be recognized. Very often, it's getting the right question; that is, if you can conceive of the situation properly along with a global framework of policy, strategy and tactics, you will be able to classify it as this or that kind of problem and then do the numbers if necessary.

Most instructors probably combine the priority focus activities with those concentrating on execution, resulting in a class plan. Even though a theoretical argument can be advanced for treating content, priority and execution as three distinct chronological phases in instructor preparation, in reality these are normally intermixed, as the quotes show.

The actual sequence of these activities is probably less important than their inclusion. A step-by-step iterative process may well focus attention on objectives first, case content second, and execution next, only to go back to content next, and then to one of the others again, and so on. For most instructors, the preparation before class is a trial and error process, trying to find an approach that works well.

The Execution Focus

The third set of preparatory activities for the instructor relates to execution. The focus here is on the class plan. What do I expect to happen in class? How can I make it happen? Who should contribute in class? What is the best order for the discussion, decision first and then analysis? Vice versa? How much time is necessary for discussion of the various case components? Should I leave the class unstructured? What teaching aids are available that I could bring to class? The responses to questions of this type are vital to effective instructor preparation.

The class plan reflects the content and priority work done and makes these explicit in terms of a student assignment, a time plan, a board plan and a call list all summarized on the Case Teaching Plan. Contingencies may be allowed for in the plan. Many instructors commit these class plans to paper, others prefer to keep them in their heads. Not all plans contain the same elements nor the same details. The reality is, however, that every instructor will have to be ready to deal with issues like: which person is going to speak, when and about what?

One of the tasks facing the instructor may be to prepare a student assignment for the following class. The current class under preparation will also have a student assignment given out previously. Thus designing student assignments is part of the execution task although, for some instructors, if assignments are given out at the beginning of a course, they may not be a major daily concern.

Student Assignments. In case teaching, student assignments are normally used to identify the case scheduled for a particular class, and, possibly, specific questions related to that case. Additional readings may also be called for in the same assignment. When such assignments are communicated to students and what form they take vary in practice.

Typically, the instructor assigns one case per class per course. Sometimes if the case falls in the 3, 3, 3 level of difficulty, it may be assigned over two or three class periods. Often the assignment for the next class is given in the preceding class. Frequently, however, assignment sheets are distributed at the beginning of the course or at intervals during the term; when these are used, the assignment given in class is likely to be very brief.

Normally, student assignments will reflect the expectations of the instructor and the kinds of learning goals that have been established. Assignment questions should be consistent with the course objectives and may be customized for each class. They may be used to start class discussion or to introduce key concepts.

Chris likes varied assignments.

Chris: The assignment questions I normally use vary during my course. In the beginning, they will be fairly specific and directed towards the right kind of analysis and ways to uncover the problems in the case. In the middle part of the course, the assignment questions may be closer to what I think are the five or six major topics of the case. Towards the end of the course, assignments will be more like, "If you were in the position of the decision maker, what would you do?"

Numerous variations can be used in preparing assignments. Mark has an interesting twist.

Mark: For a special three or four class section of my finance course which is very quantitative, I have a little gimmick. I give each student the assignment sheet and a sealed envelope. The students first try to answer the first part of the assignment and when they think they have an answer to the question, then they open the envelope. The envelope will do some of their homework for them because these are long, complicated cases, and allows them to proceed and finish the assignment more quickly then if they had to do it without a crutch. That has worked very well. I really get two preparations out of them. They first try to structure the problem and figure out how to set it up. They are then able to compare their approach with mine. I do most of the analysis and they have a little bit to do at the end to get some resolution on the issue. Students think it's fun. It's like a game.

Ian presents further variations that he has used with executive program students.

Ian: Another thing we do in executive programs, that we don't do in our degree programs, is that we will manipulate a heavy or medium case through the assignment to make it a little lighter so executives can prepare it in a reasonable length of time. For example, we might give the executive five assignment questions which can be used for guidance. The idea is not necessarily to sit down and answer each of the questions, but to help move preparation along faster. Another thing we might do to lighten the executives' load is to give some of the numbers predigested. In the assignment sheet we give some of the numbers worked out. For example, we do two-thirds of the numbers and let them do the rest, or we do three columns of numbers and leave the fourth one which requires a little massaging of the first three columns. Another thing we'll do for the executives, especially in the short programs, is to give them a very complete assignment sheet. It has the purpose and objective of the class, as well as the assignment.

There seems to be a continuing theme within these comments on assignments. Assignments are used to bridge instructor case analysis and student case analysis, and to bridge instructor expectations for class discussion and student learning progress.

The standard three assignment questions which can be asked for almost all cases are:

1. If you were in the position of... (the decision maker) in the case, what would be your analysis of... (this decision, problem, issue, challenge or opportunity)?

2. What decision would you take and why?

3. What would be your action/implementation plan?

The kind of assignment given with a case can significantly influence the student's preparation and the subsequent class. Take, for example, a case describing a merger proposal. The following assignment questions could substantially change the use of this case.

1. If you were the president of the target company, would you accept the merger proposal?

2. What is your prediction of the potential future market share and sales volume for the merged company?

3. Prepare a communication plan for the major stakeholders in the target company on the assumption that: (a) you intend to accept the merger proposal; (b) you intend to reject the merger proposal.

4. If these two organizations merged, what synergies might be expected and what would be your estimate of total potential savings?

5. Try to find out as much as possible from public sources what led to this merger proposal.

Clearly, these assignment questions may not all be used in the same course. Variation in case assignments allows the same case to be used for a variety of purposes and courses.

The Time Plan. Some instructors consider it useful to prepare a detailed time plan for each class, identifying not only how much time should be assigned to various activities in class, but also, possibly, the topic sequence which shall be followed during that time.

Chris: I think about what I'd like to see happen. I divide the class into 15-20 minute intervals. I want to know what it is that ought to be happening in those intervals. These are major topics we'll be covering. This is just to ensure that I don't get too bogged down in any one point and not get to points 3, 4, and 5 that I think are important. Under each of these, I'll think about some probing questions that I'll want to ask. Too much structure gets in the way of the students. But no structure at all, they find frustrating. So it's a fine balance between when structure is needed and when it's not. I try hard to hit that balance. For me, it's the freedom to allow people to roam within 15 minute blocks but not to roam for an hour. So I plan out sections of the class, but I don't say that within a section, we're going from point A to B to C. This is up to the student.

Steve: I tend to develop a time sequence. Maybe the first 5-10 minutes I want to make sure we get the problem defined or lay out some of the facts. I have points along the way or benchmarks that tell me how far I am into the class and where I want to get to. I have to keep an eye on the clock so that I don't end up running far over on one spot. I try and lay out a time sequence assigning so much time there and so much time here and so on. It doesn't always work, but it's a guideline.

Eric: I teach the class in a goal-oriented way. I don't give a damn about the clock. That is, I don't teach to fill an hour and 20 minutes. I used to have a very careful time sequence written out on my teaching plans; question 1 - 15 minutes, question 3 - 5 1/2, minutes. I found that unsatisfying because I got too worried about where I was in my time sequence and not enough listening to the class. So now I have a series of questions that I want to cover and some notion of where I'd like to end up. But I don't worry about whether I end up there or not. I work through covering the content of each part of my building of the analysis.

The Board Plan. Every instructor needs to come to terms with his or her recording role in class. "Do I include in my role the job of 'class discussion secretary'?" If the answer is no, then it is safe to assume that no record of class comments will be made. We have encountered numerous attempts by instructors to have a scribe record on the board the comments of various class members. Invariably, the scribe falls behind or fails to record what the instructor would like to see on the board. If the scribe is another faculty member or an assistant, resource costs increase significantly. If the scribe is a student volunteer or conscript, that individual loses the opportunity to participate in the class discussion. For these reasons instructors normally include the recording task within their teaching role.

Most instructors believe it is helpful, at least for themselves, and normally as well for their participants, to maintain a visual record of key points made during the class. There are some cases, particularly in the organizational area, where few points need to be visually recorded. The disadvantages of recording are: 1) it slows down the discussion; and 2) it is not possible to record everything. Therefore, the instructor has to be selective and "reward" some students by recognizing their contribution while ignoring others. The positive aspects of recording is that a combination of audio and visual reinforcement provides a common reference and easier recall throughout the discussion. Given that most instructors like to record comments made during class, the board plan becomes a potential preparation issue.

Some instructors like to plan ahead what they will record on the board. The location of certain comments may be predetermined, such as analysis on the left and recommendations on the right. Some teachers will even predetermine the color of chalk or marker which will be used.

Ross: I set a precise plan and structure for the case discussion. I believe in a lot of board space, and I believe in a logical progression through the case, and I like to write out from left to right on the board through the case. I must have a visual feel of what will be on the board.

Paul: I would never think about teaching a case without a complete set of notes. My notes start with a summary of case facts, organized very often in the way I'll write things on the board. My notes contain board plans where things will go as they are developed in class.

Barney: My notes on a new case will even go to the point of writing down: On board one, I will have this; and on board two, I will have that; and I'll slide that board across and that will reveal this; and at the end, I can pull the board back and we're back to the starting point. In that sense, I guess that's very directive. If there is a very important issue in the case that the students are not bringing up on their own accord, they will see a blank space on the board and wonder what should be there. That's maybe going a little bit too far, but at times that has happened. I remember one instance where the discussion was beautifully organized, as I had planned it. However, the students had totally omitted one factor that I thought was really the crucial issue in the case. And there was a big empty space on the board. After we had gone pretty well all the way through, I said, "Well, what do you think? Do you think we really understand this situation?" One of the students said, "Obviously we don't with that great big space on the board." They hummed and hawed and finally filled it in.

Robert's use of electronic projection requires extensive planning.

Robert: In my class preparation, I have allotted so much time to each of the questions on the agenda and have prepared numbered slides that contain analysis, commentary, assumptions, etc. My slides are a skeleton of what should be said. All I have done is organize the board in my slides long before I go to class. I have the slides sequenced in numbered groups along with some hidden slides that contain supplementary information; things they should   remember but perhaps don't or that I've asked people to read in the library but they probably haven't.

The amount of effort that goes into preparing these slides and the order and the timing is enormous. In preparation for any given class, I've got complete flexibility to change the sequence, try something new, rearrange my teaching plan (slides). I print out a new timetable and slide order and away we go. It's much easier than trying to shift notes around with arrows and cutting and pasting. Using the electronics is now my style. I won't go back to using the board.

Walt and Bob want to be flexible in their classes and so appear to develop broader plans.

Walt: When I sit down and prepare for class, I will first of all plan the rough flow of the class. And then within this rough flow, I will detail what I'm going to do by deciding what I'm going to write on the board, on what board, and approximately when; also what questions I'm going to ask; who I'm going to ask. But I'm very reactive and instinctive, and I rarely stick to this preparation. I develop extensive notes, bring them into class, but generally never look at them.

Bob: The reason why so much time is involved in case preparation is because I want to be ready to go wherever the discussion goes. If I was preparing a lecture, I could prepare a good lecture in four hours and have complete control of the sequencing of what occurs when; interject enough humor to keep students interested; know when to put in something that is slightly outrageous so that if a person is dozing, it will get attention. With half a brain, I can anticipate all the hostile questions that will be asked at the end of the lecture. With the other half of the brain, I can be prepared to answer them in a way which allows me to maintain my self-respect in view of the students' questions. In the case method, you're not in control. The vehicle is the students' vehicle, unlike the lecture. Influencing the process of that method in a way that is productive is much more difficult.

These statements on developing the class plan are illustrative of a continuum from high to low structure. There are several factors which influence where an instructor might want to be on this continuum: the kind of case, the position in the course or the type of student involved. A further and significant determinant is the instructor's orientation and experience. Bill talks about the transition in approaches to planning that occur with experience.

Bill: I remember when I was first starting in teaching, I used to prepare the hell out of cases technically. It's a natural tendency if you've done that to try to push the class discussion in your direction. As I get older, I am more concerned with the role of running the class. Certainly understanding the case technically, but more for purposes of pacing and timing in the classroom than for the purpose of what the students are going to say. And I believe I am more successful as a teacher now because I'm paying much more attention to that, which also means I'm paying more attention to what the students are saying and I'm trying to link across students.

Mark has a very simple approach.

Mark: I'll have a piece of paper every day that says "Teaching Plan" and sometimes it only has two lines on it. One is the first sentence I'm going to say in class and the other line is, "Listen and pray."

Call Lists. Call lists are used to identify persons whom the instructor wishes to call on during the class discussion. Some of the purposes of a call list are the following:

1. To make sure everyone in the class participates at least once during the course.

2. To identify students with particular skills and experiences that are relevant to a specific case situation.

3. To ensure that, with a particularly difficult case, the right person starts.

4. To establish class norms. For example, "It's not a good idea to come to my class without being prepared. I'll call on you!"

5. To check student skills development. For example, "I want to check how well John opens a class. I need a reading on how well Angela is prepared." Or, "I wonder what kind of a job Maiko can do to summarize the discussion at the end of the class."

6. To have a name available when no one volunteers to start the class.

There is no agreement as to whether instructors should use a call list. Nor should there be. Those who choose to use them presumably capitalize on some of the above purposes. Those who choose not to use them presumably rely on and encourage voluntary class participation. Even though a person's name may appear on a call list, the instructor may still wait to see whether this person will volunteer during a regular class discussion. Thus, some instructors use call lists to give preference to some people when several students wish to participate simultaneously during the classroom discussion.

Teaching Aids. The instructor may wish to identify, search for and arrange for a variety of teaching aids before class. Teaching aids such as samples, photographs, clippings, articles, web pages, annual reports, ads or videos can help augment the reality of a case and stimulate class discussion

Samples of company products can be brought to class and passed around. They are an extremely simple but effective way of reinforcing the reality of the case. Similarly, if samples are not possible to obtain, photographs may help. If the instructor brings, or encourages students to bring, newspaper and magazine clippings to class, these can be put on a notice board and may provide new information on problems and organizations discussed in class. These aids and others, such as articles, annual reports and company ads, are not usually the types of things that make or break the case, but they show that the instructor cares and wants to make the class as interesting and relevant as possible.

Films and videos can be used to present information traditionally committed to paper. Aside from their visual appeal, they may offer a more realistic understanding of the company situation. Chapter 8 on case use variations will cover in more detail alternatives or supplements to paper-based cases. In addition, videos can easily be made when special visitors are invited to class. These videos can be shown in subsequent classes and generate further insights into the case as well as substantial interest among participants.

Teaching Meetings. Just as small group discussion is a part of the students' preparation task, many instructors find it helpful to talk over their case analyses and class plans with colleagues. More formalized teaching group meetings can be used in those courses having multiple sections and several faculty. Chris outlined the evolving operation of his teaching group (see also teacher training in Chapter 10).

Chris: In our first year teaching group, we now meet together the day we teach the class. Previously, we met each week and discussed the cases for the next week. I found people really were not at the stage of tactics for what we wanted to do in the classroom. We have some good teaching notes now for course segments and cases that tell you what's going to happen. Why have meetings to do that? People can read them. The critical time is after your preparation and the morning before class. We can now talk about what we ought to do. Here's what the right hand board should look like. These are the kinds of discussions we're having now. This is really the fine tuning. This is where you can save somebody from a blunder. For example, how are you going to make the transition from here to there? Certain questions at certain times are important for us to raise.

These meetings are now daily. We all teach the same case on the same day, although in different sections and at different times. We meet at 7:30 in the morning for an hour. For me, I've got the case in my mind and I want to test some ideas, some of the classroom strategies. You can't do this sort of thing a week in advance.

Another thing I do, and some would say it's a waste of time, is if I have a case that I haven't taught before, I'll sit in on someone else's class. Even now, nine years into this process, I find it very useful. I've discovered that some of those new cases go quite well for me because of that excitement, sitting through it once, being on edge before I go to my class. I'm not sitting in to evaluate. It's more difficult now that I've been promoted. People see me more as an evaluator. This observation is the best preparation I can have. There are other younger faculty who, if they have a 1:00 class and I have a 8:30 class, I'll ask to come and observe in my class. They won't. I can't imagine why they don't. It seems like such a valuable opportunity. For me, it's an easy way to learn how to teach a case.

Beginning and Ending Class. Thus far, most comments have addressed preparation for the case discussion portion of the class. How the class begins and how it ends also require preparatory work. On the assumption that a good start is half the battle, most instructors carefully prepare the beginning.

Kim: I like to have the opening lines for the class figured out exactly and will write down announcements and comments verbatim. Also, my planning for the first 15-20 minutes of the class is likely to be precise. Once I start with case discussion itself, it is more difficult to make precise time assignments to individual aspects of the case. I also try to make the concluding portion of class time specific again. Knowing how much time will be taken at the end gives me the cue to stop the case discussion so that I'll be sure to finish the class on time. For some classes the ending portion of class may require 10-15 minutes, in others, 3-4 minutes. Here again, my preparation and class plan for these times will be very detailed.

Les: I religiously prepare the start of class by noting points relating to three issues. One, I note the assignments for the next one or two classes. If there is anything peculiar or difficult about the cases, I will comment on them. I always am prepared to tell students, prior to their preparation of a case, whether or not the case has been used in the past as an exam or report. Hopefully, they can do a little extra in their preparation and see how far they get. Two, I write on my class plan: Questions/Issues/Comments. Here I reflect on details that students might be thinking about regarding past classes, the course in general, current events, or for that matter anything they may want to raise. I also prepare any questions or comments that I might have for them. Announcements and past case discussion updates fall in this second point. Three, I prepare the agenda for the class and how I'm going to introduce the case for discussion, and talk about any of the assigned readings.

More than anything else with this kind of beginning preparation, I'm trying not to leave any loose ends or tangents. I want to make sure everyone knows where we are, where we've been and where we're going.

In the next chapter, the beginning of a class will be discussed further.

The conclusion to a case class, like the start, is a transition phase. Some instructors like it if students summarize the case, although most feel summarizing is a difficult role to ask a student to perform. Other instructors like to summarize the case and its key points themselves, perhaps commenting also on strengths and weaknesses evident in the class discussion of the case. Those who strongly believe in non-directive behavior prefer to leave the responsibility for evaluation of what happened in class and why on the shoulders of the participants and do not summarize or comment. The next chapter will present various ways of ending class. Some types of closure, such as summarizing the key points and lessons derived from the case, generalizing, or lecturing about the case will call for detailed preparation. Many instructors will have transparencies or handouts ready ahead of time for this purpose.

Other forms of closure will be more spontaneous, depending on what happened or didn't happen in the classroom. Typical, for example, is when instructors wish to finish class with some kind of performance feedback. Obviously, the exact comments cannot be determined ahead of time, although it is wise to allow time for that type of closure.

THE CASE TEACHING PLAN

The Case Teaching Plan in Exhibit 4-2 provides a valuable one page summary of the instructor's preparation for a specific class in which a case will be taught. Like the Case Preparation Chart for students, it provides the road map for the class. It is not a substitute for the teaching note, but the final step in instructor preparation. It indicates the what, when, who, and how of the coming class. The main headings at the top deal with time, agenda and participants.

Time

Time refers to the anticipated time in minutes that may be spent on the various class agenda items. The total time cannot exceed the class time available. It is reasonable to indicate time estimates for each agenda item as a range, such as 5-8 minutes.

Agenda

Agenda items are potential topic areas or activities on which time will be spent during the class. Some instructors put this agenda, but seldom the time allocated to it, on the board before class. Not all agenda items listed need to occur in every class.

1. *Introduction* refers to greetings to the class and announcement of the agenda.

2. *Next/Other Classes* refers to the assignment(s) for the next class(es) and any special reminders the instructor may wish to give. Other classes refer to classes already completed, or some material or issues carried over from the last class. This section provides the instructor with the opportunity to place this class in the context of the course and the course in the context of the program.

Exhibit 4-2
CASE TEACHING PLAN

Case Title: *Course/Program:*   *Date:*

Time	**Agenda**	**Participants**

Time   **Agenda**   **Participants**

___   1. Introduction

Preference Participant List	
1.	5.
2.	6.
3.	7.
4.	8.

___   2. Next/Other Classes

___   3. Comments, Questions   **Volunteer (V) / Call List**

___   4. Reading Discussion   V   or _____

___   5. Case Introduction   V   or _____

___   6. Teaching Aids

___   7. Assignment Questions

___   1 _____   V   or _____

___   2 _____   V   or _____

___   3 _____   V   or _____

___   4 _____   V   or _____

___   8. Conclusion

___   Total

Board Plan

Issues	*Analysis*	*Decision Criteria*
Analysis	*Alternatives*	*Action/Implementation*
		Missing Info/Assumptions

Teaching With Cases, © 1998, Richard Ivey School of Business

3. *Comments, Concerns* provides an opportunity for participants and the instructor to bring up news items that may be relevant to previous classes, the current one or future ones; or matters pertaining to the course or a specific class. It may also give an opportunity for participants to bring up any non course specific matter which they believe relevant for the class or the program.

4. *Reading Discussion* deals with the additional readings assigned for the class. The instructor may invite questions from participants, or may ask questions, or provide a small lecture reinforcing key points.

5. *Case Introduction* is the period just before the issue in the case is addressed. It provides an opportunity for the instructor to place the case in an industry or personal perspective. Questions like, "Has anyone worked in this industry, organization or faced this kind of decision" are part of this phase. It can be seen as a second opportunity to put the case in context of the course or program and integrate it with work done by other instructors in other courses.

6. *Teaching Aids* may include a video, samples, photos, advertisements, financial report or other material relevant to the organization, product, service or decision in the case.

7. *Assignment Questions* are the ones given in the student assignment before class. If the questions are lengthy, they may be shortened.

8. *Conclusion* refers to the ending of the class envisaged by the instructor. It refers to the priority plan of the instructor. If only three concluding points can be made, what should they be and in what order? Will the

instructor summarize, talk about what happened with respect to the decision or refer to the next class coming?

Participants

The right hand side of the Case Teaching Plan relates to who will be expected to talk in class and when.

The *Preference List* identifies those participants the instructor will call on when a choice among volunteers occurs. That is, when a number of participants wish to get in the discussion, these are the ones that in this class the instructor will give preference to. This list may contain participants who seldom speak, but does not have to be used exclusively that way. A preference list is important for instructors who believe that all members in the class should participate at some time during their course. It removes any degree of uncertainty in the classroom when options exist among volunteer participants.

The *Volunteer or Call List* underneath the preference list is different. V means that the instructor will ask for volunteers for that part of the class. Typically, the first opportunity for instructor initiated class discussion is in the section (4) Reading Discussion. The call list identifies the class member(s) who will be asked to address the specific topic under discussion. The other opportunities to ask volunteers or call on people occur in (5) Case Introduction, (7) Assignment Questions or the case discussion. If the V for volunteer is circled in the Case Teaching Plan, the preference list can be used to select from among volunteers. If a call list is used, the names of the people on the call list will normally not repeat in the preference list.

The Board Plan

The bottom of the Case Teaching Plan is reserved for the board plan. Those instructors who like to visualize what the end result of the discussion recording task will be can use this as their miniaturized overview. The headings are suggestions only. Some instructor will actually write key case points in specific places on the board plan. Others prefer headings only.

All of the blank space on the Case Teaching Plan provides the instructor with the opportunity to fill in comments specific to this class and case. The Case Teaching Plan in Exhibit 4-2, when magnified on a photocopier at a setting of 155%, becomes a letter size sheet which can be used for every class. It gives an early overview of the class which becomes a part of the teaching note file for the next time the case is taught. Whereas most of the teaching note is likely to remain the same, the Case Teaching Plan details will change every time the case is taught.

Our experience has been that the Case Teaching Plan is a valuable aid at the end of the case preparation as well as for the class session itself.

CONCLUSION

Some may worry that an exhaustive preparation can only lead to a very directive and structured teaching approach. Afsaneh Nahavandi testifies to the opposite.

The best, most exciting, most challenging, most spontaneous learning experiences for me and for my students have come when I was thoroughly prepared... The magic of being prepared is that I can either leave all the preparations behind or draw from them at will. The thorough preparation gives me the confidence I need to be creative and improvise as needed to challenge my students and involve them in the topic (202).

Sound preparation is the ultimate prerequisite for effective case teaching and learning. It can also boost the instructor's confidence and morale, important ingredients of successful teaching. The time has now come to go to class. The course has been planned, cases selected, the participants have their assignment prepared, and the trained instructor has concluded the preparation. The performance can begin.

classroom process

The ultimate action place of teaching with cases is the classroom, where the results of planning and preparation will show. Since what happens in the classroom is by no means a standard process or procedure, it is useful to reinforce process variability at the start. Variation may depend on the objectives of the class, the subject matter, the type of case, the place in the sequence of classes, what happened in previous classes, or other classes in other courses taken simultaneously by the same participants. In addition, variation between classes will depend on the teaching style and mood of the instructor, the mood of the participants, the time of year, the weather, the political and economic news and, surely, other factors a teacher may be able to identify or guess at under the circumstances. That there is no such a thing as a standard case class which can be used as an objective model is unfortunate for those who seek imitation, and delightful for innovative teachers.

Even though a standard case class does not exist, we will create one, because many case classes do have some phases in common. From a discussion standpoint it is useful to have a reference base from which variations can be contrasted. Thus, this chapter will start with the description of such a reference class, followed by a discussion of its major phases in chronological order. Since the focus of teaching with cases lies on managing the participative process, we will present a detailed discussion with emphasis on both the instructor's and participant's role therein. Finally, since a significant variant between instructors is the style employed by each, a discussion of teaching styles will form the conclusion.

THE REFERENCE CLASS

The following description of an actual class will be used as a reference for further detailed discussion. It is not meant to be an ideal model.

Professor Jones walks into his class about 5 minutes before the 1:00 p.m. starting time. He checks to see if the board needs cleaning, if the overhead projector works, and exchanges a few pleasantries with the participants already in the class. He removes a newspaper article from the notice board on the side wall (it refers to some current happenings in an industry discussed during a previous class) and positions himself near the center of the class to start promptly at 1:00 p.m.

"Good Afternoon," he starts off and most of the class responds good-naturedly. "I am happy to see that you won the basketball game last night, I'm expecting equally superior performance on the management court in this class today. Before we start the case discussion itself, let us settle a few things first." Professor Jones then discusses where the material for some future classes can be obtained and what special arrangements have been made for the coming field trip. He also explains how in this class he wishes to make sure that everybody understands the readings assigned along with the case, and that he wishes to start the class off with any issues arising from these readings. At this point, about five minutes have passed in the class.

The next 10 minutes are devoted to a discussion of the readings. One student wants an explanation of a particular point on page 542 and the professor asks if anyone in class can answer it. Three volunteer and the professor chooses one, who gives a reasonable explanation. When no further difficulties with the readings are indicated, the professor asks three different participants questions covering the main aspects of the readings. After each answer, he asks if anyone else in the class has anything to add to the answer given. In two cases, others in the class comment, mostly in a qualifying way.

Professor Jones then comments briefly on the origin of the case, explaining that a former student happened to sit next to him on an airplane and how they had discussed the course of Professor Jones. Professor Jones had mentioned the difficulties of obtaining new materials on a particular subject and the former student had replied, "That's a coincidence, that is just the problem I'm working on right now. Would you like me to send you information on it?"

Professor Jones then smiles at the class and says, "If there's anything wrong with this case, blame the airline." Then he asks if someone wishes to start the class. The remaining 65 minutes of the class are devoted to the case discussion.

Four people indicate they are ready to start by raising their hands. Professor Jones chooses the one who has participated least in his course so far, and she starts the class by saying, "This is the key decision that needs to be made. If I were the manager under these circumstances, I would concentrate on this decision because. . ."

She then takes about 5 minutes to explain her reasons and also indicates how she would decide. While she speaks, Professor Jones records her points in summary form on the board. When she finishes, Professor Jones asks her if she has anything more to say. She says, "Oh, yes, there's one point I skipped over." And she recounts it.

Professor Jones then turns to the class and already a dozen hands or so are up in the air to indicate they wish to comment. Professor Jones nods to one and that person proceeds to disagree strongly with the key decision identified by the first person. Professor Jones records this counter position on the other side of the board. Before he has a chance to turn away from the board, someone else starts to speak, and the discussion in the class proceeds for about 5 minutes on the class' own initiative, with Professor Jones continuing to record additional points on the board.

It is apparent that a significant segment of the class is in one camp, while the other seems to agree with the first speaker. Professor Jones then says, "Well, it seems we have reached an impasse, here. If we cannot agree on the issue which needs resolution, there's not much point in going on. Is there any additional information, not yet brought out, which might help in resolving this? I want to hear from someone who has not spoken up so far."

Three persons volunteer and each brings additional information from the case supporting the view of the person who started the class. The last person to speak refers to the balance sheet and income statement of the company and Professor Jones uses the overhead projector and financial statement transparencies he has in his file (in case they are required) to allow the participant to comment. This way they can also easily be checked by the rest of the class.

Professor Jones asks if the class agrees on the proper problem definition, and when the class agrees, he asks what alternatives can be seriously considered. Various class members offer four alternatives and Professor Jones records these on another board. Discussion then centers on the pros and cons of each and appropriate decision criteria to evaluate these alternatives.

During this period, Professor Jones continues to record new points on the board, asks for clarification, occasionally repeats exactly what someone has said and asks, "Is this what you said?" And, at other times, he paraphrases remarks and asks, "Is this what you intend to say?"

To one student who has already participated four times and appears anxious to break into the discussion, waving his hands energetically and emitting mumbling noises to interrupt others, Professor Jones indicates with a placating hand movement to "cool it." Occasionally, Professor Jones asks someone who does not have a hand up if he or she agrees or disagrees with a particular point but, for the most part, the volunteers have their say. Professor Jones makes sure that people from all parts of the amphitheater classroom have a chance to participate.

Professor Jones moves continually from the board to the center of the room and, occasionally, to one side or another. Once he moves to the very back of the room, asking all to look at the board and to see if they can come up with a conclusion.

About 10 minutes are left by the time the four alternatives have been discussed, and Professor Jones asks which one appears more reasonable under the circumstances. It is clear that two of the four choices are "better" according to the class in a straw vote. Professor Jones asks how one can implement each of these. Considerable discussion takes place on the implementation of the first alternative and, with about two minutes to go, Professor Jones says, "Well, I'm sorry, I had hoped we could discuss the implementation of both of these alternatives, because we might see something interesting coming out of it. Unfortunately, we are out of time and we just cannot get into that now. You have covered most of the relevant issues in this case as far as I can see, congratulations. One thing aside from how to implement the second alternative you may wish to think about, is how applicable this concept might be to other companies and other industries. I intend to focus more on this implementation stage with you in some of our future classes, because it is an area we need more practice in. Today's topic is one we will not cover specifically in any future classes, but I expect you to be able to use the concept whenever an opportunity presents itself. See you next week."

CHRONOLOGICAL PHASES
IN A CASE DISCUSSION

As can be seen from the description, the reference case class can be divided into certain chronological phases:

A. In-Class - Pre-Class

B. Pre-Case or "Warm-Up"
1. Announcements
2. Discussion of assigned readings
3. Case introduction

C. Case Discussion
1. Start
2. Issue and analysis
3. Alternatives, decision criteria and decision
4. Action/implementation plan

D. Conclusion

A closer look at each of these phases is now in order. It will become quickly evident that what Professor Jones did and what others do may be entirely different. It is useful to recognize the phases and their varied treatments, if for no other reason than identifying the options available to case teachers.

A. In-Class - Pre-Class

Professor Jones had a personal habit of arriving a few minutes early in class, just to make sure that: (1) he was not late and (2) he did not need to spend class time doing things that could be done before class. Clearing the board, re-arranging the furniture, removing debris, working on the notice board, checking the overhead projector, checking the temperature and air quality in the room, and similar tasks are all non-student contact activities which fall into this phase.

He also liked to chat with a few people to catch the "gossip" or class news and to show his interest in what the group was doing and how they fared.

Some instructors like to use this pre-class period to help them in making up their minds whom to call on first. Other instructors have already decided on their call list as part of their Case Teaching Plan.

B. Pre-Case or "Warm-Up"

For many case teachers, case discussion does not start immediately as the first item of business on the class agenda. They use greetings, announcements, stories or other means to gain class attention. This warm-up can be divided into three parts: (1) greetings, announcements, general comments, and follow-up to previous classes; (2) discussion of assigned readings and theoretical concepts; and (3) introduction to the case. All three may not be present in all classes, but each plays a specific role.

1. Announcements. When a professor wishes to start a class, whether a pre-class phase occurred or not, there is usually considerable noise; people are chatting with one another. Some means need to be found to gain the group's attention and to get down to business. Some professors yell loudly, "Are you ready to go?" Some whistle, some turn on the overhead projector, some just start talking, some use greetings, some just stand and wait. Whatever means are used, it is evident that information from the professor to the class, and vice versa, is not likely to flow without class attention and silence. Professor Jones used a traditional greeting, which the class expected as a signal. He also quickly followed it up with a good news item of interest to the group, the recent basketball victory. He then quickly turned the discussion to future course related topics.

Doug concurs with this approach:

Doug: I think the class has to be ready. You walk in, put down your books and walk up to the board, face the class, and say, "Hey." But people aren't really settled in yet. They haven't even started to listen. So the first task in class is to get them in a listening mood. Some instructors tell jokes. What I prefer to do is talk about something that relates to the section as a whole. It might be an exam coming up. It might be where we are going in the course and where we've been. If a student comes up and says, "May I please make an announcement?" half my job is done because it relates to the class and they're listening to their colleague. I don't think there is anything magic about that. It is standard procedure among public speakers.

The pre-case phase may also be a good time to review some points arising out of previous classes, follow-up to previous cases, or theoretical issues.

Kim thinks the warm-up is the appropriate time for future assignments:

Kim: In some courses, it is normal for the instructor to give the assignment for the next class as part of the current class. I learned from hard experience that the best time to give the assignment out is at the beginning of the class, rather than at the end. I found that time pressure at the end of a case class may make it very difficult to squeeze your assignment in before the class leaves.

Professor Jones also used the preliminary part of the warm-up to announce his intentions for the class, "Discussion of readings first."

2. Discussion of Assigned Readings. Professor Jones used the second part of the warm-up phase to discuss the readings assigned along with the case. He used two means to check understanding: the opportunity for students to ask questions as well as to ask questions himself. His expectation was that any further deficiencies in theoretical understanding would be caught in the case discussion. Other instructors may ask for hand-ins at this point, have a discussion of assigned questions, use a quick quiz, or any other means at their disposal to satisfy themselves that understanding of theory exists.

3. Case Introduction. Professor Jones was able to use a personal anecdote to introduce the case and also draw the participant's attention to his own authorship of the case, implying his own interest and commitment to it. For those who teach their own cases, this introduction is always an available ploy. Since most teachers use cases written by others, they may wish to use other means of reinforcing the necessity for careful attention to the upcoming case discussion. They may wish to review the last few classes to show the sequence leading up to this particular case. They may wish to refer to statements in the press identifying the case problem as an important one for management, or appeal to the group's pride, "Last year's class couldn't make head or tail out of this case, let's see if you can do better."

> **Roger:** Frequently, I start the class off by making some kind of summary: where the case fits in the course sequence, reviewing what we did yesterday, and what the purpose of today's case is.

The instructor may also wish to provide a framework within which discussion is to be carried out. This preview could include some indication as to roughly how much time is available for discussion.

> **Kim:** I sometimes say, "In the last few classes, we've had some difficulty getting onto decision making and implementation planning. Therefore, I suggest that we spend about 20 minutes on analysis of this case, then move

to alternatives for the next 20, and use the last half-hour for decision and implementation planning."

Along with a planned preview of the case discussion, reinforcement of the importance of the case to the course, the program, management, or society is probably the second aim of this "warm-up" phase and it can be accomplished in a variety of ways.

We like the idea of asking during the case introduction which participants in the class have worked in this industry, in this company, or on a similar problem. Then we ask them to explain some of their recollections of their experience thereby providing a framework of appreciation for the other participants in the class. Since most cases tend to provide few data on the industry as a whole, the processes commonly used and the challenges faced by managers, this kind of case introduction not only reinforces the importance of the case and its key issues, but also allows class participants to learn from each other more about the larger context. Participants who tend to be shy about class participation find this a comfortable opportunity to speak in class.

C. The Case Discussion

A "normal" case discussion is supposed to follow more or less the typical decision making model discussed in Chapter 3 of *Learning With Cases*. This model includes:

a) defining the issue;
b) analyzing the case data with focus on causes and effects as well as constraints and opportunities;
c) generating alternatives;
d) selecting decision criteria;
e) analyzing and evaluating alternatives;
f) selecting the preferred alternative; and
g) developing an action and implementation plan.

Many students like to announce their decision at the start, therefore, the class discussion does not always proceed as the decision making model would. (Fully prepared, the students should have covered all phases in the model prior to class. Therefore, the class is not intended to be a sample of the decision making model). Also, since ease of implementation should be a consideration in the attractiveness of various alternatives, (difficulty to implement cuts down on practicability), implementation considerations need to be discussed before a final decision on the better alternatives is taken. Nevertheless, in many case classes, implementation discussion is left to the end of class, on the assumption that action/implementation planning will not be so difficult as to make the preferred alternative(s) impractical.

Since the central thrust in many case discussions is a resolution of the specific decision or problem in the organization, four distinct phases in a case class discussion are (1) start, (2) issue and analysis, (3) alternatives, decision criteria and decision and (4) action/implementation plan.

1. Start.   Starting the case discussion implies the professor will ask someone a question and will allocate a certain amount of time to that individual. Professor Jones asked for a volunteer, asked an open question, and was prepared to let the participant continue until she felt she had no more to say.

Others have commented on the start.

Eric: It is important for me to call on people to start every day to avoid the volunteer syndrome. You got to have a little bit of tension: If you're not prepared, you're going to be embarrassed.

Sam: I almost never call on someone to start the class. My feeling is that these are big people and it's their money. I believe they will learn more if they participate and I tell them this, but I don't go and chase them.

A second concern in starting the case discussion is what is the starting question?

Kim: There are two major types of questions with which to start a class. The extremes are directive and non-directive. A typical directive question is, "How much profit do you think this company will make next year?" A typical non-directive question is, "What would you like to talk about?"

Chris elaborates on the non-directive start.

Chris: I'm now near the end of the course. I've got to be ready to go wherever the person who starts wants to go. Today, I said, "Bill, the case is yours." I didn't even say, "Where do you want to go?" I've got the class to the point where I just say, "Bill, start us today." In my mind, I know there are some things we ought to cover. But I'm ready to go. He doesn't even ask, "Do you want the analysis first or the plan of action first?" Bill knows he's got about 10-15 minutes at the beginning to give it his best shot.

We feel strongly that if the class has been given specific questions as part of the case assignment, those questions need to be discussed in class. Thus, suppose the first question in class is, "If you were in the position of Angela Martins, what would be your analysis of the sales shortfall in the Eastern part of the country?" Then it is perfectly reasonable and desirable to make that the opening question for class discussion. Instructors who do not believe the case assignment questions need to be discussed in class had better communicate this to the class to avoid frustration and confusion.

Of course there is a general understanding that it is possible for participants and the instructor to raise points outside of the questions assigned. There is a difference whether these extra points and insights are in addition to the assignment questions or are a substitute for them.

2. Issue and Analysis. At some stage of the class discussion, normally, but not always, in the early stages, considerable discussion takes place to identify the exact nature of the issue, problem or decision in the case. Discussion of alternatives and implementation is rather meaningless without common agreement in the class that the right issue is being addressed. For this reason, Professor Jones in our reference class forced the class to resolve its differences before allowing further discussion. In some cases, the task of identifying the prime decision or problem is trivial and need not consume much time. In others, the central educational issue may well be the proper identification of the correct problem. How much time to allot to this phase will, therefore, depend on the objectives the instructor has for the class and the nature of the case.

Analysis can start with developing a clear understanding of why the issue arose. The importance/urgency matrix can next be used to place the issue or decision in context. Discussion of the immediate issue(s) and basic issue(s) permits the class to distinguish between the challenge of the decision maker in the case and the reason for the inclusion of the case in the course. Further analytical work in most cases will be both quantitative and qualitative. The framework and theoretical concepts of the specific course are expected to tie into the analysis of the case. "Time-outs" to depart from the case and go back to earlier classes and concepts are usual. If the case is of the type where something did not work out as planned, the fishbone or cause and effect diagram can provide a suitable framework for establishing potential root causes. The prime purpose of the case analysis section of the class is to ensure that any alternatives which are subsequently generated are appropriate for the decision or issue under consideration. The medical analysis equivalent is diagnosis before prescription.

3. Alternatives, Decision Criteria and Decision. A significant part of any case class deals with the discussion of alternatives. Sometimes, even before the decision or problem is clearly identified, alternatives or solutions are already proposed by the class members. Normally, at least two, and sometimes up to a dozen alternatives are advanced by participants. The larger the number of alternatives, the greater the need is for narrowing or shortening this list before serious discussion of the merits of the most important ones can take place.

Any time a list needs to be made in class, such as for alternatives, or decision criteria, it is useful to ensure that all potential possibilities are listed before discussion of appropriateness or advantages/disadvantages can begin. Thus, the instructor can say, "Let me get the full set of options down first, before we start discussing them." Otherwise, someone will prepare an alternative with or without a lot of supporting arguments, and then someone else will start to argue with the pros and cons. Under this scenario it is quite possible that a much better alternative not yet identified gets a short or no discussion while some worthless options take up valuable class time.

A listing of decision criteria usually follows on the heels of an alternative listing. Criteria subsequently need to be separated into quantitative and qualitative categories. *Learning With Cases* gives a list of common decision criteria in Chapter 3. Next, both the quantitative and qualitative lists need to be prioritized. It is most unusual for everyone in class to be in full agreement with such rankings. Therefore, it is better to ask one participant to provide a ranking and then to ask, "How many agree with this ranking?" and "How many disagree?" Then ask one of those who disagree to provide their own ranking. It is also useful to ask if the quantitative criteria should outweigh the qualitative ones or vice versa. If this is done well, it can then form the basis for alternative evaluation.

The list of alternatives can be reduced in a variety of ways. One, ask for a class vote on each alternative and discuss only the more popular ones. Two, ask the class to distinguish between the alternatives. That is, ask which apply specifically to the situation versus good ideas which should be carried out regardless of the particular situation at hand. For example, in one case where a significant rise in raw material prices is forecast, students typically suggest changing package size. In this particular case, this suggestion in itself may be a reasonable auxiliary action, but it will not solve the raw material price increase.

Also, to narrow the number of alternatives, an instructor can ask which alternatives are based on an assumption with low probability of success. In the price situation above, finding a substitute material is frequently another alternative proposed. The relevant question that needs to be asked is, "What is the probability that a substitute exists and that it is available at a lower cost than the increased price of the raw material?"

Further, which alternatives can be eliminated because there are others already identified which appear to have superior pay-off?

For the same example discussed above, the raw material is currently purchased from the parent company in England at an advantageous price. The alternative of purchasing it elsewhere in Great Britain and obtaining a better price is not very realistic, given the specific circumstances.

It is also possible to discuss one attractive alternative in some depth and thus establish a "reference base" alternative, against which others can be compared.

For example, in the above case, continuing to buy from the parent company will cost the subsidiary about $40,000 per year more. Therefore, any other alternative, to be attractive, will have to cost less, and the size of the problem is clearly identified. It is a $40,000 problem, not a $400,000 one, or a $4,000,000 one. Therefore, the solutions have to fit that problem. A joint venture to start American manufacture, for example, is not realistic because the current problem is only a $40,000 problem.

After the narrowing down of alternatives, the serious examination of the two or three most attractive can begin.

Some instructors prefer to have certain board space reserved for alternatives; others don't. It is useful to record the key alternatives and their pros and cons on the board, or overhead projector or flip chart, for the group to see, so that discussion can be more reasonably managed.

Discussion during this stage should normally focus on one alternative at a time, with the instructor recording the key points, pros and cons, for each, so that subsequent class comparison between alternatives is possible.

It may well be that in any case more than one alternative is fully reasonable, even after careful examination. Such was the situation in the class of Professor Jones. It is usually wise to ask participants to state their reasons for their choice, so that their line of logic is reasonable. The argument of, "The key objective is to lower cost, and alternative 'B' appears to have the best chance of achieving a significantly lower cost," is logical. However, "Alternative 'B' is better because delivery is faster," is not reasonable, under these circumstances.

It is during the alternatives discussion stage that relevant data from the case normally need to be brought in to bolster the pros and cons of each alternative as well as the key decision criteria. The instructor may well ask the class to check back to specific pages in the case and may have transparencies available with diagrams, charts, statements, or calculations which can be shown on the overhead projector.

Toward the end of this phase it is usually necessary to reach a conclusion as to the "best alternative(s)." Class consensus may be obvious, or may be solicited by question, "How many believe this to be the best alternative?" or an individual may be asked to make a choice and others to agree or disagree.

If part of the objective of this class is to discuss an action/implementation plan, sufficient time should be left, a problem Professor Jones could not quite resolve.

4. Action/Implementation Plan. Discussion of action/ implementation often receives scant attention in case classes, because many instructors believe proper identification and analysis of the problem and discussion of theory are more important. Also, since implementation is logically a discussion area restricted to the end of the class, a race with the clock is frequently lost by implementation. Such was the case with Professor Jones who admitted to the class his own inability to manage time better.

Since an action/implementation plan, including deadlines, is better viewed as an integral whole, it is usually preferable to have a person who agrees with the preferred alternative provide a whole action/implementation plan rather than just one or two steps. Then, others may advance an alternative action/implementation plan, or suggest additional or different steps and deadlines. Since ease, cost and time of implementation are obvious decision criteria for any alternative, the opportunity to revisit the list of alternatives once an action/implementation plan runs into trouble needs to be foreseen.

Instructors who believe that the ability to prepare a decent action/implementation plan is a valuable skill to be learned by their course participants had better be prepared to set a significant amount of class time aside for discussion of this phase. They would do well to emphasize to participants in their case assignment that they expect to discuss a serious action/implementation plan, so that participants can prepare properly. A hastily conceived action/implementation plan in class cobbled together from about a dozen contributors is likely to fall significantly short of its quality goal. What is worse, is that a half-baked plan may give the participants the idea that this is a decent effort and set an undesirable standard of expectations.

D. Conclusion

"Oh, I see my time's up. I look forward to our next class," is probably the shortest but not the least likely conclusion an instructor can give to the end of a case class. Like the class start, it is a transition phase, which can be used to conclude the case and provide a transition to subsequent classes as well as a continuation in the sequence so far completed.

Some instructors prefer that students summarize the case. Most feel that asking a student to summarize is a difficult role to perform. Some instructors like to summarize the case and its key points themselves, perhaps commenting also on strengths and weaknesses in the class discussion of the case. Those who strongly believe in non-directive behavior prefer to leave the responsibility for evaluation of what happened in class and why on the shoulders of the participants and do not summarize or comment. Professor Jones was rather noncommittal and passed very quickly from the case, just warning that the topic would not be repeated.

It is also possible in these final moments to cover theory, reinforce earlier classes, preview subsequent ones, and to give the participants a lift at the end of the class. Often, relatively strong feelings may have emerged and some humorous remarks or quiet discussion can provide a calming influence before the session ends.

Most instructors feel the need for some type of closure at the end of a class. It is difficult, in their opinion, to walk away leaving the discussion completely in the open. The answers to the question, "How do you end a class?" show there are many useful things that instructors can do to help students develop a broader understanding from specific case situations and to enrich their learning experience. For example, instructors may wish to provide some conceptual input in the form of a lecture to review some important points raised in the discussion; highlight certain aspects of the case; raise questions regarding some points missed; or indicate some pitfalls with each of the alternatives identified. Among other ways to end class, Gordon likes to keep it short:

> **Gordon:** Since we don't get enough time in class, I normally leave the students with what I call a "mind bender." It's an open question having something to do with the managerial issue in the case.

At times, Dave wishes to finish class with some kind of performance feedback:

Dave: I don't have a solid way of ending classes. Sometimes, I can say to the students, "You did a great job; any board of directors would be proud of your performance." There will be some classes where it is important to compliment the class on the basis of a job well done. Those kind of compliments have to be sincerely placed. I'll usually have one class where I have to tell them they did a crappy job. Nine times out of ten, it's not a function of the case or my ability in class, but of their work load which was just too much and everyone screwed off at the wrong time.

Considerable controversy exists as to whether instructors should summarize at the end of the class or not. The instructor's personal teaching style and philosophy are reflected a great deal in the following opinions.

Chris: I don't spend much time summarizing at the end of class. Given that, I like to peak the class with 10-15 minutes left — they really do their own summarizing. This last part of class is important. But my role is not that important.

Bob: I am willing to make summaries, but not all the time, because summaries are not always helpful. Often, my summaries will take the form of sharpening questions. For example, summaries are not helpful when students don't yet know all the parameters of a particular question or issue. When the class has done such a good job, a summary from me would be futile. In those cases, I will very quickly tell them that we have done a very good job.

Roberto: From my experience (and I have taught in Mexico, Argentina, Portugal, in addition to Spain), Latin participants do not expect from the professor just the experience of going through a case. They expect more. Once the regular case discussion is over, I take ten or fifteen more minutes and give what research has been done, almost like the theory. It's always at the end. I have this in writing and distribute it to the group. Then afterwards I like to ask the students,

"Knowing the theory, is this helping you? What would you do now?" I am interested in how the class changes because of the fact they now have a framework.

There is the related question as to whether the summarizing or the generalizing should be done case by case or only at the end of a series of cases or segment of the course.

Don: It depends. I'm not a lesson-a-day believer. I'm not sure that a summary of certain types of cases is enormously functional. Sometimes the summary is apparent as the discussion reaches closure. I do think, however, that after sections or subsections of the course, it's enormously useful for the instructor to endeavor to relate the cases to each other and to the concepts underlying the section. Now in the best of all worlds, with some stimulation, the students will be able to do that. But this is asking a lot from students. You will get a little of it from very good students. But most of this falls upon the instructor.

There seems to be a consensus that executive programs have a greater need for summaries than degree programs. The following quote underlines the basis for this opinion:

Ian: In executive program classes, I think the instructor has more of a responsibility for pulling the discussion all together. Sooner or later the instructor has to summarize or pull it together more than in an MBA class. There's another good reason. Usually one case per topic area or situation is about all that can be covered in a short executive program. In the MBA class, there may be five classes on that topic and if the students don't get it today, so what? The class runs right up to the bell, and then everybody leaves, and tomorrow they know they're going to come back and, even though it's another case, it's going to be the same general subject area, and maybe they can pick up something from yesterday and tie it back in. Not so on the executive programs. The instructor has to go on to a completely different topic tomorrow. So our better executive program faculty spend five or ten minutes in the class summarizing the class discussion where they might never do that, or rarely do that, in the MBA class.

There are two further ways of ending class which, although often relished by students, should be handled with care. One is for the instructor to provide his or her own solution to the case and the other is to tell the class what the company actually did. The first approach may be risky in several ways. A few students may reject or challenge the instructor's solution in an unproductive fashion while a large number may accept it as the "correct" one. Also, if students expect the instructor to provide "the answer" at the end of the class, it may well demotivate them to search extensively for their own alternatives and turn them towards trying to predict which alternative the instructor will favor. That is not the purpose of the case method. It would be wise for the instructor, when offering an opinion about a case, to caution students that it is an opinion and not the answer. Some instructors prefer to state such opinions informally after class is over.

Sometimes, especially when an instructor has written the case, there may be great temptation to reveal what the company actually did. Of course, confidences and disguises should never be violated and students should understand that the company's decision was not necessarily the best solution. Also, news of this sort tends to provide closure to the case. Some case instructors insist that the mind keeps working away on unresolved problems much longer than on situations where the instructor has told students what actually happened in the company. Finally, it implies that the instructor is privy to additional information the student does not have about the situation. The idea that "all of us enter the situation with equal information, let us explore it together" does not really hold.

We believe it is useful to remind students shortly after class to take no more than five minutes to record and summarize their key observations, insights or generalizations on their Case Preparation Chart (see *Learning With Cases*, Chapter 5).

MANAGING THE PARTICIPATIVE PROCESS

Throughout the discussion phases the instructor faces a variety of issues not necessarily related to the specific case, but concerned with managing the participative process according to the Class Teaching Plan. These issues will be discussed next. All of them focus on what the instructor can do in the classroom. They deal with topics such as encouraging participation, dealing with participation problems, dealing with material problems, moving in the classroom, linking contributions, recording contributions, pushing for decision and implementation, managing time and sequence, maintaining order and dealing with trade-offs.

Encouraging Participation

There are many ways in which an instructor can deal with the management of participation in the classroom. The choice of whom to call on first and what to pose as the starting question have been discussed previously.

The decision on whom to call on and whom to give preference to during the remainder of the discussion phases needs further coverage.

Bert: When there is more than one hand up in class, whom do you call on? The one having it up the longest? The one waving frantically? The person who hasn't recently spoken? The person who told you the previous evening, "I'm going to really be ready today?" All of these pass through your mind as you're looking over the people. Again, I think it has to be related to what you're trying to accomplish. For those hands that are up in the air, I believe it's useful to know something about their prior responsiveness in class and their backgrounds. I'm willing to give up some progress with the discussion for the sake of that person who hasn't participated but who now has his or her hand up, particularly if this person is among those fifteen students who are running a B- or C in participation. I always try to get them in if their hand goes up.

For Andy, the use of volunteers versus selected students presents no dilemma.

Andy: I give them a chance to volunteer first. If the hands aren't up when the previous speaker is through talking, then I call them. I don't typically go into class with a call list.

Roger gives calling on students an explicit preference:

Roger: You've got to call on students. In my opinion, you can't depend on volunteers only, because the people who volunteer incline to be the best in the class. And you can get a completely erroneous idea of where the class stands if you rely on volunteers exclusively. If I could, I would call on people all the time. But this is impossible as you cannot ignore completely the people raising their hands.

Instructors who have prepared a Case Teaching Plan obviously would not have the difficulty that these previously quoted instructors seem to have regarding volunteers and call lists.

Dealing with Participation Problems

Part of the instructor's task in managing participation is to deal with four types of normal problems: low, poor, overactive and dysfunctional participation.

In this chapter, the focus will lie with what the instructor might do in the classroom about these problems. Further follow-up on an individual or small group basis in the office may be required. Low participation is unlikely to be resolved adequately by classroom measures alone.

Low Participation. Kim starts with the experience of low participators' negative feelings.

> **Kim:** In any class, there will always be some people who participate little or not at all. In an 80-minute class, it is difficult to bring in more than 30 people into the discussion in a meaningful way. Therefore, if the class size is larger than this, a number of people can obviously not participate. The problem is to prevent the same people from not participating in every class. Part of the difficulty is that with a participative method like the case method, any repetitive non-participant can become a dropout or an isolate and feelings of non-involvement and frustration begin. Some may try to "psych themselves up" to participate in a class. If they succeed, they will probably feet better. If they do not, they will probably feel worse. In the latter case, a spiral may start to occur to the point that individuals may find it becomes impossible to work; every class becomes a mountain of trouble and real feelings of depression occur.

The correlation between ability and willingness to participate is not always obvious. Many poor students volunteer frequently, while the good ones sit silently. There are a number of things that instructors can do in class to help low or non-participators. Again, students have different motives and knowing your students can help tremendously.

> **George:** I think people are very different. People respond to different stimuli and I like to try to find out what's the right thing. For some, it's a carrot; for some it's a stick; for some it's waking them up and getting their attention; for some it's just priming the pump and getting them started. Somebody who hasn't talked at all, after he's called on once or twice,

may turn into a very useful contributor. I will embarrass someone if I think it will do something. I will make someone mad. I've done all of those things over the years.

Nick: With the non-talkers, I do a few things. First I usually make a practice to scan during discussions for any new hands that are up. Another thing I do is watch for interest on the part of habitual non-participators. Quite often, these people are as involved as anyone. They are just afraid to get in there. I'll watch for them and try to catch them at a point when it looks like they've got something on the tip of their tongue. If I don't call on them directly, I'll look at them momentarily giving them ample opportunity to speak. Now, thirdly, cold calls can certainly help. This next year, I'm going to use them more as follow-ons; that is, after someone has made the opening contribution, ask someone else what they think. I'm going to use this for non-participators. I'm convinced because I've seen it so many times that as much as they may dread it, it is a very welcome shove into the cold water. Finally, if some are not talking by mid-semester, I usually call them in my office to discuss their difficulties.

Kim: Here are some of the more unusual things I have tried to get non-participators in the class to speak up.

1. After about three classes in the course, I have asked that only those who haven't had a chance to speak up in class yet to carry the discussion. It's not a huge success, it can probably only be done relatively early into a course, and it certainly pinpoints the individuals involved, which may well carry some heavy penalties. What do you do if no one speaks up? Are you going to start pointing a finger?

2. I have put all of the names of people in the class in a hat and had someone draw names to establish the order of participation. It tends to create a bit of a strained discussion, because it lacks the spontaneity and natural flow of a more volunteer based discussion.

3. I have walked into class and said, "Everyone is going to make at least one statement about this case, and it may not be a repetition of what anyone else has said, nor repetition of a case fact without an evaluation or implication attached." Then I would start off at the beginning of one row and keep going for about five to eight participants in sequence, before jumping into a different section in class, even a different direction along that row. This has worked reasonably well, except you tend to run out of board space (because you are recording something for everyone) and comments run the full gamut from problem definition through analysis, alternatives, etc. to implementation. Sequence will be non-existent. The net result, generally, is a fairly good assessment of almost everything in the case, but disorganized. The last time I did it, one student played games and moved seats, so I deliberately ignored him and left him to the very last. He then atoned for fooling around by making some excellent broad concluding remarks that neatly tied the previous comments together.

4. I have asked students themselves to choose their own successor after their own participation. When I tried this, I allowed others to volunteer, and I wonder if it would work differently if no one was allowed to indicate they were ready to continue the discussion.

On reflection, it may well be that the real benefit of these kinds of efforts lies more with the reinforcement that participation is important, than with the technique itself.

Poor Participation. It is possible for people to participate, but not in the desired spirit and quality. People may not have prepared properly and remarks may be shallow or off the mark. As discussed in Chapter 4, the instructor must indicate the quality of work expected and insist that the class live up to these norms. Regular acceptance of poor quality participation will bring the whole class down to a mediocre level. At times, it may be necessary to resort to hard stands. For example:

George: Some years ago, if we went through a policy case and I didn't think the class had come prepared and I didn't think they had done a good job, chances were I'd say, "This is what we have not done today. You've got the case again tomorrow; now let's go get the job done."

Rick: I think it's useful to walk out of a class once a year. I've really come to that conclusion. What to do with a class when they're poorly prepared and down? Well, one weak preparation is OK. But if they're really going that badly, why prolong the agony? I'll walk out. After twenty minutes, I'll say, "Hey, I worked my butt off to be prepared and I'm here to do some work. You're obviously not. So why waste everybody's time?" and walk out.

Paul: In the first year course, I don't really worry very much about student feelings. I guess I'm pretty harsh with them. I call on them cold. I will take a student who I don't think is working as hard as he should be or whom I haven't heard from, and I'll stay with him. If he gives me a straight up reply like, "I was ill last night," then I'll say, "Fine" and move on. But if he gives me a weak response like, "Well, I didn't get very far," then I'll come right back and say, "Well, how far did you get?" No matter what he says, I'll stay with him for an hour and a half and even when he's got nothing left, I'll use his name. "Tell Mr. so-and-so what the issue is, help him out." Then I'll ask Mr. so-and-so what he thinks. I'll stick right with him. Then you just can count on it, just like the sun coming up, the very next class, I'll walk in and call on him again and he'd better have done a better job preparing. The same goes for the student who was ill.

Earl: Until about three years ago, I used to get mad, angry, visibly annoyed if the students were not prepared. And I quit doing that and to my benefit because I think I came across looking petty when I did that. Now I take the humorous approach without any clear annoyance, but it's obviously a put-down.

Jeff takes a softer line:

Jeff: I'm aware that the students are not as well prepared for class as they ought to be. So, I consciously spend ten minutes of every class dragging out what the issues are along with the fundamentals. I typically walk in and ask the students what the case is, what is it about, and tell them I've forgotten about this or that. I will often deliberately misstate or misconstrue something just as a way of trying to keep the attention of all of the class.

Overactive Participation. Just as it is possible to have underactive participants, it is possible to have overactive participants. It is normally much easier to deal with the latter than the former.

Kim: The verbose students will get on the nerves of the class and frequently the class itself will jump on individuals like this and calm them down over time. Instructors may ignore hands that are outstretched and may invite certain individuals to come to the office to ask them to tone down a bit. It is useful to point out to these individuals that every student has a responsibility and opportunity to participate and that, if they take too large a chunk of class time, others are automatically excluded.

Brad uses a blunt approach:

Brad: I tell the person who talks too much to shut up. I'll say it right in front of the class. I'll say, "Alright, I've heard enough from you. I realize you want to participate. That's fine. You can make three comments in a class and then it's game over. Pick them."

It seems, however, that executives are much kinder to one another than regular students and one cannot rely on them to do their own disciplining.

Don: In an MBA class, the loud vocal types aren't much of a problem. First of all, I have the privilege of only selectively calling on them. Secondly, in a class that stays together for a long time, peer group pressure begins to silence the loud mouths whose content per minute is reasonably low. In an executive education session where you're dealing with people who aren't going to be together too long, there I think you do have to be more aware of potential monopolists when it comes to air time. You have to be prepared either not to call on them or somehow humorously cut them off.

Dysfunctional Participation. We refer here to empty, irrelevant, or out of place comments which may creep into the discussion. Again, each class should have some of its own discipline to handle such comments. When the instructor is trying to keep discussion to a certain point or certain area, it is proper to request that each participant concentrate on this area only. One may even ask, "Is it to this point that you're talking?" before allowing anyone to speak. If a point is relevant but out of sequence, it is easy to say, "Let's come back to that point later."

Dealing with dysfunctional participators nonetheless can be difficult.

Steve: I had a couple of students this year... I just lived in trepidation every time their hands came up. I really wasn't sure what was going to come out, but I could rest assured it wasn't going to be anything I wanted to hear. I feared we would suddenly find ourselves deflected off somewhere. I became very reluctant to let them participate. I probably shouldn't have, but I found at times I just couldn't cope. The question or the comment was often so convoluted that either I couldn't understand it, or the rest of the class couldn't understand it. I tried talking to them separately. But it continued. In class I just couldn't ignore it. Right there in front of me, this hand has been waving for 25 minutes. It's losing blood, turning white. Everyone can see I'm moving everywhere but there. You've either got to work with them individually or ignore them entirely. When I ignore people, I think I've failed. I should be able to get to the point of helping anybody participate well in class. When I have to neglect them purposely, I've failed.

Eric stresses the need to be flexible.

Eric: If the first time a student speaks and it's not relevant you slow him down and say, "Jim, it's interesting, but it would be more effective it you could tie it to some data. Where's the evidence to support your notion? Can we look in the exhibits here?" Jim says, "Gee, I haven't done it." I say, "Okay, that's fine. Can anybody help us with the numbers? No. Fine. Well, maybe this point isn't worth pursuing, Jim. Let's get back to the theme." If it happens again, it seems to me you become less patient. I say, "Come on Jim, it's not valuable to take up our time with your opinions, either you've prepared the case or you haven't." The third time, I'll call him at home and tell him I don't want him talking in class anymore. He is out. But you have to know enough about your students so that when some poor soul who hasn't spoken all year raises a hand and starts out in something that is clearly empty, doesn't have quite the analytic rigor, this is when you let it go. The skill in being a teacher is when and when not to enforce your own rules. It has to be credible to the class. For example, it might be Jim's first contribution this year and he's "scared skinny," but we're not going to beat him up versus here's somebody who's a hot shot, talked a lot of times, and you go in there and say, "Cut it out, we don't want to hear this from you." So you can't go in with a role that's consistent for every person, every course, every institution.

To help minimize problems related to participation, Nick says:

Nick: I tell students that the secret to effective participation in a case discussion is to listen and think at the same time. By thinking, you're able to keep updating, re-formulating, re-constituting parts of your own analysis. And by listening, you're able to have both the input to do that and also to monitor, to get the timing right and trace what you're thinking about, so that you can participate. This seems to have an impact on them. One of the ways of thinking about doing that is just to keep in mind that most people only talk about one fifth as fast as they think. Therefore, you've got a lot of time to fill the dead space as people are talking.

Dealing With Material Related Problems

There are potential problems related to case materials that unsuspecting instructors should be aware of. These include: missing information and assumptions, questions in class by participants, ending class early, and case quality issues.

Missing Information and Assumptions. It is very difficult to find a perfect case. Thus, naturally, the participants will read and understand cases differently. They are forced to live with the reality that all desirable information may not be provided. It then becomes natural for students to come to class unprepared or frustrated because they think they did not have the necessary information. The instructors reply must be, "Why is the missing information so important to you, and how would it affect your decision? Secondly, what assumptions could you make that might be reasonable under the circumstances? And thirdly, would this information normally be available to the decision maker in this organization?"

Forecasts are a typical example. It is easy for participants to say, "The quality of this forecast is lousy, therefore, I cannot make any plans." It may well be very difficult to make good forecasts and good planning may have to allow for many contingencies.

Missing information and assumptions are an integral part of the case method. In Chapter 3 in *Learning With Cases*, suggestions are made for participants on how to deal with missing information and assumptions. The following comments are in addition to those already identified for participants.

Missing information should be labelled: missing relevant information. By definition a case is but a summary of a real life situation with lots of information missing. One possibility is that relevant information may be missing because the case writer inadvertently or deliberately left it out of the case. If it has been deliberately left out of the case, it may be at the request of the managers and the company from which the case was obtained or it may have been done for educational reasons. The other possibility is that the information was not available to the decision maker in real life either.

These are quite different sets of reasons. If the information was available to the decision maker in real life, but is not included in the case, the case writer may be asked to do a revision of the case. An alternative is to include the information as part of the assignment with the case, "Assume that last year's actual sales amounted to 750,000 units priced at $12 each." If the relevant information was deliberately excluded for educational purposes, the instructor may have to explain the reason in class, "The reason I did not give you last year's actual sales in units and average price was because I wanted you to use secondary data to estimate them and to show you how close you could come to the real number." If the data were not made available at the request of the organization where the case was written, an explanation can easily be given in class.

Should the data not have been available to the decision maker in the case, participants can be asked whether this is reasonable, whether the data might be obtainable, where it could be found, how much time and cost it would require to collect it and how it would affect the analysis or decision in the case.

Arguments that missing information prevents a participant from doing a decent preparation is a popular one with participants who like to have any excuse for avoiding a decent individual preparation. A fact of life is that few decision makers ever have all of the facts they would like to have before making a decision. Therefore, the role of assumptions in case preparation and discussion is a vital one.

Chapter 3 in *Learning With Cases* contains five types of assumptions which occur frequently. The context and "normal state of affairs" assumptions (#1 and #2) normally need little reinforcement with the group of participants who have collectively significant work experience. For groups without work experience they may not be so obvious. Assumption #3, the decision criterion assumption, almost always needs to be made explicitly. If a class participant does not volunteer it on his or her own, the instructor will have to pull it out of him or her.

Assumption #4, the "if-then" assumption, assuming that the alternative chosen will work perfectly, needs a fall-back position. "What would you do if your meeting with the president did not work out as planned?" is a standard counter question which can be raised by the instructor or a class participant. "Does everybody agree with this?" is a good way to elicit a class response to this kind of assumptions. The "perfect person" assumption (#5) can be handled in a similar manner as assumption #4.

Assumptions can and should be challenged on the basis of their reasonableness given the case context and their relevance in view of the issue under consideration. Hidden assumptions, ones that are never explicitly stated, may prevent the suggestion or selection of alternatives for consideration and lead to an unsatisfactory solution. "I assumed this alternative was too expensive and, therefore, never suggested it," is one example of a potential hidden assumption. Both the instructor and the class need to make such hidden assumptions explicit.

Francis explains her approach to differing assumptions.

Francis: I have a philosophy and I make it very explicit to the students in the beginning of the course. I tell the students, "Look, I think what we want to do is be explicit about our assumptions. They are all going to be a little different. Now being different isn't necessarily something we have to worry about. We only have to worry about them in those situations in which the decision you are going to make is sensitive to that different assumption." So I take somebody and say, "You tell us what you've done, what your assumptions are." If it's the beginning of the year, we may lay it out in detail on the board. If it's half way through the course, we may just put up her conclusions and assumptions. Then, basically, I say, "Let's use this as a base. If you don't like what you see, here is your chance. Let's talk about what we have to change. Let's first of all determine whether in fact what we are arguing about is worth arguing about. If not, let's move on."

I think you have to go through that several times with them. You're going to have to expect some initial confusion, some initial wrestling but the decision making is critical. Only if we are differing on the critical stuff should we talk about whether we should be differing.

Questions in Class by Participants. Kim reflects on questions related to case materials that are brought into class by participants.

Kim: The case material can generate questions in the mind of the students. I should not pass over questions that are pertinent. However, I should not be led into wasting time with questions of little interest for the class as a whole. Students are very adept at wasting time in class. Perhaps one of the favorite games is to ask questions to the instructor, "In your opinion or in your experience...?" or "Can you tell us a little more about this organization?" The types of questions are endless. It's easy to spend 10 to 20 minutes a class fielding questions of this sort, particularly on cases written by me. Normally, these are straight delaying tactics by students anxious to keep me talking instead of jumping in themselves. Instructors who give in regularly to this temptation may well find themselves short of time to do more important things in class.

On the other hand, it is possible the instructor may find him or herself in the position of having to say, "I don't know." Frankly, when using cases, the possibility that instructors do not know is substantially increased. The case method deals with a tremendous amount of institutional information. It is unreasonable to presume that an instructor would be fully knowledgeable with all aspects of every case. Insofar as such information might reasonably not be known by the teacher, an "I don't know" in class is totally legitimate. If, on the other hand, it reflects improper preparation on the part of the teacher, students may well question why the instructor is allowed to get away with improper preparation and why they are not. For instances of the first kind, the class can itself be relied on to provide the insight or the information.

Ending Class Early. Every once in a while, a student will crack a case wide open at the beginning of the class with super analysis and a logical conclusion. It may appear that there's little need for further discussion given the extensive job done by the individual. Such a presentation may prove to be a springboard for a better discussion than would have occurred without it. However, once the class has been given an opportunity to discuss the presentation and once it's clear that no one can come up with better ideas, there may not be much need to have a further discussion on this particular issue. It is possible to discuss the case to death. Occasionally, when a class has done an excellent job of discussing all the relevant issues with a case, it is possible to finish class early.

Case Quality Issues. There is another type of difficulty with some cases, which might be termed "quality issues." The quality of the language, spelling, grammatical constructions may not be good, turning off readers, preventing them from doing a sound preparation. The language may be misleading, so that a segment of the class sees it one way, while others have a different interpretation. Dates, numbers, and other facts may be confusing or contradictory. In one part of the case, it says last year's sales were $5 million; in another, $9 million, for example. There may be a legitimate reason for some of these differences in facts. Actual company documents may contain mistakes. (This latter issue should not be confused with different opinions expressed by characters in the case; such differing opinions are always a fact of life.) Insofar as these problems are a result of improper case writing, class participants should be shielded from those as much as possible. The best place to catch them is at the time of material selection for a course. Avoid using cases like this. Any problems which arise during class need to be dealt with quickly by the instructor, "I had not realized this was a problem; let's resolve it right now. I will make every effort possible to ensure that others using this case in the future won't face the same problem."

After class the instructor then tries to communicate the problems to the case author. If such efforts are unsuccessful, and the instructor still wishes to use the case again, corrections can be noted on the assignment sheet or on an addendum page to the case. Under no circumstances should instructors make any changes to cases not written by themselves.

Instructor Movement

In the reference class discussion, Professor Jones moved throughout the classroom, although he spent most of his time at the board or near the center of the room. What are the advantages and disadvantages of moving around and what body messages are sent? Effective use of the body can assist the instructor in performing almost all of the various tasks identified in this section. Some instructors have given considerable thought to movement in the classroom.

Eric: I also use my body, the way I move in class, to move the class. I stand at the back of class a lot, totally outside, and watch. I move toward people, away from people. Block people off. I try to use my physical presence in class as well as the board to lend order and energy to the discussion. If I want the session to slow down, I slow down. If I want it to speed up, I speed up. If I'm upset with what's going on, I stand in the center of the room and yell and scream. If I like what's going on, I sit in the back and let it go for 10 minutes and don't say a word, just point to people. If I think it needs to be balanced one way or the other, I know what people will say in class, so I'll look for a call pattern that has a physical dimension to it; i.e., move the focus of discussion around the room, for example.

Gordon: I am very careful about where I position myself in the classroom. For example, if you approach a student who is contributing, he or she will tend to finish off, conclude quickly. Whereas if you move away, he is more likely to continue on with the point and develop a new one or go off on a tangent. You can also involve other students in the discussion by positioning yourself close to them and then ask them to pick up the point that's been developed by the previous student.

I use my hands to signal a lot. It's almost like half of what is said is non-verbal. With a nod of the head or a hand movement, I indicate another person to pick up the point. A substantial portion of the people I intend to involve speak without ever being called by their names.

The instructor not only sends non-verbal signals, but also receives them. By paying attention to little things such as eye contact, noise level, body attitudes or side remarks, the instructor may realize it is time to re-orient the discussion, to change the pace or to conclude.

Linking Contributions

In addition to eliciting participation, the instructor must somehow link contributions. Some people find it hard to think on their feet.

Dave: The key skill in the classroom that I don't think very many people have is to be able to respond to what the students say. A student may talk for 4-5 minutes and there may be a dozen things you can respond to. Picking the right one, so that you can move the discussion in the way you want and also in the way that tells the student has made an important point worth expanding on, is a key skill.

Nick: The teacher can learn to listen selectively so that he or she can be thinking. For example, I can often tell when people are coming to the end of a statement by the drift on how they are speaking. What I do at these times is step out to figure out where I want to go next with the discussion while the speaker is holding forth. In some cases, I stop listening altogether and rely only on modulations to tell me when they're about to close. Usually, I pick it up in the last

4-5 words as to how they're ending and I project back to their earlier points and know how to respond. Occasionally, a student will just stop cold and mess up my plan. If a response is required from me, I'll just have to say, "I'm sorry, I wasn't listening."

The instructor may be involved in linking not only a point of discussion to another point, but one class to another class, one course section to another, one course to other courses, and even one course to a total program. In doing so, the professor supplies the glue that makes the whole thing stick together. Eric and Harry talk about case to case linking:

Eric: In complex teaching like this, I think it's critical for students to have it clear in their mind every day where they are on this intellectual journey they're taking. Besides outlines and notes on the course, I spend time at the beginning and the end of every week to state, "Here's where we've been, here's where we're going." It's like a broken record. It's a linking so that they have confidence that there is some kind of method to the madness. The minute they get lost in case by case, however exciting the case by case is, they're gone. So maybe I sacrifice some of the drama, some of the lively elements, to make sure it has continuity.

Harry: One of my teaching techniques, and I'm sure everybody uses it, is to keep raising old cases. I try to remember who took what position in certain cases, and I am familiar enough with some cases to recognize some positions. And I try to keep track of who those students were who took those positions. It really impresses a student to say, "So and so over here took such and such a position in such and such a case, now tell me about that again, relate it to this situation." If you can do some of that, you get a lot more learning going on, because suddenly they're beginning to think, "There's something to what's going on; somebody's listening to what I'm saying," and students are making some conclusion.

Sometimes the bridging is provided by the students themselves. Bruce refers to the interface between courses and encourages professors to bring in the discussion that form of linkage.

> **Bruce:** Sometimes you don't know what is on students' minds because they are taking a lot of other courses which you don't always know about. Very often there is an interface between what they are learning in control, finance or organizational behavior. They can see some interesting parallels among the cases and they want to bring that into class. That's part of what a school which focuses on general management should be encouraging. Now a suggestion here is that one ought to know what is being taught in other classes; but it is not always possible.

Probably the most normal way of relating contributions as well as inducing participation is by asking appropriate questions.

Questions and the way they are asked by the instructor convey to the participant what role the instructor wishes to play. A minimum of questions conveys a non-directive preference as do questions which ask for clarification, "Do you mean? Can you repeat this? Please explain this further? Did I hear you correctly?" Other questions are meant to expand, "Do you wish to add to your argument? Are there other points you wish to make?"

Other questions focus on logic, "Why do you believe this is (not) possible? Why is the sales manager having difficulties? If this is the key problem, how will this alternative solve it? Why can this be done overnight?"

Please note that the way questions are asked will also send a message. A firm tone and aggressive body stance convey quite a different message from a gentle tone and a relaxed body language.

Andy does not worry about the number of questions he asks:

Andy: I just keep raising questions. I try to get them to differ with others. I think a primary job of a case oriented discussion is to try to promote a fight, figuratively speaking. I feel learning begins when differences of opinion arise. So I'm in there trying to promote fights and to be the policeman so they don't kill each other.

Larry provides a different perspective:

Larry: To me, the very first rule of teaching is: don't hurt. An instructor can use his or her questions as a shepherd's staff or as a club. He or she should take care to use them as a gentle prod, not as an instrument of wrath, anger or punishment.

Recording Contributions

A significant task for the instructor involves the recording of comments made in class. The usual record reinforces the importance of points made, provides a reference to new comments, and focuses class attention. Various devices such as black or white or electronic boards, flipcharts, overhead projectors or screens may be used during this process. How well the instructor records may affect the quality of class discussion.

The Board. Boards are probably the most common recording means available for case discussion. They can serve a number of functions. The most important are: a focal point where class comments are recorded; a tool to structure the discussion; a reinforcer; and a way of putting across points, calculations or explanations.

Eric: My teaching plans require careful, explicit attention to what the boards are going to look like, what's going to be up there in detail, what goes first and where. The board is the most effective way to direct the non-directive class, to lend order while at the same time giving freedom to allow the students to organize their thinking. Good use of the board is a way to organize, to motivate, to move and have a sense of progression... Often when I summarize a point on the board, I'll come back to the person and say, "Is that right? Have I got what you said right?" It's clear that everybody knows I'm manipulating them, that I'm taking what they say and building on it so I can get the class going. Some of them are delighted, "Did I say that? It's fabulous. Sounds super." Sometimes they'll get annoyed and say, "No. I didn't say that. You put that out of context. It goes under strategy." Somebody else says, "No, that's not right." Now we have a debate and the board becomes the focus.

If the board works right, it gives you continuity. They kid me about my board plan. I love it. The basic analysis is the same everyday. They know that performance goes on the left and context goes on the right. They know it. They'll laugh and say, "Hey, you forgot it or you got it in the wrong place." I'll smile and say, "No, I think I got it right." They say, "Yes, you're right; that's how we did it yesterday." This is a nice way to have continuity. They'll even begin to gesture and point to the board. I tend to write in a totally illegible way which doesn't seem to affect anything because it's impressionistic on the board; it's not substantive. I write in three dimensions because I write on top of things. At the end of class, my board is a disaster.

Earl: I frequently assume the role of the scribe. I say, "I'll just record today." They soon take the responsibility for getting the right numbers up as quickly as possible and correcting their own mistakes quickly, challenging their own numbers, because they know that I'm not going to. However, I don't like to leave the room with bad numbers on the board. If we're running short of time, I'll be more directive.

As part of the recording function, one question is whether the instructor should put on the board the student's own words or summarize and interpret these words, like Eric does. Once again, it depends on what the instructor is trying to achieve. Many instructors like to be exact in their reporting for fear of biases or too much interference. For these people, recording is merely a means for keeping the key elements of the discussion before the class. Nonetheless, it should be recognized that by recording something that has been said, implicit reinforcement takes place.

> **Kim:** It is always necessary to use some form of shorthand because there is never enough time and space to record comments verbatim. Even with shorthand, very few boards are large enough to be able to handle a whole class. For this reason, it will be necessary to put ideas down and erase them again, or hide them behind boards if sliding boards are available. Knowing this, the instructor may be subconsciously trying to economize on board space. This may well mean that refusing to put an idea down, that seems not to have much merit, appears to be attractive. Even a momentary hesitation will signal to the class that here is something the instructor may not be too keen on putting down. If the instructor wishes to encourage the class to take issue with the point raised, the class had better be aware of this desire. A comment like, "All I will do is record ideas on the board, you are responsible for evaluating them," is useful under these circumstances.

It is useful to plan and work out ahead of time any charts, diagrams or calculations required on the board to avoid embarrassing situations. Colors can be used to highlight and relate important points by underlining and circling them in the same color.

Legibility of the comments on the board and an understanding of the shorthand used by the instructor are important, even though Eric downplayed this aspect in his earlier quote. It is a good idea for the instructor, occasionally, to walk to the back of the class and look at the board to see if it is possible to read what has been put down. Don is well aware of his weaknesses in this area:

Don: My board work is largely for my own edification, since no one can read my writing. However, I can refer to it and it helps me keep track of where we are.

Chris finds writing on the board time consuming:

Chris: It's hard to be at the board and leading the discussion. Every time you go to the board and you're writing, you've lost something. It's dead time. I use the board early to get the analysis out, the problem definition up, the alternatives out. Then, as we start to evaluate alternatives and get a plan of action, I'm pointing to the board, but not writing very much.

However, instructors don't always realize how much time is required for the students to take proper notes. By writing the major points on the board, it enables the teacher to hold down his or her own speed to the rest of the class.

Finally, another disadvantage of the board is that the instructor needs to turn his or her back on the class. The overhead projector or electronic projection gets around part of this problem.

Overhead and Electronic Projectors. Many of the comments which apply to the board use also apply to the overhead or electronic projector. In addition to enabling the instructor to face the class continually, the overhead projector has other distinctive attributes over the board.

The instructor is able to use materials prepared ahead of time, which is a great advantage, especially for people with bad writing, and therefore, speed up the process. Both handle colors easily. It is not necessary to erase comments already made. It is possible to go back and review all of the recordings for a total class and even to distribute them to the students, allowing them to concentrate in class on the discussion, instead of on their notes. In hotels, or other such locations where it is practically impossible to get a decent board, it may well be the only reasonable alternative, provided a large enough screen is available. There are no limits as to how sophisticated one can be in his or her use of charts and slides. Clint explains how he uses overhead transparencies to create participation.

> **Clint:** We do two things. We use blank transparencies and pass them out for students to show certain transactions or numbers on and then take them up in class. We also tell the students early on that everything should be prepared in a fashion so that we can take a picture of it. So I will have my assistant be available at the start of any class to make copies of the students' preparation and then we'll use their work on the overhead in the class discussion. So it's very seldom I have prepared transparencies. In fact, at least in accounting, during the first week or two of school, everybody's work is flashed up at least once. This is one way of breaking the ice. Everybody is forced to participate in this fashion. They will explain and defend their work. I think one of the worst things a professor can do is to put his or her own answers up. Then you are up there trying to defend your work instead of the students defending it.

Barney warns against using too many instructor prepared overheads.

> **Barney:** Relying on overheads is the greatest way to kill the whole learning process for students. They immediately stop putting out and sit back for you to put out. I even had one professor tell me, "I'm going to give a full class lecture on this section of the course because I've got some good overheads!" Of course, there is a time for overheads and I use them when I want to deliver information.

The overhead is not a panacea, however. It is difficult to stare at the light and the class at the same time; and it draws the attention of the students somewhat excessively to the front of the class when they should be focussing on each other. It works better at focussing on specific points than at providing a global picture for a discussion.

Robert discusses his use of electronic projection.

Robert: For my teaching in first year finance, I go through how everything fits together for the 50 classes in terms of building blocks and sequence and priority. I start by showing the learning objectives, using electronic projection. I show what we're going to try to get out of our discussion and the objectives are prioritized. I just talk my way through each of the points. The next slide I put up is the class agenda; question by question or topic by topic. I start by asking the question(s). For example, "How would you approach this class of problem?" We would spend maybe 10 minutes talking around the class, how students would do it, what they would do first, next and why. When I feel like the time is up, we move on.

My slides are a skeleton of what should be said. You have to have a good memory to be really effective in doing this. You have to remember that Heather said this and John said that and be able to relate them. I economize and efficiently use the class time which allows me more time to focus on who is saying what and the process of exchange. Writing on an overhead or a board takes a lot of time as well as it diverts my attention to what to write and where to record it.

I never give my slides to students even though they constantly ask. I do, however, make available any of the supplemental information I would lecture about or material that I have summarized or something like mechanical calculations. These materials are just information delivery and so, instead of people writing madly, I just hand it to them and I talk to it. It doesn't destroy the class. This practice is no different than your not giving a teaching note to the students — you don't and I don't either. My slides are my teaching notes and I don't hand them out.

The agenda really sets the pace for the class and helps students to determine the sequence of events and exchanges. As we go through the agenda they know what's coming next. I do everything by question format. I don't want to spend time talking about case facts so I tell them on the slides what the facts are. Then I just raise the questions and provoke discussions around meaning and interpretations. Each one of the questions naturally leads into another one. It is the design of those questions that automatically moves us from one topic to another. Very rarely do students move ahead of where we are in the discussion. I can sense when they start to get "antsy" and we move on. It's the design of the questions that is important and that's how you solve business problems. This, essentially, is what consultants do. They ask questions and one question leads to another. That's all I'm doing here and we're just walking through the questions. It takes a lot of expertise and thought but if you set it up right you won't be jumping around.

When students come for counseling I use the slides to walk through and help clarify student thinking and understanding. Sometimes I just set-up my note book for them and they can just walk through the case. Foreign students in particular find a big difference when they see things on the screen. They can see the terms and there are no mistakes, you're not writing short-hand, they can see what the terms mean. Reading someone else's writing in a foreign language is very difficulty if you're not accustomed to it.

Pushing for Decision and Implementation

One of the key goals of the case method is to train participants to make decisions; that is, find solutions to problems on the basis of their analysis. Since participants are frequently inclined to avoid making decisions, some special initiative on the part of the instructor may be required to push them from analysis to decisions and from there to implementation planning. Logically, decision making and action/implementation planning fall near the end of the class. They are, therefore, subject to the greatest danger of lack of time to treat them seriously. Most instructors set aside a certain amount of time to give students some exercise in these very important phases.

One way of providing an action orientation to the class from its very beginning is achieved by using "backward chaining," that is, by asking for action first and then backing into the analysis which would support that course of action. Nick explains when and how he uses backward chaining:

> **Nick:** When I have a case that is very much decision oriented in mechanistic terms, I usually start with the decision. I will stay with the initial participant not just to get the decision in a cursory way, but really wringing him or her dry in terms of analysis and support and how he or she used the data in the case. The discussion is then opened up and I try as quickly as possible to isolate opposing views. I even ask for someone who has an opposing view. The balance of the discussion is then focussed on the elements of the decision: to work on facts and assumptions, to flesh-out judgements, to work on decision criteria and to arrive at a decision given an analysis of alternatives. With an expository case where the decision may be secondary, the primary objective is to get an understanding of the concept. I want to build the discussion around some point of tension that will expose the concept. Although a decision may be a starting point, it is only a jumping-off point.

Quite often, several alternatives have been raised during the course of the discussion. No single decision may have been reached by the end and no attempt made to come to a specific conclusion. The instructor's plan may be to leave the discussion open so that students will think further about the case and come to their own conclusions.

However, to facilitate a confrontation of views on an issue or to heighten students' commitment to their opinions, the instructor may force the class to make a decision by asking for a vote. Sometimes a vote at both the beginning and the end will show the effect of the discussion on the class.

Managing Time and Sequence

Since only a limited amount of time is available for every class, it is particularly important to manage time well. The use of a time schedule, within limits, can help provide some type of control over the rate of discussion (see Chapter 4). Still, the instructor has to exert judgement repeatedly as to whether to push the class to move on to the next topic or to explore further the one being discussed. A number of instructors find it effective to control the class rather closely on the time dimension.

> **Earl:** I run a fast paced class. There are no twenty minute monologues. It's much more a bang, bang sort of thing. I can tell you before the class what I'm going to talk about and roughly how long. I will very seldom get deflected from that. That's because the case fits into some sort of idea of what I'm trying to do and what I'm not trying to do. So if the students want to go in a direction that may be a perfectly good direction, except it doesn't relate to where I'm trying to go to, I don't let them go. It's not an open-ended totally uncontrolled discussion, that's for sure. In terms of the topics and sequence, it's pretty tightly controlled.

Eric talks further about sequencing:

> **Eric:** Good teaching, in my view, is where you start together, work on a topic together, and build up to the next one and

the next one, and everybody has a sense that the class goes up. This requires the right teaching questions, the right board plan and a sense of discipline, both in getting the details, evidence, facts and descriptions sorted out from the opinions. It may require comments such as, "Jim, I understand this is an interesting issue, but lets set it aside for a moment because we're still on the description of the short term strategy. When we get to the long term strategy, we'll come back to you." This level of control in the class, that level of direction, is critical.

Don identifies some elements of the price that the advocates of tight control in terms of time have to pay:

Don: Some people know exactly what they want to do in class and they do it in a very effective, orderly way. There is, however, a cost. There is a little less spontaneity and provocativeness associated with the classroom session. So I might achieve the spontaneity and provocativeness at the cost of the systematic coverage.

In reference to pacing, Earl notes:

Earl: In the beginning, the pace is slow because I'm calling on people and they're giving long comments. The first person can go ten minutes. Then the pace accelerates as we define problems, and generate and evaluate some of the alternatives. Then I'm really probing, I'm pushing and pulling hard. I'm asking for evidence. If someone really needs to take a long time to say something, he is really frustrated by me. I won't allow him to take three or four minutes to say something I think could be said in thirty seconds. I'll be impatient. Every body sign I have is one of impatience at that point. There are some people who just can't say it in thirty seconds. They've got to have five minutes just to make sure they've got it right. And I'm standing there with 30-40 hands up and we're moving, getting right to the point. Now momentum stops, this person slows us down. These people have trouble with me. But I think most students would say they would rather have me in on the side of a faster than slower pace. Nonetheless, it's a problem. But for me, it fits my style. Somehow, students will have to adapt.

Eventually we make a decision and discuss implementation. In each class, there is a peak. Some people like to peak at the end of class. I like to peak, if there's a peak in terms of where the real interest of the case is and you bring it all together, with about fifteen minutes to go so that you can ride the peak for a while with a high level of discussion and understanding.

Maintaining Order

There has to be a reasonable degree of class discipline. Not all participants can talk at the same time. People must listen to the speaker of the moment. Without order in the classroom, it is impossible to run a decent case discussion. The role of the instructor can be compared here to the role of an orchestra conductor. It includes turning up the volume on the quiet ones, and toning the class down so that all can hear, as well as discouraging side discussions which might create noise.

Kim: In some countries the noise level in class tends to be higher than elsewhere. In South America, for example, on executive programs, I have found the total noise level high. There is a tendency to carry on side discussions, to snap fingers, to talk simultaneously and to emit sympathetic and unsympathetic noises. It can be fun, but there is a threshold beyond which case discussion cannot go.

Dealing with Trade-offs

The number of tasks the instructor performs during a case discussion is large. The objectives are multiple and varied. Thus, an instructor is concerned not only with the list of tasks and problems already identified but also with all of the normal tasks and objectives of any teacher in any circumstance. It all adds up to a very complex task, and consequently, a continual facing up to trade-offs right in the classroom. The difficulty is that many of the tasks have conflicting aims. For example, any time taken by the instructor to speak has to be taken from the students' participative time. An instructor who uses a great deal of control for the sake of efficiency may take away from the student the responsibility for learning. An instructor who plays an active role in cutting off discussion and orchestrating discussion may not encourage the class to do its own discipline. An instructor who wishes to use up time to discuss theory in class may not permit the students sufficient time to do problem solving or decision making or implementation planning. The instructor must, therefore, know how to manage trade-offs. These trade-offs are far from simple and can only be resolved in a total program and course philosophy. It is reasonable to do certain things in one class because in a previous class other aspects have been highlighted. Glenn states the frustration of trying to deal with trade-offs.

> **Glenn:** I have about four things competing for my attention as I run the class: What's being said now; what someone just said previously; where I want to go next; and how much time to be used. This is all jamming around in my head to the point where sometimes I don't listen closely enough to the most important thing, which is what that person is saying right now. These four kinds of competing dimensions, the now activity, the past, the future, and time, make a very dynamic environment from the standpoint that you give control, or at least are willing to allow the class some control over where they want to go, what they want to say, who wants to say it, and how much interaction you allow to go on there. In addition to all the technical analytical kind of stuff you bring in with your own analysis of the case, it just gets hot and heavy down there in the pit,

or at least, from my point of view it does. Also to keep those four or five balls in the air all at the same time while trying to be somewhat empathetic in terms of your listening ability so you can pick up on the two or three key words, that's hard!

Professor C. Roland Christenson's comments provide a thought provoking conclusion to this section on managing the participative process.

From my earliest attempts to analyze what discussion teachers, myself included, actually do, I have observed that we spend the bulk of our classroom time posing questions to students, listening to their replies, and making some sort of response — not always a further question. The time we invest in these activities would, by itself, recommend studying them, but I discern a further stimulus: teachers who treat questioning, listening, and responding as skills to master with reasoned care also gain the ability to influence aspects of the discussion process — mood, tone, pace, culture, and abstraction level — that otherwise seem untouchable (153).

CASE TEACHING STYLES

References have been made several times to case teaching styles. Most often the references have been in the form of, "My philosophy is, my role in class is to, depending on that I'll be this, my approach is to..." In reflecting on these personal statements, there are two aspects worth noting. On the one hand, some people seem to have a consistent style in at least some areas of teaching with cases. For example, in the preparation for class chapter, Les always prepares his three points to start the class. Eric said he calls on people to start every class. Sam said he almost never calls on someone to start the class. On the other hand, several people have qualified their ideas and experiences with the phrase "it depends"; that is, depending on the students, the case, the course, the program, the time of day, the time of year... instructors engage in one of a number of roles and styles. For example, Ian feels that he should summarize at the end of executive program classes more so than MBA classes. Chris' style apparently changes from the start of the course to the end. At the end, his approach is to go wherever the students want to go in the class discussion.

In highlighting case teaching styles in a separate section, we are not trying to convince anyone that one style is better or worse than another, nor that in certain circumstances a certain style is preferable. However, style is an important element in teaching with cases because it ties the various roles together in a logical whole. It will be up to each instructor to identify those styles that seem worth trying. Besides, a label or a title on a set of behaviors can in itself be helpful.

Dooley and Skinner have identified a variety of case teaching styles and some of the reasons why instructors might wish to adopt one over another.

One Extreme

The range of pedagogic philosophies employed in the case method is bounded, on the one hand, by the belief that learning is a self-acquired process. This is the philosophy that contends, in the words of Charles Gragg: "Wisdom can't be told." The student learns what he or she wants to learn and is ready to learn; the student must take full responsibility for his or her own learning. Any external elements — such as books, instructors, texts, principles, the articulated wisdom of others — can help or hurt the learning process, depending largely on whether the student is receptive to them, and perceives them as useful. But each individual can learn only at his or her own pace, in his or her own way, and according to his or her own needs.

The professor who subscribes to these assumptions believes that in a case discussion the instructor, at best, can help as a classroom traffic officer, keeping everyone from talking at once, reporting/recording the flow of analysis and conclusions. At worst, the instructor can be a foreign, intrusive, divisive element. The instructor can interfere in the learning process — can fall into the trap of assuming an understanding of what the student wants to learn and is ready to learn. But since all students are "on different tracks," the instructor inevitably gets in the way of many of them. When the professor says, "I'm going to help," he or she begins to deny the student some part of the responsibility for learning, creating student dependency instead of self-development.

According to this philosophy an instructor can offer modest assistance to students as they undergo an intensely personalized experience; the instructor who attempts to play an active role inevitably will impede, perhaps even destroy, the learning process for at least some percentage of the class. Responsibility cannot be shared. Either the student accepts the responsibility for his or her own learning, or goes to the other extreme of saying: "Here I am, instructor. Educate me."

The Other Extreme

At the other extreme is the pedagogic philosophy that the instructor is the decisive element in the learning process, that the instructor's knowledge and wisdom place him or her on "center stage," that the ultimate responsibility for making sure that the class is "effective," that "students learn something," is the instructor's. People of this persuasion believe that for the professor to play other than a dominant role, to take refuge in questions when there are answers, to act as if his or her experience, judgement and insights are not superior to those of the students, is to pervert the teaching process and the basic tenets of professorial responsibility. Wisdom can be told, and the professor should do the telling. "That's what professors are paid to do."

Time is viewed as precious. The instructor's job is to make sure maximum imparting of knowledge is achieved in the time available. When leading case discussions, the professor must maintain control, identify, and then lead students through the important aspects of a case, without letting time be wasted in fruitless arguments between uninformed and inexperienced students who have not yet learned to approach problems systematically, rigorously and efficiently. Letting students "muddle around" and master concepts themselves perhaps may be appropriate for occasional, brief intervals, but a little of this is sufficient. The instructor then must impart knowledge efficiently by showing students how to approach and handle the topic correctly. The professor constantly must make clear where he or she stands, and impart continuous feedback as to whether each student who speaks is right or wrong, and why. The instructor instructs. The student absorbs.

A Middle-Ground Viewpoint

There is a middle-ground philosophy. Here the notion is that while the instructor is not the decisive element in the learning process, and must not try to play that role, he or she nonetheless should help substantially in the learning process, and can do so without removing the student's ultimate sense of responsibility for learning. The instructor can build bridges and linkages from other courses, from case to case, and from class to class; he or she can help make the classes interesting and challenging and meaningful; can add perspective; can interject color, fun, spark and focus. And in making these contributions, the instructor can help the learning process, as long as he or she does not: (a) dominate by playing too active a role and taking too much time; (b) remove responsibility from the student for analysis and conclusions; or (c) insist upon his or her approach or conclusions. The instructor must not provide the "right answer." That is the students' task.

Varying Roles of Students and Instructors

Growing out of such differences in objectives and pedagogic philosophy, understandably divergent views arise regarding instructor and student roles. The choice lies anywhere within the vast range bounded, on the one hand, by a completely nondirective role for the instructor and, on the other hand, by a completely dominating, directive role. Correspondingly, the role assigned to the student can vary from intense activity to total passivity, with the student in the latter instance being expected only to absorb the wisdom being spoken by the instructor.

Most instructors with whom we are familiar embrace a technique somewhere between these two extremes. Some play all of these roles from time to time, depending upon the specific objectives of the individual class session. The array of alternative pedagogic roles is great. For purposes of illustration, we will "label" and describe four of the many different instructional approaches practiced under the case method.

The "Facilitator" Instructor

In the "Facilitator" method... the instructor leads off most class sessions with little or no introduction or "warm-up." He or she assumes that the students have prepared the case carefully, see its relevance, are interested in it, and ready to discuss it, but that doing so is their responsibility. The professor also assumes that students will recall what has occurred in prior sessions and will draw on that for perspective, if needed.

Given these premises, the instructor's classroom role is largely nondirective, leaving responsibility primarily with the students. The instructor may write on the board various data, issues, questions, principles, ideas, generalizations, concepts, and analyses that are offered by the students. But in doing so he or she plays merely the role of a recording secretary. The instructor shows no partiality, reveals no judgements or sentiments, gives no hints of judging "right" or "wrong," "good" or "bad," in the flow of student ideas. These are judgements for the students to make. The instructor even attempts to assure that his or her body movements and facial expressions are nonobtrusive.

At the end of the class the instructor may or may not ask some student to summarize the flow of thoughts, analyses and conclusions. Different students are likely to carry away quite different "lessons" from the class experience. But the instructor's goal was not to impart "the answer," rather to create an atmosphere in which each student could arrive at his or her "answer."

The "Coach" Instructor

In the "Coach" approach the instructor plays a more active role than the Facilitator, assuming a limited measure of responsibility for conduct of the class. He or she takes on the tasks of: (a) motivating and developing interest and generating a sense of the importance of the case and its issues; (b) linking the particular case to other facets of the course; and (c) taking active responsibility for the progress of the case analysis by probing, questioning, lifting up unsolved issues, challenging students' logic and evidence, giving them feedback, summarizing, and so on.

What the "Coach" instructor does not assume responsibility for is the quality of the students' analysis, for the correctness or incorrectness of student conclusions. These are student responsibilities. If the professor/Coach assumes any role in the final summary, it is a shared responsibility, building upon what the students themselves have contributed. Such contributions are offered as being "possibly helpful" rather than presented as "the gospel" buttressed by the instructor's superior knowledge, wisdom and experience.

The "Quarterback" Instructor

In the "Quarterback" approach, the professor makes the subtle but important transition from the role of a coach (who attempts to help students "play their own game") to a "Quarterback" who "calls the signals," makes the crucial decisions about what is to be done, by whom and when; and plays a key role in "making things happen." There is no question about who is "in charge." Nor is there any question about who is responsible if, at the end of the game, the results are disappointing. "Poor execution" by the players perhaps can explain a few "broken plays," but if the entire offensive game goes badly, the Quarterback must have "called it wrong."

The "Demonstrator" Instructor

In the "Demonstrator" approach, the assumption is that the instructor can do a vastly more efficient job of case analysis than the students, and that observing a demonstration of such expertise can be a valuable learning experience. After "being shown," students may be able to emulate the Demonstrator and do an effective job on their own, should a similar situation confront them in the future.

The instructor is the "doer." Usually employing something close to a traditional lecture, the instructor demonstrates; clarifies; performs the analysis; "walks" the students through the case facts, exhibits and figure work. The instructor identifies the critical problems; establishes the priorities; takes the "case apart;" presents the "correct" solution. Blind alleys are avoided by a simple expedient: the instructor denies students access to them.

Under this approach the student's role is largely passive. While the instructor is "demonstrating," the students listen, take notes, speak only if necessary to communicate that they have lost sight of their guide.

Still Other Forms of Instructorship

These four varieties of case instructorship represent only an illustrative sample of the pedagogic arsenal available to the teacher. Depending on preferences, convictions, talents, and ego-needs, instructors also may act as Prod, Referee, Dance

Master, Choreographer, Prosecutor, Evangelist, Judge, Conductor, Soothsayer. Other options include: Lion Tamer ("Students, you're the ones who are going to go through the paces, but I'll decide what paces you go through, and when, and how, and for how long. I'll crack the whip - you jump."); District Attorney ("I'll ask the questions; you answer the questions that I ask."); Senior Airline Captain ("O.K. co-pilots, so long as you stick to the general flight plan that I have prescribed, you can do most of the flying; but I'll take over during the closing minutes of the flight to correct any navigational errors that you have made, bring us in for a safe landing, and button everything up properly."); Will Rogers ("I'll say funny things to make you laugh — but there will be an important 'bite' to each of my witticisms."); Aesop ("There's a moral to each of these cases — figure out what it is and remember it. If you need help, I'll make the 'fable' explicit") (283-288).

CONCLUSION

This chapter discussed a number of considerations related to case teaching and reviewed a large array of techniques and processes used in the classroom. In conclusion, Kim's comments provide some thoughtful insight into where the instructor's priorities should lie.

Kim: To my mind, the process becomes a natural one over time. If it had to stay a totally conscious one, it would drive us nuts. You'd be continually asking, "Am I doing the right thing in the classroom right now?" versus trying to solve the issue at hand. How I perform as a teacher in the classroom has to be secondary to the questions, "Are they concentrating on the problem? Are we solving the issue?" What students are getting the brownie points, or whether in the end I'm looking like a hero should be well down in terms of my personal priorities. Now, if I'm doing certain things in the classroom that are highly dysfunctional in terms of the overall learning process, that becomes a

different kind of an issue. From what I've seen, most
teachers who, one, have some reasonable student interest,
and two, have that problem solving orientation, can only go
so far wrong. You recognize you've got to keep quiet a
reasonable amount of the time, let students talk, and set up
an environment that they feel ready to talk in. That's
fundamental to cases and I don't think needs to be worked
out to the infinite degree all the time.

I think you can go overboard in process, where you
continually experiment, "Do I roll my sleeves up to three-
quarters?" or "Is there any effect if I roll them up above the
elbow?"

I don't think there is a best way of teaching. We complement
each other. It would be very boring if all of us did the
inevitable thing in the classroom. Then we'd become
teaching machines.

class evaluation

The class is over, but the instructor's task is not. The habit of a regular evaluation after each case class is an essential part of standard case teaching. Class evaluation has six components: (1) participant evaluation, (2) Case Teaching Plan evaluation, (3) material evaluation, (4) personal evaluation, (5) class assessment and (6) teaching note evaluation and revision. It is our experience that many instructors engage in some, but not all of these activities. The after class review need not be overly time consuming, but the discipline of this review, shortly after every class, is important.

PARTICIPANT EVALUATION

The first focus of evaluation after class is on assessing student performance. How well participants contribute in the large group discussion is the question.

Whether class contribution by participants counts towards a course grade and what is considered a contribution have already been discussed in Chapter 3 on course planning. Therefore, the concern here is on when and how case teachers evaluate contribution, assuming some form of recognition is given to class participation. It should be noted here, however, that experienced case instructors make a habit of evaluating class participation regardless of whether credit is granted. Their purpose is to ensure that all participants over the length of the workshop, seminar, course or program are involved in the learning process. By noting who is strong and who is weak allows them to deal with each person appropriately.

When to Evaluate Class Participation

The first issue concerns when to evaluate contribution to class discussion. Recording evaluation during the class stifles the flow of discussion, produces added anxiety for students and distracts instructors from managing effective discussion and exchange. The common practice for most case instructors is to evaluate classroom contribution as soon after class as possible.

Les: I tell my students that I am not available for anybody or anything for 10-15 minutes following the class. I go back to my office and rewind the tape, so to speak, and then replay the discussion in my mind. Who was not there? Who opened the discussion and with what? Who else got in? Who offered important chunks of analysis? And so on.

Chris: I come back to my office immediately after every class. There, I have the students' names on a grading list and I put down a mark about how well they did. I record whether it was a negative, good, extra good or a super contribution.

Alan: I reflect on the class immediately afterward, and I think about what was said, who said it, and hope that, if it was good or bad, it will stand out in my mind. I put down explicit grades for what people did, so that I can look across a string of participation grades and tell people, if they ask, "It looks like you're doing about such and such in participation." In a reasonable class, I'll get about 25 people out of 55 into the discussion and, of those, I'll be able to recall about 20. I'll miss a few, but hopefully, not the same ones every time.

How To Evaluate

A number of people had some interesting ways and means to evaluate participation.

Steve: When I started out, I tried to keep track of everybody who participated. I discovered that in the course of the class, I just couldn't keep track of everybody. It became impossible. I got wrapped up in what was going on. I decided what was important was to keep track of the people who moved a particular class forward; the people who gave what I found were the key pieces of contribution that advanced our analysis. Coupled with that, I noted the people that I thought really threw us off track. I decided I would just look after these tails. I set up the criterion that, during the course of the term, I expected each student to end up in the positive tail two or three times. I should have thought enough of their comments to record them.

Glenn: I'm not at all satisfied that I have highly reliable measures. My system uses a big seating chart of the class. I run off as many as I need, say four or five during the year. Each participant has a box a couple of inches square on this chart and I make myself some really short notes in these boxes immediately after each class. I use numbers, from 1 to 4, with 4 as excellent. I also record if people were absent. I'll give people a negative evaluation if they made a negative contribution. I'm hardest in my evaluation on people who are not prepared.

Lou: After every class, I sit down and go through the class list. Basically, I decide whether the person participated, and whether it was particularly strong or weak. I know it's not overly scientific but I record this. Then, at the end of the year, I add up the quantities. What I'm really looking for is a ranking. Then I look at each individual student. I readjust this ranking by whether I feel a person has fewer entries, but those few were really good. And then, my final tally is a gut, subjective feel. I ask, "Was this person good or bad?" Then,

I must admit, I determine whether this grade will hurt or harm the student. Unless it was a flagrant disregard for participation, I will not normally let participation grades fail a student. I would definitely let participation drop a student's grade overall. If a student had outstanding participation and one bad exam, I'll reduce the value of that exam. It's a matter of trying to pretend I'm scientific by putting the check marks in after class, and then letting my guts sort it out afterwards.

Les: The school has classroom layout sheets prepared on letter size paper. I have students print their name in the appropriate box at the start of the course and then I put this sheet inside a plastic cover. I often record, with a different transparency pen color, three or four classes in a row before I put the participation assessment into the more formal and permanent register. Then I can wipe off the plastic cover and start over again.

The easiest part to measure is attendance. People in my classes are conspicuous by their absence. The second easiest part to measure is who started the class, who was the first speaker. The third level of assessment is, did I call on the person or did the person volunteer. From my point of view, it's better if students take the initiative to join the conversation. The fourth level of assessment is to determine who got into the discussion and who didn't. This determination is measuring the quantity of contribution. The fifth level of assessment is making a judgement on the quality of the contribution. And that's what it is, a pure judgement regarding what value the contribution had for the learning of the class.

I try to be very sensitive to people who want to volunteer but if, for a host of reasons, I didn't get them into the conversation I make an "I" notation in the register which means "interested." It's not their problem they didn't participate, it's mine. A string of "I's" in the register says I'm the problem and I had better be more aware of this person.

Likewise, a string of blanks on the register, meaning present but silent, says it's possibly time for me to call on such a person to check the level of preparation and quality of contribution.

Obviously, no one standard exists for how to evaluate and grade class participation. Whatever system an instructor chooses to use, it should be consistent, as objective as possible and shared with the students.

CASE TEACHING PLAN EVALUATION

It is useful to review the Case Teaching Plan for a few minutes after each case class. Was the agenda the right one? Were the estimated times realistic? Was the participation plan sensible? Did the board plan work out? Adding notes to the Case Teaching Plan provides a valuable reference for the future.

The Agenda

The review of the agenda deals with the extent to which the agenda was covered. What additional items came up that could have been added to the agenda originally? Were all of the case questions or main topic areas of the case discussed adequately? Once we got into the case discussion, did we answer the assignment questions? The instructor needs to determine whether a rearrangement of the agenda items and possibly the sequence of case questions would produce better results.

The Time Plan

The time plan review is clearly connected to the agenda review. Did the class go according to plan? Where were the largest time deviations and why did they occur? Was the original time plan unrealistic or did something happen in this class that disrupted the time plan? If the time plan was disrupted, was it better the way it really went or the way it was expected to go? Given that most instructors tend to be ambitious in their time plans and given that the participative process is difficult to control at best, time plan deviations are to be expected. In view of the learning objectives for the class and the course, it should be possible to review the time spent on the main agenda items afterwards and make a judgement whether full educational value was obtained for the time spent.

The Participation Plan

The review of the participation plan will reveal how many of the preference list volunteers actually participated. It may also allow for reflection whether the split between call list and volunteers was appropriate at various stages of the class discussion. Might it have been better to call on participants or to ask for volunteers? Aside from this split, the number of participants to be called as part of each agenda item needs to be reviewed. Would it have been better to call on a different participant for this particular question? Would it have been better to let participants with industry knowledge or problem familiarity get into the discussion earlier or later? Who did not get a chance to participate even though they were on the call list? The participation plan review provides important input for the next case discussion participation plan.

The Board Plan

The board plan review allows the instructor to reflect on how good the original board plan was and where deviations occurred. Was there enough space for criteria definition and was it in the right location? Similar questions can be asked for each segment of the board plan. Some instructors make a habit of going to the back of the class after each case class to make a quick judgement whether the board was legible, logical and fit the visual image originally intended.

Conclusion

It should be reinforced that the review of the Case Teaching Plan is likely to identify substantial deviations in a number of areas. Furthermore, perfect adherence to the Case Teaching Plan in every aspect is not the goal of the class. This may well create a rigidity not realistic in good case teaching and learning. The review after class must also recognize that any deviations from plan may have occurred because the original plan was not a good one. Sticking to a poor plan is not a good option. Furthermore, even if the original plan was a good one, unforeseen events may happen in class. For example, the majority of the class may have significant trouble understanding the assigned reading when the instructor believed it to be self-explanatory. Or, a participant who has not yet spoken up in class starts to talk and slowly covers some relatively minor points, but the instructor wishes to encourage him or her to the maximum extent possible. Or, a news item covers a key topic area in the course and all class participants want to talk about it. Or, a case exhibit needs a lot of explanation in class. Or, as the discussion progresses, it becomes clear that a theory covered earlier in the course is still not clear and needs to be reviewed. Or, a participant comes up with a novel alternative heretofore not identified in the teaching note.

Any of these kinds of occurrences makes it difficult to cover the agenda, time, participation or board plan as intended. Part of the instructor's judgement at review time is whether these were random events that could have been predicted and incorporated in the plan, or should be considered in a future plan, since the class was a better one because of the deviations.

MATERIAL EVALUATION

Assessing the quality of the case after teaching it is no easy task.

Barney: I don't ask the students to evaluate my cases. Some instructors do. I simply try to figure out if the case generated the discussion that I thought was appropriate for the concepts I wanted to deal with. It's difficult to tell sometimes because the class may not have been well prepared for a number of reasons. They may have had a previous class which interfered with the one that followed. Or, you may discover that you should have covered some prerequisite material before using the case. So, if the discussion doesn't do what you want it to do, you don't automatically throw out the case. I may have done a lousy job of leading the class. Any time a class doesn't get excited around concepts, and when I don't see students discovering ideas and going from step to step and arguing with one another about issues, I know I have to think carefully about that class and whether the case might be the problem.

Sid: I have real difficulty in picking a winner prior to using a case in the classroom. When I have just had a tough class, that is, with a lot of effort on my part to force the students constantly to look at this and look at that, then the case may be inappropriate. It is just not doing the job. Maybe it's too early in the course. Maybe it's too complicated and too much to ask a student to do in a reasonable length of time. Maybe it's just tough, because although everything is there, it's written in such a way that several little things destroy its credibility. For example, numbers are misplaced, or there is a direct misunderstanding between two parts of the case.

Les: With each new case it takes me three iterations to determine whether the case has educational value. The first time through, I'm just barely one step ahead of the students regarding understanding, analysis and appropriate decisions. Sometimes I don't really hear what they are saying because I'm unconsciously committed to my own views. The second time through, I am much less concerned about analysis because I feel much better about the fit of the case in the course sequence. I know what's coming next and am more flexible in listening to the discussion. The third time through, I don't worry about the case content — I know it will come out in the discussion. I don't worry about the fit, it works. The third time through I can really focus on the discussion process: Who is saying what? What's the emotional tone? Who's struggling and why? Who's got some experiences we all need to hear? It's after the third iteration that I can make a good judgement on whether the case is a "keeper."

It is also necessary to review the case in combination with the assignment questions. Would the case have been better with a different set of assignment questions?

The reading, handouts, or participant data gathering tasks from outside sources also need consideration. Were these helpful to the case and the course, or did they not add enough educational value for the time required?

PERSONAL EVALUATION

One of the most difficult evaluations an instructor must wrestle with is the one of self-evaluation. "How good was my own performance in class?" It is so much easier, if things went wrong, to blame the materials or the students. It is another matter to be objective enough to be able to assess one's own role in relation to the total process. How much of the time was I talking? How many topic areas did I introduce? How much of the discussion was directed at me, as opposed to others in the classroom? Did I have the feeling that getting comments out was like pulling teeth? Was my mood right for this class? Was my preparation adequate? Could it have been better? In retrospect, would I conduct the class differently if I had a chance to do it over again? If I had to rank my performance on a scale from 1 to 10, where would I fall? Would someone I know have done a better job of that class, and why? Did I learn anything in that class?

If we could ever learn to be totally honest with ourselves, answers to such questions might be reasonably objective. Without recognition that the teacher's performance is an important ingredient in evaluating total class performance, one may easily come to the wrong conclusions.

CLASS ASSESSMENT

The next step in the after class review concerns itself with the quality of the class just taught and the implications of this class in the context of the course as a whole.

Most instructors can generally tell after a class is over whether or not the class was successful. Several people expressed views on this topic.

Dave: I think it's a good class when the discussion has made progress, when there has been some disagreement that students have been able to resolve and when there has been lots of participation. I don't like people shooting from the hip or giving the one-liners. I want people to make points and try to relate their points to other people's points. When this happens in a class they're making some progress.

Sam: I measure class success by the amount of electricity: when there's a lot of active participation, when the ideas from the student are moving fast, and if those ideas seem to be related to the material. Now, if you have to drag responses out of people and they don't sound very excited while they are saying it, and it doesn't provoke any controversy, then it's not a good class discussion.

Paul: I judge a class by whether there are lots of hands up, whether they are anxious and interested in participating, and whether they come running down after the class is over to talk about the case. I listen to what they are saying to each other as they walk out of the room. I read their faces. I talk to students at coffee and try to find out how things are going. There are lots of little signs you have to look for.

Les: For me, what happens after class is a good indication of whether the students learned and got excited. Do they continue to discuss the case among themselves? Do they come to me to argue it further? Do they talk about it over coffee, lunch, drinks or dinner?

Tom: A few years ago we had a new instructor here who had a special class evaluation sheet prepared for the students. It asked the students for comments about the case, the instructor, the extra readings and anything else they wish to comment about. The feedback was anonymous and voluntary. These sheets were handed out at the beginning of every class and handed back at the end. I had misgivings about the procedure because it turned the focus of the students on evaluating the educational process, rather than on learning. I believe that was serious not only for that instructor's class, but also for mine.

In assessing a particular class, Jack offers an interesting summary:

Jack: There are about five "ifs" and if all five are met, you've had a good class.

One "if" is obviously students who were motivated, caring, concerned and at least willing to give it a half-way decent effort.

Two, and equally important, is "if" you've got good preparation.

A third is "if" the case itself really truly was important and relevant and real and critical. I tell my students at the beginning of the course, "I'll experiment and we'll blow a few, but, to the best of my intentions and knowledge, I'm never going to give one single case in this course that is not of major critical importance to the key person in it or to the company."

A fourth is that "if" there was an atmosphere of freedom in the classroom: freedom to fail, freedom to risk, freedom to experiment. When students put up their hands and got shot down in flames, they were not ashamed with me or their peers. Of course, they were a little bit. But I try to say to students that if you don't get shot down at least once a week in this classroom, having said something that turns out to be completely and totally wrong, you're like a skier who never falls down. This is what this classroom is all about. You're going to see me make an ass of myself a few times. But this is what we're all about. So the atmosphere has to be one of seriousness about the case and about the analysis, but not serious in terms of the individuals, the personalities. I say sometimes, "Look, we got to build a brick wall and I want everybody to put on a few bricks. If you don't like the other guy's brick, take it off. But we're all in this together. No one person is going to do it. It's a team thing. Part of this also is don't be afraid to ask questions or to say after we've been in class for 45 minutes, 'As far as I'm concerned, we're totally wasting our time.' I want that atmosphere of freedom to challenge me or the discussion. If we talk about the wrong thing in this class for 80 minutes, don't blame it on me. It's your class."

The last "if" is that I really want the atmosphere to have been one of fun in the classroom, but at the same time one of involvement, of concern, of seriousness. I want the fun to be the way a good baseball team can kid each other, but, boy, when they're on the field, they play ball.

Now my presumption is "if" you haven't met those five things, that class at the end of 80 minutes is going to be just as dissatisfied as you are. They don't feel they've made breakthroughs; they haven't discovered the excitement in the case; they're confused about it; and they don't really see it in a clear and understanding way. They were looking at that clock just the way you were.

The class review also leads to a consideration of the course implications. If the class did not cover some points as well as it should have, is there an opportunity for reinforcement in later classes? If certain theoretical concepts covered earlier in the course were still not fully understood, should earlier classes have been taught differently?

The Teaching Note Review and Revision

There is no better time to review the case teaching note than right after the class has been taught. Are changes required under any of the headings of the standard teaching note? (See teaching note discussion in Class Preparation, Chapter 4.) At a minimum, instructors need to put the reviewed Case Teaching Plan in the teaching note file as input for the next time the case is taught. The Case Teaching Plan review may result in changes to the teaching note or future plans for this particular case or other cases.

For new cases, especially after the first class, substantial revisions to the teaching note may be required to fill gaps that have been exposed by the first class. For most instructors the teaching note grows with each teaching of the case and becomes a valuable record and document of the experimentation that has taken place with the case over time. Even the inclusion of notes like: "I don't think the class was as well prepared as it could have been because most students were busy preparing for an exam in another course" may affect the future use and timing of this case.

CONCLUSION

The after class review forms an integral part of the case preparation, class teaching, after class review cycle that repeats itself every time an educator teaches a case. If class participation is a valued part of the course objectives, participant evaluation, whether for credit or not, is the first step. The temptation to go no further is strong. Most teachers are short of time. Even the few minutes to review the Case Teaching Plan, the case, one's own contribution, the class and the course and to make changes to the teaching note are often difficult to come by. Yet, these steps are essential to the continuous improvement of the case teacher. Making the after class review a habit removes the discretionary decision aspect of "will I review or won't I?" thereby becoming an automatic reinforcer of self-improvement. The collection of after class reviews for each course builds the basics for course planning for the next round and for improved teaching performance.

The checklist below is a useful reminder of the key topic areas to be reviewed.

1. Participant Evaluation
   Who contributed? How well?

2. Case Teaching Plan Review
   Agenda, time plan, participation plan, board plan.

3. Material Review
   Case, readings and other materials

4. Personal Assessment
   Instructor's contribution

5. Class/Course Review
   Course implications

6. Teaching Note Review/Revision
   Additions, deletions, changes

feedback and counseling

Feedback and counseling are an integral part of the case teaching/learning process. The prime focus will be on instructor feedback to students on their class participation and on counseling those who are experiencing difficulties in participation. Additional topics will include the use of case exams and feedback from students to the instructor on the course.

FEEDBACK ON CLASS CONTRIBUTION

Informal Feedback

Informal feedback on class contribution can start during the case discussion itself. Positive body language, supportive head nodding, appreciative murmurs, writing comments on the board or overhead in exactly the same words as the participant used and keeping other participants quiet, while giving the individual a chance to take the time necessary to explain ideas fully, are all forms of positive feedback in class.

Some instructors thank participants once they have finished speaking, others say, "This was a great start," or "Your comments were very helpful," or "Well done." Other instructors are wary of such evaluative comments in class, lest the absence of them conveys the opposite meaning. Moreover, these teachers believe their role in class is to be less evaluative and more facilitative. Therefore, they prefer other participants in the class to indicate whether they agree or disagree with the comments made by one of their class members.

Unfortunately, most participants find it more difficult to praise star performers than to disagree with those who are less able. Thus, even the noise level in class may rise when one judged to be inferior chooses to participate and chronic time wasters may well generate derogatory comments from their unsympathetic peers. Lack of negative feedback from classmates can, therefore, be interpreted as neutral or positive. Willingness of peers to reinforce points made and to enlarge upon them is already a positive reinforcer. Students who come to see the instructor in his or her office and say, "I haven't a clue on how well I'm doing in your class participation" are, therefore, not telling the truth or are inordinately insensitive to all of the ever present signs during the case discussion.

During the summary or conclusion phase of the class, the instructor has the option of reviewing the most significant contributions made and single out certain participants, much as an orchestra conductor may recognize the contribution of certain musicians to the rendering of a particular piece of music. Asking the individuals to stand up and take a bow is not the normal routine in case discussion, but "Paula's quantitative analysis really got it off to a great start," or "Peter's suggestion that a much less expensive alternative might be available put us on a totally different track" are typical ways in which an instructor can give positive feedback in class.

The time period right after class, while participants have not yet left the room, may present an opportunity to nod to a participant and say, "Good job" or something similar. Giving feedback can be extended to the hallway outside the classroom, the coffee area, the lounge area, the cafeteria or any other student gathering place between classes.

The office feedback session as opposed to the counseling session may be initiated by the teacher or the participant. Some instructors invite all class participants to drop by any time they wish. Others may have sign-up sheets or even discourage such participant initiated visits. These face-to-face sessions, when they do occur, provide a great opportunity for frank exchanges. A participant indicates the prime purpose of the visit is to receive an opinion from the teacher. "How well am I doing in participation in your class?" This question comes in a variety of phrasings and is offered with a great range of intonations. The most standard reply for most teachers is, "Well, how well do you think you are doing?" Since instructors have to keep track of all participants in the class, it is much easier for the student to monitor his or her own progress.

Throwing the ball back into the participant's court is a good tactic. It forces the casual student to do some serious thinking and also to reflect on taking responsibility for one's own evaluation in a case method context. Moreover, the instructor may learn some insights into this person. Finally, agreement with the participant's own assessment will help shorten the interview and disagreement can be focussed on specific aspects. Should any counseling be required, it can be done on the spot or left for another time.

Formal Feedback

A number of the interviewees believe formal feedback on contribution to class discussion should be given, just as it normally is on written work.

George: I have given each of the students an individual memo in which I tried to give them a verbal summary of my impression of them in terms of participation. I use phrases like, "Participation shows interest and preparation for class. You probably have a good knowledge of finance, but a little trouble getting to the point in participation." I believe this sort of feedback is more valuable than just giving a straight grade.

Sam: I try to give feedback on participation performance and encourage my colleagues to do the same. I give a midterm participation grade indicating where each student is at relative to others at this point.

After every class I come back to my office and I grade every student on a five-point scale. Those that say nothing get 0; those that say something spectacular get 4. About a third of the students in any class session get 0; there may be one or two 4's, three or four 3's, lots of 2's and some 1's. I just add up the numbers and rank the class on this basis. I post this ranking by student number on my office door and then I try to give lots of verbal feedback when students come and ask or when I ask students to come and have a chat.

Les: In my experience, there are some general categories of participation that students seem to sort themselves into. For me it's a matrix of low to high quantity and low to high quality:

QUALITY⟍QUANTITY	LOW	HIGH
LOW	I	II
HIGH	III	IV

Low quantity means students have participated in less than half the sessions and high quantity would be participation in more than half. Low quality ranges from minor, brief comments having little substance to small parts of the analysis and some interpretative comments. High quality means significant value added contributions that seem to advance the understanding of the class and that other students in their own commentary keep referring to.

I prepare a personal letter for each student that indicates my judgements on the quality and quantity of participation. The letter also contains some advice on what students might consider doing with the feedback. The advice for the low quantity contributor is something like, "While quantity is not everything, we need to have active and wide discussions to collect the wisdom of the group. I would like to see you be more active in our class discussions." The advice for the high quantity contributor is, "While quantity is not everything, we need to have active and wide discussions to collect the wisdom of the group. You are contributing your share and I urge you to continue." For the low quality contributor the suggestions are, "My advice is to stay in the conversation longer when you have the floor and string a series of your views together with the case evidence in moving the discussions to a new level," or "When you choose to contribute, you add considerably to our discussions. I would just like to see you contribute more of the same." High quality statements include, "Your contributions are strong and add value to the class discussion. Keep up the good work," and "Your contributions are memorable and add considerable value to the class discussion. We will all benefit if you continue to offer your insights."

COUNSELING

At times almost every instructor finds him or herself in a counseling role with students. For the case teacher, the need for this role is almost guaranteed given the subjective nature of the case learning and teaching process. Although students develop ways and means of coping with ambiguity, case based learning can generate particular frustrations and anxieties. The greatest counseling challenges deal with participation in class discussion.

Contribution to Class Discussion Counseling

Frequently, students who have difficulty with participation in case classes will seek out the instructor to discuss their problems.

Les: In all of my student counseling, I'm positive on participation. Participation is an opportunity not a problem. I suggest they experiment continuously. Start with the "chip-in" variety of comments, ask good questions, open the class, debate the issues and alternatives, summarize the class, practice a variety of strategies in each of their courses on a day-to-day basis.

Steve and Ron try to help students with their frustrations and anxieties.

Steve: I tell students, "I don't mind if you bring up the wrong point, because sometimes this is a counterpoint, a good focus for what we are doing. If you go down the wrong track, I'm not going to punish you for class participation." Students seem to feel they have to get to the right answer. They don't want to participate, unless they have got the right answer. I say, "No! No! Give us your answer, and if it's wrong we'll get it out on the floor and you'll be able to see from listening to people why it's wrong. If you are right, you're golden. Sometimes you do me a great service by putting that wrong answer out because there are 12 or 15 people in that class that agree with you 100%. In fact, if it never comes out, they are all going to walk out of class with a note of doubt in their mind that the class was wrong. There's no punishment for being wrong. The floor doesn't open. You don't get swallowed. You don't end up with a big X on your forehead." You've got to get this across early in counseling. It's the process of participating that is important, not so much for the answer, but for getting into the discussion and defending ideas.

Ron: I have been surprised with the number of students I have called to my office, or those who have come in on their own, who still are not prepared to talk about their problems. They seem uneasy and frightened. When I get someone like this, I reflect a little about why they might have difficulty talking about it. I will talk about problems, whether they are personal or related to the classroom. Frequently, when I've been reasonably sure of my grounds, I've said to the student, "Look, it seems to me you are not being totally honest with me or yourself. There are some signs that you have other problems." I have found consistently a couple of things happen when I'm taking the risk to share my hypothesis and to say that I am concerned. First of all, in a large number of cases, you are not only right, but the students are relieved. They then feel able to ask for your help, if they need it, and make progress. They also have told me after reaching that point of another explanation. They say that in spite of hearing our comments in the beginning of the year about the kind of school we run and about the method, they still have been skeptical about it. They still do not believe that the professor will, in fact, help them, care about how they did, maintain confidences and spend the time. They will say, "It's a first time a professor called me in because I might be in difficulty, not because I was in difficulty." It's only after you've taken the big leap that they'll say, "Now I believe you, because you went to the extra step of watching, listening, and now I feel I can trust you a little." This explanation has been both personally satisfying, and tremendously demoralizing and scary about the place a university is. The students in their educational experience have been really turned into cynics about motives and about the needs of the faculty and their objectives. It's a bitter sweet kind of comment.

Kim: Almost all of the serious counseling I find myself doing deals with problems in classroom participation. For a number of students it becomes a vicious circle. They become concerned about participation, try to do something about it, fail, feel worse about failing, try again, fail again and feel worse yet. That chain needs to be broken. I will say to such a student, "Let's both agree that neither you or I are satisfied about your participation in my class. Now, I'm only one instructor and I have only limited information. You have a lot more. Let's both engage in some detective work to find out why there is any problem at all. So far, all we have identified is the symptom. We don't know the cause." Then I ask the student to reflect over the next 48 hours on the following points: Is the student having general participation problems, or only in my class? Is the student participating in small group discussions? Is the student generally quiet? Is the student afraid of talking up in a large group? Is the student afraid to talk for fear of saying something stupid? Is the fear of talking in class based on a lack of adequate preparation? Would the student prefer to be called in class or would he or she be more comfortable with volunteering? Then, within 48 hours we will have another session with some answers to these questions. Normally, it's a lack of participation in all courses, a feeling of depression and some signs of an inferiority complex. A typical argument is, "There are so many others so much brighter than me who can say it so much better." The obvious answer to that one is that the purpose of the class is not to have the most efficient process for solving the company's problems. And it is important that everyone tries to solve the problem or decision at hand. Only through participation can students become part of that process.

It is an unrealistic assumption that someone with such problems will turn into a high participator. I find that setting some reasonable goals and a regular feedback system is important under such circumstances. So, we use such simple agreements as, "Within the next three days, you will put your hand up at least once a day in one of your classes. Whether the instructor recognizes you or not is not your decision. Whether your hand goes up or not is." I may have the student drop by at the end of each day to tell me whether the hand was up or not. Sometimes, I may wait for the end of the three day period. Using little steps at a time is an effective way of proceeding. The interval has to be short to be effective. You cannot say, "Come back in another two

months and we'll see whether there has been any change."
If there is no progress in the short interval, sit down and
discuss why not. I also find I keep talking about what cases
are all about, why it is important to talk in class and what
some of the simple signs are of good class participation. I do
not wish to give the impression that this is a simple process,
nor that it is always successful. That students appreciate
such help is abundantly clear.

Counseling sessions may not only benefit the student,
but also the instructor. Valuable feedback may be obtained
as to what is going on in class, whether study groups are
working well, whether certain instructor mannerisms are
disturbing to the students and whether the material is
being fully understood. This kind of contact may also help
the participant by identifying individual problem areas
and helping plan remedial action.

The challenge for instructors during the counseling
sessions in the first instance is to diagnose the possible
causes of student concerns and then to pursue some
possible remedies with them.

The basic point in participant counseling is that the
teacher does not have all the answers. However, the
teachers must have the right questions. The participant
plays a key role in the diagnosis and eventual prescription
of remedial action. The non or ineffective participation
issue can be viewed as a typical quality problem in
operations. When things do not work out as planned, the
cause and effect or fishbone diagram provides a useful
framework for attacking the problem. Therefore, in Exhibit
7-1 we have constructed a comprehensive diagnostic guide
to assist in the detection work of identifying the prime
causes for inadequate participation by an individual class
member.

Exhibit 7-1
CAUSE AND EFFECT DIAGRAM FOR INDIVIDUAL INEFFECTIVE CLASS PARTICIPATION

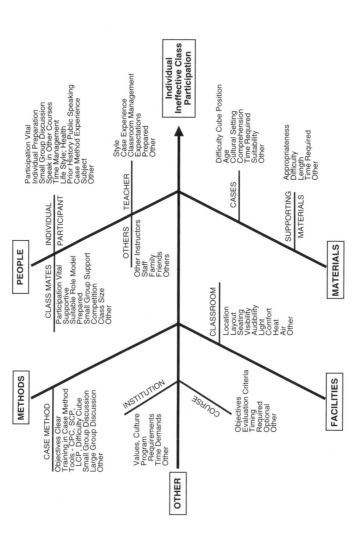

Teaching with Cases, © 1998, Richard Ivey School of Business

It will be useful to enlarge this diagram to at least twice its size and to give a copy of this sheet to the individual participant who needs counseling. Explain that on this sheet are the most common causes for non-participation and invite the participant to help you diagnose why he or she is having difficulties. Then proceed across the chart. It is a good idea to start with the physical facility, a fairly neutral starting point to put the individual at ease and to start the sharing of information process. Most of the material on the bottom and left hand side of the chart is easier to address than the people category on the top right hand side. Involving the participant in the diagnostic and prescriptive process enhances the likelihood that remedial action will be effective.

Our experience is that most non-participators (1) honestly do not believe that participation is that important, (2) have significant concerns or difficulties about speaking up in a large class and have a history of not speaking in public, (3) have course understanding deficiencies and (4) have difficulties in understanding the case method. The favorable part is that they recognize there is a problem when they come in for counseling.

The following pages will address these most common issues. The assumption will be made that most instructors will be able to deal with most of the other items on the cause and effect diagram by themselves or with the aid of medical, psychological, or student counseling support.

1. The realization that class participation is vital. Ironically, participants who have done very well academically in educational programs or courses where memory played a significant role often find it difficult to adjust to the participatory requirements of case discussion. They are convinced that the final exam will reward their ability to memorize and often are not convinced that participation is vital to their success in a case course. Aside from the arguments already advanced in the quotes such as "participation counts for a significant part of the course grade" and "you are not contributing to the learning of your classmates," there is an even more fundamental reason for each person to participate in class.

The parallel lies in sports. No athlete can become successful without practice. The would-be tennis player can watch all the greats of the tennis world on television or videos and attend numerous lectures on tennis technique, however, sooner or later, the individual needs to hold a tennis racquet and needs to learn how to hit the ball. For the case method, the small group and the large group discussion are the practice sessions. Some instructors say the small group is the practice and the large group discussion is the game.

The key point is that the individual who knows he or she will not be playing the game or even participate in practice and who will only be a spectator will not be as motivated as the one who will participate. It gets boring sitting in class and just listening to others. Lethargy sets in. Why read the case carefully when you know you are not going to be tested on it? Preparation slips. Small group attendance slips and participation is minor. The mind wanders in class, "The only reason I'm here is that attendance is required, but I am sure not learning very much." This attitude is a spiral to trouble.

Therefore, the first concern in counseling has to deal with the participant's recognition that class participation is not just for grades; it is the driver behind the learning process. The participant who is ready to participate all the time prepares better, listens more actively to others, feels part of the process and accepts that he or she is responsible for learning. Truly, it is a process of learning by doing and learning by teaching others.

2. Speaking up in a large class. A significant percentage of participants are not comfortable speaking up in a large group. Even those convinced of the vital nature of class participation find it difficult to face up to the implication, "You must speak up in class." Frequently, such participants make up their mind to participate in a particular class and then find they cannot. They return home and every successive failure lowers their self-esteem. This spiral is also dangerous. It is important to pull the individual out of it as soon as possible because the negative feelings spill over onto the course, the program, the institution and life in general.

Let us assume at this stage that the individual is at least comfortable with the course content and the decision model of the case method. Let us also assume that the individual does not need professional advice from a psychologist, psychiatrist or similarly trained counsellor and is willing to work on remedial action with the course instructor and/or other teachers.

Identification of the fear of public speaking is the first step to recovery. The second step requires the will to do something about it. The participant's knowledge of self and preferences become particularly relevant. "Are you the kind of person that can motivate yourself or do you need other reinforcers?" is a good question to ask. "I am willing to help as are other instructors, but would you prefer it to be a classmate instead?" Here are some standard options that can be offered:

1. "You agree to make sure you will raise your hand at least once in each case class you have over the next week. You cannot control whether you will be

recognized, but you can control whether your hand goes up. Make a record for a week whether your hand goes up and whether you were recognized and did speak in class. After one week come and see me. Let's set an appointment right now and we'll talk about how it went."

2. "I can arrange for myself and other instructors to call on you in class if you feel raising your hand is too tough right now."

3. "You may volunteer to start a class of mine or someone else's. At the start you can say exactly what you prepared without having to worry about what other people in class have said."

4. "You may volunteer for a presentation in my class or someone else's course."

5. "You may make a deal with a classmate, particularly someone who wants to participate more. Whoever participates more in a week wins a small reward from the other: some money, a drink, a snack, a movie or whatever. The point here is that a fellow student is watching you in class and you know it and you are doing the same for the other."

6. "You may just try to participate over the next week and then come back to see me. If it doesn't work we'll figure something else out."

The important points are:

1. Let the participant decide on what he or she believes will work.

2. Make the participant realize he or she now has an ally on the faculty who is willing and anxious to help.

3. A process of improvement has started. One visit to the office is very seldom enough to accomplish a turnaround.

4. The process of talking about the fears and feelings associated with public speaking allows the individual to face his or her challenge.

Our experience with hundreds of students is that the great majority find a way to cope and become reasonable participators. They are most grateful for the assistance and find all kinds of benefits beyond the passing of an individual course.

3. Lack of course understanding. It is entirely possible that participants do not wish to speak in class because they do not understand the course material. Therefore, to avoid personal embarrassment by a public display of their ignorance, they remain silent. Lack of course understanding should be comfortable territory for most instructors. The diagnostic process will require identification of where in the course difficulties arise and what the causes could be, including inadequate preparation.

Allowing individuals to provide a few hand-ins on specific topic areas to prove their understanding can help build their skills to the required level. Alternative readings or a tutor are other options.

4. The decision making model in the case method. A fairly high percentage of non-participators have difficulty with the process of analyzing and solving a case. They go through repeated readings and underlinings of the case but lack a logical process for the next steps. Such individuals often have difficulty even with the Short Cycle Process, the immediate/basic issue identification and the importance/ urgency matrix.

Walking these participants through the Short and Long Cycle Process as documented in *Learning With Cases* may be particularly helpful. Having them hand in Case Preparation Charts is a useful reinforcer. Reviewing opening paragraphs of cases and having them talk about the decision, the kind of analysis and criteria that might be appropriate, is also helpful. Often, such individuals are quite willing to spend the necessary time, but lack the tools.

A non-participant who comes in for counseling normally recognizes that he or she has a problem. The most potent counseling challenge of all is dealing with the participant who is afraid to speak in class, lacks some course understanding and does not understand the case analysis process. For this individual the solution begins with work on the course concepts and the case analysis process. There is no point in class participation if potential contribution content is not adequate. Time will be a major concern because such a compound problem may not be solvable before the course is over. We have not experienced many of this type and hope you will not either.

CASE EXAMS

The two common written modes of evaluating student performance are case exams and reports. In this chapter, the focus will be on how people use case exams. In Chapter 8, case reports are highlighted as a special variation in the use of cases. One of the issues in using cases for exams is how to select the appropriate case in the first place.

Bruce: A good final exam should be designed to test learning of concepts you have specifically emphasized. That leads to one of the problems with a lot of case exams. It is difficult to find a case which exactly covers what you are looking for. It should cover some of the same issues raised in class, but the situation should be different. Sometimes, using a brand new case for an exam can also be a good way of testing it out for future class reviews.

Nick: You need a case that separates the poorer grades from the excellent, one that will provide an opportunity for people who really know their stuff to demonstrate it.

For instructors using a significant number of cases in their courses, the use of case exams makes a lot of sense. Since case exams tend to "burn" cases, because so many written student analyses with grading comments on them will get out into the system, instructors may not be too anxious to use their best cases for exams. It is certainly good practice not to use the same case for exams in consecutive semesters or years. Also, the grading of case exams is a time consuming and messy job, compared to some other exam options. Thus, the decision to use cases for exams is a significant one.

Grading Exams

A second issue concerns the exam grading process and who does it. A variety of comments on this topic follow:

John: I spend a lot of time beforehand making sure that I know what the case will test and what I think are the dimensions of a good answer. Then I break out the dimensions in a grading key. The grading key has various points awarded. I always mark some of my own papers, but I always get help with my larger classes. I review the few papers I looked at with my grader's first batch, and see if they correspond. I let my class know there will be a grader helping me.

Kim: As each case is different, it is difficult to state the minimum acceptable level of demonstrated knowledge and ability in specific terms. However, I indicate several grading criteria that will be applied.

To be considered acceptable an examination:

1. Must identify and analyze at least 80% of the major problems in the case.

2. Should identify the key assumptions based on information in the case situation - recognizing that different and sound assumptions will be made by different people on the basis of the same information.

3. Must demonstrate that the correct method was used when any analytical tool was applied. Since all exams will be open-book, obtaining a partially or completely correct answer will increase the grade accordingly.

4. Must demonstrate that arguments used to accept or reject any alternate solution are consistent with the assumptions and calculations made, and are consistent with the prior interpretations of case information.

Lou: In marking my exams I need some sort of numerical guide. I do allocate marks to specific areas, not necessarily point by point. If the student has well thought out recommendations that seem to come from the analysis and is addressing the problems, that's not a specific number, it's simply very good. Therefore, if I allocate 10 marks for a recommendation, this paper will be somewhere between 7 and 10, depending on how it struck me. So, I take away some of the subjectivity with particular numbers.

Glenn: I develop a framework of what I am looking for beforehand based on the teaching notes and my ideas about what was important. Then I read between half a dozen and ten papers, flushing out my framework from that and developing a scheme. The students are told, in general, the background analysis counts for 30% and the analysis of alternatives and implementation is another 70%. I split that down more finely into blocks of 5 to 10 points, and go through grading keeping a running tally of how people perform in certain areas. If I were extremely conscientious, I'd go back over the papers, but I don't. I go back over the worst papers and a couple of the best ones, and that's how I generate a score for people. So I've got a framework that says how much implementation is worth. For example, 10 points, but not that X is worth 2 points and something else 2 points, all adding up to 10. I make a subjective evaluation of how they handle the implementation with some reference to a sublist of ideas.

The grading of a case exam is a time consuming task. It may take anywhere from 20-40 minutes per paper, on the average, assuming a 2-4 hour examination period. Despite serious efforts to develop evaluation schemes, much of the grading is still subjective. Thus, there may be a significant gap in perception between what the instructor reads and what the student thinks he or she said. In view of this, it is no wonder that instructor preference might well be to use someone else to do the exam grading. It seems to be a feeling of duty and responsibility, rather than a love of grading, that keeps most case instructors at the task of grading their own exams.

> **Alan:** Until last year I did my own marking and feedback. Then, last fall, I just got inundated by other things. I had a marker and it was not satisfactory. This year, I'll go back to doing my own. The students feel that you care more. You have a better feel for where the students are, both individually and as a group. When a student comes along and says, "I don't understand these comments," you can be right there.

If case examinations are to be handed back to students, then every effort should be made to do so quickly. Ideally, it should be obvious from the reading of the comments on the paper why a student received a particular grade. Sometimes, instructors may wish to schedule a special class session to discuss the case and its grading, and hand back the exam at the end of such a session. If the time gap between writing and return is too great, most students will have forgotten the contents of the case, making explanatory comments more difficult without their re-reading the case. Complaints are then almost totally grade centered, without any reference to content.

> **Kim:** I strongly believe that instructors using case exams during the term, and which will be handed back to students, need to do the grading themselves. I must admit that I don't like it, because it takes so much time and I see all of my own mistakes coming back to me. I tell my students that I will do the grading, but that I will not write extensive comments on every single paper. I explain that this would slow me down too much and, in the case of repetitive comments, become too frustrating. Thus, I will tell them at the time of the exam writing that they will receive their exams back within a week. I will schedule a feedback session in which I will comment on the common problems and errors encountered. On the papers I will only single out uncommon problems and concerns. I will, however, use extensive crosses and tick marks on individual points throughout the paper.
>
> I have always admired those people who can develop beautiful grading sheets with individual grades for every single point made. I have tried to use them, but have always found it difficult to stick to them. So I use a much broader scheme which asks, "Does this student make sense?" If the answer is yes, the only thing which needs to be determined is how good the paper really is. If the answer is no, no amount of individual point totalling will make the whole an acceptable paper.

In Chapter 6 in *Learning With Cases* various types of exams and student instructions for them are discussed. Exhibit 7-2 provides a typical written case outline and Exhibit 7-3 a list of typical case exam evaluation criteria. The weighting decided upon by the instructor for each of the six categories identified in Exhibit 7-3 may be shared with the class before the exam. Both of these exhibits tie logically into the Case Preparation Chart. We have found that for very short exams the Case Preparation Chart itself can be used as the hand-in. Even in longer exams students often hand in their Case Preparation Chart in addition to the exam itself.

Exhibit 7-2
TYPICAL CASE EXAM OUTLINE
(May vary depending on the case,
the course, and the instructor)

1. **Executive Summary**
    (Brief — one page summary of the main conclusions)

2. **Decision or Issue Definition**
    (Key decisions or issues to be addressed)

3. **Analysis of the Decision or Issue(s)**
    (Importance/Urgency, Causes and Effects,
    Constraints/ Opportunities)

4. **Alternatives/Analysis**
    (Identification, decision criteria, advantages,
    disadvantages, quantitative, qualitative analysis)

5. **Recommendations**
    (Preferred alternatives, predicted outcomes, action
    and implementation plan)

6. **Exhibits**

Exhibit 7-3
TYPICAL CASE EXAM EVALUATION CRITERIA
(May vary depending on the case,
the course, and the instructor)

1. **Identification of Issue(s)**

2. **Issue Analysis**
   Importance/Urgency, Causes and Effects,
   Constraints/Opportunities

3. **Alternatives/Analysis**
   • Analysis of alternatives provided
   • Generation of other alternatives, of decision criteria
   • Qualitative and quantitative analysis

4. **Recommendations**
   • Legitimacy of chosen alternatives
   • Reasonableness of predicted options
   • Feasibility of action/implementation plan

5. **Logic**
   Congruence between analysis and recommendation

6. **Presentation**
   Quality of language, appropriate use of exhibits,
   organization of the exam.

Written Case Analysis Counseling

Sometimes students are not satisfied with the feedback they receive on written work. Each instructor has a way of handling irate or disappointed students. For some it is as simple as, "Tough! Try harder next time." For others it's, "Let's sit down and take a good look at this."

Bill likes to separate the issue of grades from actual performance.

Bill: I will start off by telling a student, "Tell me what grade you want. Grades are not in short supply." Once students get over the grade hurdle, discussion can proceed on the case issues at hand.

For Robin the strategy of feedback on written material is more deliberate.

Robin: First of all, I won't see a student for 48 hours after returning an exam or report. The student must get over his or her emotional upset. Sometimes, I'll make exceptions, but not often. If a person is extremely upset, I've got to see him or her on that pretext, although we won't discuss the paper. But that does not occur too often. Students who wish to see me have to resubmit their paper to me in advance with a one page description of what they want to talk about. This presumes that I have been over the paper in class with them. I see this procedure performing two functions. One, I will reacquaint myself with the paper, so I am as up to date with it as the student is. Secondly, I know what he or she is upset about, so I can arrange the interview to have some mutual usefulness. Thus, the student hands in the paper with an explanation to my secretary, who makes an appointment at that time with me. I re-read the paper and make my own notes before we meet together. I hope that I can predispose the student not to be thinking merely about the grade. The grade will take care of itself because, if I find myself in error, I don't care about moving a grade.

COURSE EVALUATION
AND INSTRUCTOR FEEDBACK

Up to this point, the issues in this chapter have been presented almost exclusively from the instructor's point of view. Students, the other key stakeholders in the process, have an interest in evaluation and feedback as well.

Sometimes, instructors elicit student feedback in a random and informal manner, much like George does.

George: I am perfectly prepared at any time in a course to stop the class and get away from the case and say, "What's going on in the course? What are you learning? Are you learning anything or not?" Now, apparently some people don't like to do this because there could be a number of people holding up their hands to say, "I'm not learning a thing." And somebody else might say, "I don't think you are earning your pay." Well, if you are not prepared to take that sort of stuff, then don't do this because you are going to get some of that.

In Alan's case, sometimes informal student feedback can come at unexpected and awkward moments.

Alan: I recall a class where a hand went up and the student said, "Professor X, I expect to learn something in this program. I'm not learning a darn thing in your class, and I'm wasting my money, and I'd like to know why you're wasting my money." You know, up against the board, baby! In another class, the professor had asked, "What is the relevance of this movie we've seen to what we're talking about." The section "rep" raised his hand and said, "I think what the class wants to know is what's the relevance of anything you're teaching to what we want to know." Just that boldly! The point being, if you're not delivering the goods, they're going to tell you about it in no uncertain terms.

At most institutions and in most in-house programs, it is normal to have a formal procedure for students to evaluate seminars, workshops, courses and instructors. Every institution has its own rating forms and procedures for retrieving and using this kind of data. It is one area in which standardization has not advanced very much. Nonetheless, such feedback can form a valuable insight into course planning and execution. Considerable controversy remains as to whether good teaching ratings and effective learning go hand in hand. One professor, after receiving a devastating feedback, commented, "There is such a thing as a negative learning experience."

Whatever the merits of teaching rating systems, they can be used so that both students and faculty will be able to make a number of judgments regarding a course and its instructor. A course/instructor rating form is included in Exhibit 7-4 as a sample applicable to courses using cases.

Exhibit 7–4

Professor and Course Evaluation Questionnaire

Please mark the appropriate response to each of the following questions.

On a scale from **1 (POOR)** *to* **5 (EXCELLENT)**, *how would you rate the following aspects of the course and professor:*

		1	2	3	4	5
1.	The course overall?	☐	☐	☐	☐	☐
2.	The professor overall?	☐	☐	☐	☐	☐
3.	How clearly the professor communicated the learning objectives for the course?	☐	☐	☐	☐	☐
4.	How successfully the course achieved the stated learning objectives?	☐	☐	☐	☐	☐
5.	The contribution that cases used in the course made to your learning? (if the question is not applicable leave the response blank)	☐	☐	☐	☐	☐
6.	The contribution that the textbook and other readings assigned for the course made to your learning? (If the question is not applicable leave the response blank)	☐	☐	☐	☐	☐
7.	The contribution that projects, reports and other assignments used in the course made to your learning? (if the question is not applicable leave the response blank)	☐	☐	☐	☐	☐
8.	The contribution that other learning devices (e.g. simulations, videos, exercises, guest speakers) used in the course made to your learning? (If the question is not applicable leave the response blank)	☐	☐	☐	☐	☐
9.	The effectiveness of the professor in utilizing the diverse perspectives and experiences of the students in the class?	☐	☐	☐	☐	☐
10.	The effectiveness of the professor in providing timely and useful feedback?	☐	☐	☐	☐	☐
11.	The assistance the professor provided outside of class?	☐	☐	☐	☐	☐
12.	The effectiveness of the professor as a lecturer?	☐	☐	☐	☐	☐
13.	The effectiveness of the professor in facilitating classroom discussions?	☐	☐	☐	☐	☐

On a scale from **1 (VERY LIGHT)** *to* **5 (VERY HEAVY)**:

		1	2	3	4	5
14.	Relative to other courses at the Ivey Business School, what was the overall workload for this course?	☐	☐	☐	☐	☐

On a scale from **1 (NOT AT ALL)** *to* **5 (A GREAT DEAL)**:

		1	2	3	4	5
15.	Relative to other courses at the Ivey Business School, how much has this course contributed to your development?	☐	☐	☐	☐	☐

SCANTRON® FORM NO. F-5231-STC-L   Scantron sells that you please RECYCLE this product.   © SCANTRON CORPORATION 1998 ALL RIGHTS RESERVED   34567 F C9989-12 11 I0 9

In addition to these faculty wide, typically end of the course surveys, many instructors design their own form and collect information for their own diagnostic purposes. Bob describes his procedure:

Bob: Also, in addition to the school student survey, we have our own department survey, which we use as input to form our own judgment about our course and materials. The school survey focuses more on course content in the general sense. Our survey is designed to get specific comments on specific areas and materials. The surveys are complementary. Our survey is presented periodically during the course. We ask students not to write if they don't remember the specific case. Questionnaires are anonymous. Then we spend a day or two at the end of the term with all of the feedback and debrief the course in detail. There is a consensus that emerges in terms of what our priorities are for new kinds of materials and for new directions in the course. Then we commission one or two people to implement the steps in the new direction.

CONCLUSION

If cases are used infrequently, it is probably not wise to put too much weight on participation performance nor too much faith in any measures of assessment of the learning that transpired. Furthermore, the task of providing feedback to students regarding their performance may be seen by some instructors as so difficult that all such feedback is withheld until the end of the course and until a final grade is given. Then it is too late for corrective action by some students who may leave with less than might have been possible.

Feedback and counseling when using cases is, undoubtedly, a challenge. In almost every area of the process, the questions are easier to ask than to answer. In this chapter an attempt has been made to provide ideas and personal aids used by a number of instructors in meeting the feedback and counseling challenge.

case use variations

The focus to this point in *Teaching With Cases* has been on the standard practice of teaching with cases in a live classroom. Both the participants and the instructor have come prepared to exchange facts and opinions about the case, along with any ancillary information, in a face-to-face discussion format. It is occasionally desirable to utilize variations around this standard practice.

The most obvious reason for using cases differently is a better fit with the learning objectives. Often, a particular variation provides a change of pace to relieve the case after case routine. As well, technological developments permit instructors to teach differently, allow cases to be presented in different modes and media, and enrich the learning environment for participants. Also, a particular variation is sometimes appropriate when only a few cases are used in a course.

The following variations around the standard theme are presented in this chapter: case presentations, case reports, role plays, case format variations, visitors to class, team teaching, field trips, and interactive video conferencing.

We first describe case presentations, reports and role plays; why these variations might be selected; how to implement them effectively; and note some limitations for each. Many of our interviewees had used these particular variations and shared their experiences.

CASE PRESENTATIONS

Description

Case presentations involve the live delivery of a prepared statement by one or more students to an audience of one or more people. Chapter 6 in *Learning With Cases* describes different types of case presentations and suggestions for presenters and critic observers. Case presentations offer a variety of permutations and combinations (see Exhibit 8-1). Each instructor needs to decide which option makes more sense given his or her course objectives.

Exhibit 8-1
CASE PRESENTATION OPTION LIST

- presentation format: case competition, consultant, debate, town hall meeting, other
- post presentation format: regular class, question and answer, lecture, theory discussion, end class, other
- number per class
- size of the presenting group: one or more
- number of presenters in the group: one or more
- presenting group assigned/not assigned a point of view
- presentation notes handed/not handed in
- assign/not assign grades
- assignment/no assignment for the rest of the class
- critique group: size and number
- evaluation guide used/not used
- frequency in the course
- debrief or not debrief
- debrief immediately following presentation versus later
- video record/not video record
- presentation to class versus specific person or group
- formal/informal

Purpose

Case presentations are a popular variation because they add variety to the class routine. Whether instructors use predominantly lectures or case class discussions, Exhibit 8-2 presents a range of additional reasons why presentations provide an effective option. Several of these purposes can be achieved simultaneously.

Exhibit 8-2
CASE PRESENTATION PURPOSES

- add variety
- develop presentation skills
- develop communication skills
- experience making briefings to senior management
- emphasize action and implementation planning
- develop prioritizing skills
- develop time management skills
- practice using audio/visual supports
- increase the quality of preparation for a portion of the class.
- allow participants to teach themselves
- force participants to prepare
- practice group dynamics
- develop listening and evaluation skills in non-presenting participants
- easy way to evaluate new case material

Implementation

Instructors can be helpful in directing participant attention to particular aspects in their preparation. Participants will have to deal carefully with information management, priority assessment and the art of presentation within time constraints. Following each group member's individual preparation, a substantial amount of time will have to be spent together in the small group to reach consensus on content and how to present the group's conclusions most effectively. Often, more than one small group meeting is necessary and, in addition, one or more rehearsals can be valuable. The Case Preparation Chart provides a good outline for the completeness of the coverage in the presentation. The emphasis will normally be on the preferred alternative and its implementation.

Limitations

Case presentations have their limitations. A major concern lies with the general lack of preparation from the non-presenting members of the class and their passivity during the presentation. There is limited group learning in the third stage of the learning process and the quality of whatever learning transpires in the class rests solely with the quality of the presenting group(s). Generally the emphasis in oral presentation shifts to communication skills development versus rigorous analysis. Presenting groups spend a significant amount of preparation time in rehearsal and the development of visual supports. The equity principle says that every member of the class should get a chance to present. Invoking this principle heightens the above limitations. Also, a steady diet of case presentations becomes stale relatively quickly.

Experiences

Kevin, John and Tony have some advice in using case presentations.

Kevin: I decided that we could get some valuable experience by having the class period taken up by oral presentation of the analysis. I would announce these instances in advance and I would expect those students who wished to take advantage of this opportunity to form themselves into teams of 4-6 people to prepare for and make the presentation. I placed constraints on presentation time at around 10-15 minutes. When they went beyond, I wouldn't shut them off, but they would be downgraded for every minute they went over. Beyond this, they had complete freedom to parcel out tasks, have one or all members be involved in presenting, have one or all be involved in the analysis. This proved to be an extremely popular and useful device. Presenting groups worked very hard on this. On occasion, I would make use of video tape recording and the group could later see it along with me. I would offer my evaluation of it. At the same time, I devised a brief evaluation sheet that each member of the class filled out for each presentation and those were handed to the team at the end of the class. Sometime later the group would exchange these for my written evaluation and grade of their presentation. All group members received the same grade, and so it was up to them to police their effort.

It is typical for students in making formal presentations to try to pack in too much information. This is one of the values in having a rigorous time limit.

Lack of presentation experience is also certainly a difficulty. This manifests itself most markedly in a complete lack of appreciation or understanding of what they're doing when they stand up there. That is, they know what they intend to do, but this may be quite divorced from the reality. In that respect, I have found the video tape to be a powerful instrument. Almost literally, people will not believe it if I say that they stood there for five minutes twisting their hands; they have no recollection that they did so. Actually, to see things again that they are perfectly aware are distracting for the audience is very useful for them.

John: Anytime an individual or a group does a presentation I run off a one page memo to them stating what I think the major strengths and weaknesses were on both content and form. It's a lot of work but I figure they've put a lot of work into it. I generally have presentations near the end of the year. And if I'm going to use formal presentations, I try to get all the groups worked in. I leave it up to them regarding who does what in the group and the presentation. I would limit two groups to any one case. I also say to them that this isn't for a formal grade. It's a chance to participate and I'll consider it at the end of the year. The quiet people generally try hard to get themselves worked onto the floor and that is always a plus.

Tony: I use a very structured approach for presentations in my personnel course. I use cases only at the end of various modules in the course and divide the class first into small groups and then assign groups to either "analyst" or "critic" roles. On the "case" days I select two analyst groups to present the case and two critic groups to appraise the presentation, while the rest of the class members assume the role of board of directors and/or stockholders of the firm. Following the analysts' presentations and questions from the board, the critic groups provide their feedback.

For many years, the management communications teaching group at our school has used case presentations involving all students as a standard part of their required first year communications course. Some presentations are for practice, some for grades, some for taping and debriefing and some for a debate format. More recently, all the first year graduate program students and third year undergraduate program students engage in a four day, round-robin, case competition format of oral presentation. Each small group prepares a presentation for each of three different cases. The case presentations are made by groups to judging panels of students and faculty members simultaneously. Finalist groups are selected and they in turn compete to determine ultimate winners. Students feel some extra tension in this process and work through some of the stresses in group dynamics while gaining an opportunity to develop their presentation skills under friendly but competitive conditions.

CASE REPORTS

Description

Case reports are also a very popular variation in using cases. Here, participants either individually or in small groups submit a formal written statement of their analysis and recommendations of a particular case. Chapter 6 in *Learning With Cases* describes various types of case reports and preparation suggestions for students. As with case presentations, there are some options that instructors can choose from with respect to particular features of the case report (see Exhibit 8-3).

Exhibit 8-3
CASE REPORT OPTION LIST

- individual/ group report
- word limit / no limit
- time limit: short or long
- specific / no specific assignment
- format required: formal, informal
- suggested outline provided/ not provided
- executive summary required/ not required
- for / not for grading purposes
- grading criteria made known / not made known
- graded by instructor/others
- other sources of materials required/ not required
- handed in before/after a particular class

Purpose

Among the most important reasons for requiring a case report are the notions of a more thorough case analysis and practice in writing with clarity and impact. These objectives can be highlighted simultaneously with a range of other purposes as outlined in Exhibit 8-4.

Exhibit 8-4
WRITTEN REPORT PURPOSES

- promote rigorous case analysis
- practice using analysis and presentation tools
- simulate the typical management or consulting report
- practice using all dimensions of the Case Difficulty Cube
- assess performance
- practice time management skills
- use larger, more complex cases
- practice managing group dynamics
- practice preparation for case exams
- test newly written cases

Implementation

Individual preparation will take significantly longer for a case report than for a standard class discussion. In addition, if a small group discussion and common exhibit preparation are allowed, then a few hundred person hours of preparation may be expected. First year MBA students at our school spend upwards of 30 hours individually and in small groups on a case report assignment that is handed out on a Thursday at noon with a 48-hour deadline for submitting a typed, 1500 word statement plus exhibits.

The Case Preparation Chart that results from both individual preparation and the small group discussion, if permitted, can serve as an effective outline as well as contain the salient features of the content of the written report. The more thorough the point by point outline on the chart, the easier it is to write the final report. The grading of case reports is similar to the grading of case exams already discussed in Chapter 6. Feedback and counseling on case reports is similar to case exams as discussed in Chapter 7.

Limitations

There are some limitations and concerns when using cases for reports. Perhaps the most obvious one is the time required for students to prepare the report and for the instructor to read, evaluate and provide feedback (also discussed in Chapter 7). There are other limitations as follows:

• Participants may plagiarize and hire ghost writers.
• Participant time spent on the report may negatively impact preparation for other courses.
• Participants may try to contact managers in the organizations where the case was written.
• Collections of case reports may build, especially in student residences.
• Cases used for reports may be "burned" and not usable in regular class discussions for a few years.

Experiences

In some institutions the responsibility for a management communications program, including the writing of case reports, is assigned to a special faculty group. In others, individual teachers may choose to make a written case report part of their own course design. It is not unusual to assign two grades to a report, one for content and the other for presentation. In those institutions where case report writing is a formal program requirement, extensive manuals have been developed to explain expectations, presentation format, word limits and so on. Kevin talks about the purpose of written reports, some difficulties in writing and the fundamental requirements in effective report writing.

Kevin: A case provides a real life situation on which to base the writing exercise. It gives the student some context. With cases it's possible to say, "Now here you are, this is your situation, how are you going to respond to this?" For example, a classic case in communications centers on a letter. But the letter does not exist by itself as something that could be improved, or something that in retrospect seems to have been a mistake. There is a whole situation. The answer is not just simply, "Write a better letter." You now have the opportunity to say here is a real person, in a real situation, who faces this decision or problem. Now you look at the whole situation and see what you would do.

It amazes me how typical it is for the writer never to have thought that he or she is doing something for somebody else. It doesn't make a bit of difference how clear the writer thinks the pattern of words on the page may be, or how simple the organization. The writer is the least important reader you can imagine. It's what the reader needs to know, not what the writer chooses to tell. I have found it useful in this respect to call to people's attention what an "in-basket" looks like on the desk of a busy manager. Think that when the occupant of that desk looks at that "in-basket," all that is seen is work. Consequently, what the occupant wants to do is pick up each piece of communication to find out what it's about and to know what action needs to be taken. If the message isn't clear, then the writer has done him or herself a great disservice, because it will get put at the bottom, it will be delayed with a request for clarification, or it will convey the wrong message. People don't think about that.

I find that a great source of difficulty is that people won't recognize the need to organize in advance. They feel the organization comes while they are writing and after they've got a draft, they'll sit down with their computers and just start moving things around. This is time consuming and, generally, far less efficient than organizing in advance. I get this across as simply as I know how by saying that written communication has three separate and distinct phases. The first phase is preparation and organization. This has, as its output, a detailed outline. The second phase is writing a draft and the obvious output is the draft. The third stage is revising the draft and the result is the finished product. If these steps are all bundled into one process, you won't get good results.

The distinguishing features of a case report, as opposed to a case class discussion or an exam, are the rigorous case analysis and attention to the written presentation. As some people have said, "Reports are power tests. Exams are speed tests."

ROLE PLAYS

Description

The typical role play asks the participant to take on the persona of a case character and to respond as one might expect this case character would respond. Trying to "be like" a case character in a role play is quite different from the standard case analysis and discussion process where participants are asked to step into the position of the case character but to bring their own personality and experience to bear in their interpretation of the data and the events contained in the case. As with the oral and written presentation variations, role plays offer a number of options (see Exhibit 8-5).

Purpose

Role plays can help to bring a greater emotional quality to the standard case class discussion. Participants become more committed to case characters and to the case events. Others reasons for using role plays are listed in Exhibit 8-6 and many of these can be achieved simultaneously.

Exhibit 8-5
ROLE PLAY OPTION LIST

- spontaneous/planned
- specific format: town hall meeting, debate, buyer/ seller, negotiation, management/union bargaining
- students assigned to role: singly, in small groups, in sections, all to a role
- scripts prepared by instructor/students
- students selected/ volunteers
- debrief/not debrief
- duration: short/long
- role plays graded/ not graded
- in class/outside of class
- instructor involved in role play/ not involved

Exhibit 8-6
ROLE PLAY PURPOSES

- add variety to standard discussion class
- develop communication and listening skills
- develop negotiation, interpersonal, persuasion, and implementation skills
- practice dealing with consequences of actions
- make case analysis and recommendations more personal
- provide enjoyment in learning
- generate additional ideas and insights

Implementation

Role plays tend to be more successful if they are carefully planned. Instructors need to be clear why a role play should be used and which option should be the most appropriate to achieve the intended learning objective.

Limitations

Some cases are more conducive to role plays than others and some courses, such as organizational behavior and industrial relations, lend themselves better to role playing.

There are several other limitations that instructors should note and plan for when thinking about role play possibilities.

- Role plays are difficult to execute well.
- They can consume a lot of time.
- Participants in their roles can get off topic and away from the reality of the case.
- Role plays sometimes become a joke and are not taken seriously.
- Not enough information in the case leads to invention and fabrication of data.
- They do not always work and hence need a recovery strategy.
- Role plays can sometimes hurt people.
- Not all students make good role players.

Experiences

Terry uses a role play around a negotiation session in his course.

Terry: I wrote about a situation where I have not really one but two cases. One team has only the purchaser's view and the other only the vendor's. Then I have debates between the two teams. The purchaser has certain requirements and the vendor has certain limitations. I also enliven the debate a little by bringing in around the mid-point of the negotiation a telephone message for each. This information significantly changes their position. For example, the purchasing company thought they had an alternative source of supply, and could get equipment within a few hours though at a higher price than they had hoped to pay. However, the alternative source of supply calls up and say, "By the way, we found out that was another model we had in stock. We don't have any of what you want at all." The next closest source is a long distance away. I have found that both business executives as well as students like it very much. It's alive, they're negotiating and they're deeply involved.

We have used a debate style format in one of the sessions of our operations course at the Ivey Business School. We have groups volunteer before the class to take the affirmative position and the negative position around the resolution stemming from the case. We distribute to each of the groups the debating rules and order of the speakers and the time limits. The rest of the members of the class play the judging role in selecting the winning side in the debate.

Other cases, adaptable to group role playing, have been developed by instructors in industrial relations, with certain groups taking the union's side, others the management's position. Other cases present rich descriptions of various stakeholder groups involved in the issues and challenges and the instructor has the option of separating the class into distinct interest groups, each pushing its point of view in a "town hall meeting" style of information exchange.

A further variation on the spontaneous in class role play is the use of incident cases to elicit participants' immediate responses. The incident process is a technique often used in human resources management training programs. Basically, the incidents are presented in very short two and three paragraph cases or simply set-up and presented by the instructor right in the class. For example: "You've just seen an employee strike a supervisor. What would you do?" Or, "One of your employees has just told you that she has been sexually assaulted. How would you respond?" Or, "Your boss emerges from his office in a stumbling, unsteady manner and makes his way towards the exit to the parking lot. The distinct smell of alcohol comes to your nostrils. What would you do, how and why?" These kind of incidents provide opportunity for participants to develop a broad range of interpersonal skills including conflict resolution, giving and receiving criticism and counseling.

Professor Mary Crossan at our school talks about yet another variation of the in-class role play called improvisation.

> **Mary:** I look for opportunities in case class discussions to use improvisation techniques. In many ways it is like jazz improvisation which requires the traditional skills that people have to have to operate in an orchestra — you still have to practice, you still have to do your scales and practice the dexterity and tone required, but it's when you get into the ensemble and you're able to work in real time with what's going on that you can build on those skills. Often, in the classroom, this is the way it ought to be. You come in prepared but then you build on what happens while you're there.
>
> There is a notion in improvisation called "yes-anding." It is a way of not shutting down an idea before knowing whether the idea is a good one or not. It is stepping out a little bit. The skills of improvising through "yes-anding" can be very useful for an instructor to be able to recognize when there might be some potential gold nuggets in an apparently right-angle comment. In the conventional day-to-day classroom there is not a lot of opportunity to do this because you're constrained by time.
>
> Improvising is helpful for me just in the way I facilitate a classroom discussion. I've seen some professors teach who are so controlling, so dominating that they don't allow much ownership excitement and commitment in the classroom because the students just feel "well he/she will just tell me what it is anyway."

CASE FORMAT VARIATIONS

The three variations presented so far focus on the participant role and requirements. There are also some interesting variations in case presentation formats. On a continuum from the standard paper-based case at one end to the live case or field case experience at the other end, we can identify three other variations. Cases can be presented in (1) video, (2) electronic and (3) multimedia formats.

Video Cases

Video cases are the visual and audio equivalent of the words and data of paper cases. We are using the term video case not in the sense of a teaching aid, as reviewed in Chapter 4, but as a self-contained case that is used with or without a paper case supplement. When used by itself, a video case requires individual preparation during the video play itself and it is normal to stop the video periodically during the class to allow for further individual preparation, small group discussion and/or large group discussion.

One of the benefits of using a video case is that it reduces the preparation time. Each member of the class starts and finishes at the same time. There are also the added benefits of adding variety, more spontaneity in the class and simply better visual detail.

Video cases are in short supply because of their high cost and the added challenges involving release and disguise. Even if they are available, the analytical rigor, particularly quantitative work, may be less especially when the video case is used by itself. As well, video cases tend to take more class time for both individual preparation and discussion.

Electronic Cases

In its simplest form, the electronic case format provides the paper case data on a computer disk. The paper-based case has been supplemented with spreadsheet software and electronically conveyed data for some time. Presenting case text, data, exhibits and graphics on a CD-ROM is a natural extension.

Electronic cases allow more data to be included along with a richer presentation format to capture student interest. In this regard, students get more practice in working with the presentation dimension of the Case Difficulty Cube in terms of specifying relevant information.

One of the obvious limitations to the electronic case format is cost. Electronic cases are expensive to produce. Participants will need to purchase or have access to a computer with the necessary minimum specifications for the CD-ROM case. Investing in the necessary infra-structure in the classroom to accommodate in class use of computers also adds to the cost. As well, there are costs associated with providing a technical support structure to handle the glitches that arise. A second limitation lies more in misusing the technology itself as Jim Gallagher of Napier University, Edinburgh points out:

> ...It would be a mistake to confuse the CD *per se* with multimedia. CD is simply a distribution medium whose storage capacity is equivalent to 14 minutes of video or 250,000 pages of script. Thus, the creation of a CD-ROM-based case study is more than an extension of the paper-based case study. In its simplest form the paper-based case study could be directly transferred to CD-ROM. However, this would be a misuse of the potential of the technology. Presenting a case study in CD-ROM format must be more than this obvious extension (4).

Multimedia Cases

The multimedia case is a combination of both the video and the electronic case. Gallagher's description of multimedia is as follows:

> The essential features are the ability to link the following by hypertext: text to text, text to graphics, text to animation, text

to video (still and moving), text to audio, and any other combination of such (4).

The obvious reason to use a multimedia case is that it comes the closest to the real life situation without actually being there.

Gallagher continues:

...Concepts can be presented on screen in ways which are not possible on the page. In the same way truly interactive tutorial material can be designed so that students receive feedback to questions attempted that incorporate explanations for errors and directions for remedial work. There is also considerable scope for "what if" modeling and competitive decision-making (5).

Producing a quality multimedia case is very expensive. The added costs for student hardware, classroom wiring and technological support structure are the same as for the electronic case. Multimedia cases present even further limitations. With the increasing complexity of data and presentation modes, student preparation time expands. Release and disguise of information along with copyright infringements and obligations for both producers and users become more complicated with multimedia cases. Alexandra Freeland talks about multimedia copyright issues.

Developers and marketers of multimedia products face a maze of copyright issues. When creating their products, developers often use pre-existing content in their compilations, and, in order to avoid post-release lawsuits, need to negotiate multi-layered licensing agreements for the use of this content. A number of variables will affect these negotiations, and familiarity with them, at all stages of the licensing process, is essential. Once licensing agreements are arranged and multimedia works created, developers must also understand the scope of their rights when distributing multimedia compilations.

Users of multimedia works include individuals who browse the Web and download images and sound clips for their own personal use, or incorporate digital components into works intended only for private use. These individuals also need information about copyright, to protect their rights as users, and also to avoid violating the rights of others (2).

Jim Gallagher adds a final limiting perspective to the multimedia case.

It must be emphasized that multimedia interactive case studies should not be viewed as a replacement for traditional paper-based cases and the class discussion which they generate. Rather, they are tools which support and augment good teaching practice. Good case study development and preparation will still remain within the domain of the good case writer. But, at the end of the day the customer, the student, will ultimately dictate what we deliver (5).

The Harvard Business School, the Copenhagen Business School, the London Business School, along with many others are increasingly providing multimedia case studies. Professors Turgeon, Barbieri and Clarke at Pennsylvania State University offer an entire course electronically and at a distance.

...By using Netscape Navigator or another web browser, the students could access the course's home page and, from there, all of the cases and supporting materials. The case descriptions were organized into a series of hyper linked web pages, including text, illustrations and photographs. In contrast to the traditional hard-copy form in which cases are usually available, web-based cases can have a virtually unlimited array of exhibits (i.e., tables, graphs, illustrations, photographs) associated with text. After being digitized, the exhibits are converted to JPEG or GIF images and hyper linked to an anchor (usually an underlined word or phrase) in the text. In some cases, a link was provided to materials resident elsewhere; for example, students could access

Material Safety Data Sheets resident at a Gopher site by clicking on MSDS in the text.

In addition to the case description section of each case page, other sections usually contained study materials and assignments. The study materials contained materials for acquiring the prerequisite knowledge needed for analyzing the case or developing strategies for improving the problem situation. The assignments section included description of role playing exercises, case presentations for videotaping and downloadable documents — including Microsoft Word, Excel and Project — to be completed and submitted by individuals or groups. Also included in this section was an interactive electronic mail form with which students could communicate with the instructor and attach and send completed documents (13).

Please notice that in the description about distance education and the use of multi-media cases there is no mention of the standard small group or large group discussion and face-to-face contact between students that are part of the Three Stage Learning Process. Clearly, the potential for small and large group discussions exists with multi-media cases.

VISITORS TO CLASS

An interesting variation is to invite a visitor or visitors to attend the class. The visitor list can be quite broad as indicated by the following possibilities:

• the focal person in the case
• a representative from the organization in the case
• a person in a similar organization or in a similar industry
• an expert on the issue(s) addressed in the case
• the case writer
• a person from the same culture as represented in the case.
• a person from a different culture as represented in the case

• a guest instructor who knows how to teach the case very well or who has some special knowledge

Inviting visitors to class can add substantially to the credibility and relevance of the discussion. It becomes easier for participants to see the connection between the class discussion and the case data and the real world. If the visitor happens to be an expert in the field, participants have an opportunity to learn just what it is that experts really do. By making prior arrangements, it is possible to video tape a guest's contribution to the class and hence provide a more permanent record of the visit, just in case the guest is not available the next time the case is used. The video tape can be edited and added to the case teaching file.

Instructors need to do some careful planning in order to obtain the educational value that visitors can add. It is common, for example, to have the visitor participate in the last third or quarter of the class as opposed to the beginning. Visitors may comment on the range and depth of the discussion, field questions and outline the rest of the story, if the visitor is the focal person, or discuss the current practices, if the visitor is an expert. Visitors should be briefed before the class begins on the nature of the course, the characteristics of the participant group, the typical case discussion format, and the likelihood of hearing comments that the visitor may believe to be naive, erroneous and sometimes critical of company people or practices. Instructors will also have to decide whether to introduce the visitor to the class at the start versus the end of the class. If the introduction is at the start, it may reduce the spontaneity and range of the discussion. If at the end, it may be perceived by the participants as deceptive and unfair.

The introduction dilemma is but one of the difficulties with visitors to class. Other limitations include the risks that the visitor becomes upset with some remarks made during the discussion, the visitor bores the student or the visitor breaks the disguise of the case. In addition, this variation, like others presented earlier, takes time.

Gordon, for example, thinks that visitors take up too much time in his course.

Gordon: Given that there are a number of topics to get across as well as some examples, my feeling is that the course is pretty full and I really don't have time to bring in an outsider. There is enough reality in what we do that we don't need an outsider to provide it. We don't feel pressure from students who say, "Hey, I like your theory but let me find out somebody else's reality."

Ken has mixed feelings.

Ken: I have had some cases where experienced business people were brought in and I thought they had done a good job lecturing. But the students who were used to a more active participating role said it had been very interesting but they would rather have had a full period on the case. So, in general, I have used them to supplement a case discussion for maybe 20 minutes at the end. Also it can be awkward if the class discussion is coming along and you have to cut it short for the comments. So I don't try it very often. There is the other concern that students will be inhibited in their comments by knowing there is a visitor. Generally speaking, in a new case, I would prefer not to have the people from the company there. It also depends on the case: if the company comes out not looking too good, it may be better not to have somebody there from the company, since it can be a traumatic experience. I do not have any fixed rules about visitors in the classroom, except that the students or visitors should not be embarrassed.

With the proper reservations, inviting visitors to class can provide a departure from the normal case routine and reinforce the reality of the case.

TEAM TEACHING

Certain cases lend themselves to team teaching; that is, two or more instructors jointly conducting the classroom discussion. This variation is used most often with multidisciplinary or very complex cases.

Team teaching provides an opportunity to show the faculty as a team. Various faculty members can take on various roles, represent different functional areas, or focus on specific parts of the discussion. As an example, in one of our executive development programs, the four member faculty team all participate in the first introductory case discussion session. The participants get to see all the instructors very early in the program and the faculty have an opportunity to demonstrate the consistency of the message and the seamless nature of the program focus on the decision making process.

Team teaching is obviously an expensive use of faculty resources. As well, time, the constant limitation of discussion-based learning, becomes even more scarce with more than one person conducting the session. This case use variation requires some teaching experience that many instructors simply have not yet had the chance to acquire.

Although some instructors find it cumbersome and difficult to execute, those instructors who have tried it generally believe it is a useful device.

Dennis: Team teaching is a terrific vehicle for learning. It can be done sequentially with a minimum of effort. It allows you to tie issues very nicely. The world of business is not divided into neat compartments and I think we teach as if it were. This is a mistake. Team teaching can be an attempt to overcome this tendency.

Gary: I have done joint teaching in just about every functional area. This kind of teaching, and using the same case in different courses, is something I think we should do more of. It may allow some learning from different points of view. I remember one class where I was to team up with an organizational behavior colleague. The students came to me before class and asked, "What does organizational behavior have to do with this?" They just saw some of the techniques and couldn't see the interface. But team teaching is expensive because of the preparation time and two faculty members.

Rick: I'm still learning how to do team teaching. I guess I'm nervous enough just by myself without thinking about what we are going to do together. I've only team taught maybe half a dozen times in my life. I've only been disappointed once. And I've had some rather pleasant surprises. I've gone into team teaching situations with instructors that I didn't think were that good, that I didn't think I agreed with. When we got in there, however, positive things happened. I would say that I had to be prompted to team teach either by others or by material that was so obviously a team teaching situation that even I couldn't avoid it. I don't know why I don't do more. I think it's me. I don't mind the trade-off of time. I think team teaching can work well and the students really seem to appreciate the sessions.

Clint: I just came out of an executive program class and three of us were in the classroom together teaching the same case. Yesterday, two of us were in together. Tomorrow, three of us will be working together all day with the class.

The first time it happened spontaneously. We were in a square classroom and in the different corners. We'd move in when we wanted to focus on something and other people would move back. Actually, it works better the more spontaneous it is.

We do this most often in the more comprehensive cases. For example, this morning we went in and put on the board

Strategy, Financial Accounting, Marketing, Operations and People as headings. We started out with these and, as the class moved through the material, each of us would take a part. We always have someone in charge of the class. That person is responsible for starting the discussion and pulling the class together. We have found that the participants are usually surprised, sometimes overwhelmed on these occasions. We use this approach more in the executive programs than in our degree programs. One of the problems with the degree program is the number of sections we have to coordinate.

Ken: I don't like team teaching. I find this very hard to do on a case basis. I have done it probably five to ten times. In general, my efforts to chair a case discussion jointly have not been too successful. One of the problems is to develop a train of thought without obviously manipulating the discussion to suit your predetermined pattern of attack. It sometimes takes patience to keep a discussion flowing as you want to. And I find my colleagues too impatient to straighten out the discussion and to focus on something of interest to them. I suspect that they also find that my interventions in their line of attack, which are intended to be helpful, may be more distracting than helpful. So in essence, I don't like team teaching.

FIELD TRIPS

For decades, the operations faculty group at our school has arranged at least one, and sometimes two, field trips a year for all of the undergraduates and graduates in the first year of their program. Sometimes the trip is to the company represented in a case and it becomes a valuable supplement to the case. Sometimes the trip is to a company in the same industry represented in a case and here, the participants have a chance to see a similar process and talk about similar immediate issues and challenges. Often, the trip is to a company in an industry not represented in any case in the course. During this visit, the participants have a chance to see an unfamiliar process and to talk about a range of basic and underlying issues challenging the company personnel.

Perhaps the greatest value in field trips is the opportunity for participants to see operations in action, to feel the rhythm and pace of work and to smell the reality of molten metal, welding or canning fish. These are great reinforcements to the classroom discussions. As with visitors to class, field trips provide an opportunity to talk with practitioners and to draw the connection between the classroom discussion and the real world of work.

Field trips, like other variations take lots of time and incur some financial cost. The added limitations here include getting access to a company and making the administrative arrangements, managing generally large numbers of students during the visit and dealing with liability concerns for safety and confidentiality.

Les adds an interesting twist to his field trips for his class.

Les: I schedule in a field trip when I design the first year course for the Executive MBA Program and place it after the first three or four classes. I try, as well, to arrange this trip to the facility of one of the participants in the class and this gives the group an instant welcome while providing the hosting participant a chance to show off his or her company. There is always an assignment based on the visit. I require each participant to write for me, what I call a "Dear Boss Memorandum." In this 800 word memorandum addressed to the participant's actual boss, I ask people to raise three issues: (1) what was seen and heard; (2) what were the key learnings; and (3) what should "our" company do that we are not currently doing or what is "our" company doing that should be maintained and emphasized? The feedback I get from the participants is generally the following, "Good exercise, I've already sent this memo to my boss."

The last case use variation is interactive video conferencing. This option may include any or all of the options presented thus far but it has its own special considerations. A number of schools and universities, including ours, are conducting case discussions with students on-line from distant locations using the technology of video conferencing.

INTERACTIVE VIDEO CONFERENCING

Distance education is by no means new. Correspondence courses have been offered for many years to participants located at geographically remote sites. Decreasing costs and increasing quality of computer and communications technology has led to a major breakthrough in distance education. Computer conferencing allows geographically dispersed students to communicate asynchronously not only with instructors but also with each other. Students and instructors can electronically post messages, give assignments, send responses, or whatever and maintain a common record of the exchanges even though they are not physically present at the same time. Materials can be loaded and distributed in CD-ROM form or on network arrangements, to be shared among the students for reading, viewing and preparation.

Just as exciting, and maybe more so, is synchronous communication via video conferencing. Small groups of participants are physically present at dispersed sites and are on-line in real time with sight and sound connection to other small groups and to an instructor at a studio site. Some special challenges arise when instructors conduct interactive case discussions via video conferencing.

Our network at the Ivey Business School includes a studio at the school which has a wall with eight monitors, a space for a live small group and a podium containing a key pad to operate the various communications options available (document camera, active screen, still screen, electronic board, picture-in-picture, and various angle views of the instructor). The eight monitors carry the video and audio feeds from the distance locations spread across Canada.

In this book we are not so much interested in the technological specifications as we are in the case teaching and learning challenges and opportunities via video conferencing. We present the views of some of our colleagues who have experience in what we call the EMBA Program via video conferencing. Professors Terry Deutscher, Chris Piper, Kathleen Slaughter, John Haywood-Farmer and Paul Bishop offer their experience and advice.

Getting Started

Most people seem to agree that getting started in using video conferencing begins best with a live, face-to-face meeting of the class.

Terry: My research on video conferencing for distance learning and even for business meetings says it is important that participants and instructors know each other before going into video conferencing sessions. Everything I have experienced has reinforced that. The times when we get the class together provide the foundation for the kinds of exchange we can have for productive video conferencing. People who know each other before engaging in video conferencing do not really operate at a distance with each other. We bring the class together at the beginning of term and each faculty member teaching on the program has 12 to 16 hours of class time before moving to the video world.

Faculty Reactions

Teaching in a video conference environment is very much different than in a live class environment. Kathleen describes the key differences for her.

Kathleen: What I found very distracting the first year I taught was the tons of chit-chat going on at each site because you can see they're not paying attention. It's really not a sign of disrespect. They're just clarifying something amongst themselves. The problem is for those of us who are control freaks, it really does take your attention. For example, if I see some person leaning back in the chair with the feet sticking up on the desk, I watch. I can't help it and say to myself, "What are you doing? Who do you think you are?" They're just getting comfortable and it's not the same kind of deportment they'd have in a live classroom. It's almost like you're coming into their private little space and they want you to take them as they are. Now people do this in the live class but it's more subtle. In the live class the eyes glaze over and people are off on a side trip. I realize people aren't with me 100% of the time. But it's quite different in the video class when you watch people taking all sorts of these side trips.

Another difference is that if you call on someone in a live class and they say something to which you respond by asking, "What do you really mean by that?" you can get some interplay, a conversation going. In the video class students get in the habit of pushing the button to turn the microphone on, respond to the question and then turn the microphone off. It's almost like, "There, take that." So if you ask them something again, they go through the same routine. You lose some of the rapid fire questioning and follow-up. The repartee is not quite the same. You have to lead people into leaving their microphone on if you want to get some spontaneity in the exchange. It's all a part of painting the picture — doing a lot more talking yourself about what's happening and what your expectations are. So I think you actually talk more in staging the event.

I've spent a long time trying to figure out the really key difference between the live class and the video class. I did it by asking myself what do I do differently when I walk into the video classroom. My style is that I teach differently depending upon what the mood of the class is and I can't sense the mood of the video class. In the live class I pick up the mood and teach to it. In the video class I have a little chat with the first site that comes on when I go in while I am waiting for the others to get on line. So when you try and sense the mood, you've got one group where it's 10:00 a.m. and another at 7:00 a.m. and that alone changes the mood. Then a group comes in from a site where it's minus 23°C and they're all freezing to death and its raining somewhere else. So all the things that affect the mood are all different across the country. I never realized how much I was affected by the mood of the class until I couldn't figure out what the mood was.

Another thing is when you're with a live audience I get my energy from them. I can't get the same energy from the video audience. I think I work harder in the studio than in any other way of teaching. I have to keep my own energy level up and I can't rely on having the class give it back to me. As a matter of fact, we have a small group live in the studio and that actually makes it more difficult not less. I find when I say something that is supposed to be funny, you kind of look to see if anybody is laughing and the live group doesn't want to make any noise because they're conscious of being distracting if they're noisy. So even they don't respond and you're left with guessing whether your humor worked or not.

Terry also experienced differences.

Terry: A key disadvantage is the dependence we have on technology. Many of us, particularly our more experienced faculty, are accustomed to going into class and, as long as we don't run out of chalk, we are okay. We know our material pretty well, we are working with quite good groups and we know there is going to be a good class. Once in a long, long while the power will go out and then there is clearly no class. In the video world, we and our participants are bound together by an umbilical cord that has all this technology in it; telephone lines, codex, multiplexes. We are totally dependent on that. It isn't a question of remembering to bring a piece of chalk or checking the board or seeing if there's an extra bulb in the overhead projector. Things can go wrong in the studio that are not within our power to fix and it isn't usually a black or white, all or nothing problem. It is a phone line or a switch or we can lose a site or the quality of the transmission to a site. That puts a lot more strain on our faculty, especially the older ones, who are used to a simpler world where they can deliver by making sure they arrive on time, well prepared.

Paul sees some strengths and weaknesses in the video class.

Paul: The only difference for me is that it tends to be slower. You just can't get the one-liners in, you can't get the quick back and forth exchanges and that hurts my style. Because that's how I teach in order to keep people awake and alive and how I try to inject a lot of energy into the class. I carry on conversations with individuals in the class, joking and bantering away throughout the class — teasing them almost. It's very much harder to do in the video class. So, I find, when you speak you almost have to make a prepared statement and they respond the same way. Recognizing the difficulty of getting in and out, they have to have something significant to say or they don't start. That takes a lot of the spontaneity out of the discussion and I don't think it's as much fun. It is definitely harder work for everybody. And it simply takes more time to do what I would do in a live class.

Student Reactions

Student reactions to video conferencing cover a wide range.

Terry: The satisfaction I hear most often is the excitement of interacting at a distance with people they know and like and who otherwise are way too busy ever to be able to come together in a conventional class. The downside I hear is that it's a pretty tiring experience. In our program, for two days straight (i.e., Friday and Saturday every two weeks), they are watching live monitors with only a few other people in the room. That's a pretty enervating task.

Side conversations among students at the sites during class discussion can be both satisfying and dissatisfying for students. At times, many people find them very useful because they are able to clarify what is being said at another site or fill in background material without disrupting the rest of the class. However, to the extent that they disrupt the ability for people in that site to see and hear, they are a dissatisfaction. By and large, side conversations are seen as a strong positive.

Kathleen: The biggest dissatisfaction I've heard is the frustration of not being called on. If I'm the only one in a site with my hand up and you didn't call on me... What's the matter here? Who else has their hand up. And then the group at the particular site all start to point to the person whose hand is up. They don't realize that everybody in another site has their hands up and there are six in another site and two more in another. I almost see the people in the first site saying to the person, "You answer this one," and so only one person puts a hand up and if you don't call on him or her, the student gets frustrated.

Preparation for a Video Class

Most instructors appear to spend more time and take more care in preparing for a video class than they would for a live class.

Paul: I do a lot more work in preparation for a video class. I prepare much more carefully and this for me means I memorize the numbers so that I don't have to look at notes at all. There is something about writing on a board that allows you to "ad-lib" a lot but using the document camera you just can't do that. It is very constraining in terms of what you can write for them to look at. For that reason I do prepare much more carefully and I think my classes run on rails compared with how I wander around in a conventional classroom. I honestly think that detracts a bit from the learning experience.

There is much less access to the students before class or after class for people to ask questions or vice versa. Normally, in a class when you have an opportunity to have a coffee with them after, you can circulate around and, if you feel someone didn't understand something, you can talk to him or her. I almost go on a leap of faith that there is a transfer of learning because I'm getting much less feedback. I make assumptions more than I do in a regular class.

Terry: I try to be creative about finding ways to get interaction in the class. It's harder to do this in the video class than in my regular live class. Thinking about role plays, for example, maybe using students selectively, mini presentations on something. Using buzz groups to work for ten minutes on a particular question or issue.

I plan for more breaks in the video class. Some people still blast through the 3 hours and 45 minutes we have for our regular EMBA live class time with just one break. Some students have said there shouldn't be any long lectures by anyone without getting interaction because it's too easy just to tune out. These people grew up with pretty good television and high quality video games and so they have high expectations regarding presentations.

Kathleen: Don't wear red is something to remember. Color makes a difference. One of our colleagues has a shirt with a red strip in it. When you look at it on video it shimmers. The color red just shimmers around the outside and it looks ethereal. It is the same on the visuals. Some colors don't have the same resolution as others do.

John: First thing I would tell instructors new to video conferencing is to act normally. Don't panic! Forget about the fact you are on T.V. Forget about how you look and sound. You are not going out over national television. This is a conversation between adults just like we have in the live class. It's a telephone call with pictures.

Terry and Kathleen talked about visuals and the quality required in preparing them.

Terry: There are some obvious things about font size. We need to remember that in contrast to working with a transparency on a 10′ x 10′ (3m x 3m) screen in a live class, the transparency in the video environment is displayed on a 35″ (1m) monitor. You can't just take what might be a "busy" slide and transfer this to the monitor in the video world. Using a 28 point font with bold face is our norm. It boils down to having the same respect for our students in the video class as we do for students in the live class. So if they can't see your slide and you haven't provided a handout, there are going to be some very justifiably upset people.

Kathleen: I put much more detail on visuals and have many more visuals prepared. The interesting thing is that I don't care how sloppy my handwriting is on the live classroom board. I mean, I just write the stuff down and forget about it. In the video world I am much more conscious of it because I see it on the screen in front of me.

Managing A Video Class

Several people talked about some special challenges in conducting a case class via video conference.

John: In a live class, I typically start with a student volunteer and consciously scan the room from one side to the other specially trying to avoid blind spots. In the video studio, I tend to jump from site to site as opposed to staying with speakers within a site.

I ignore the live studio group except for their image which is on one of the monitors before me. I want all students to feel they are getting the same treatment. I do like to have the group in the studio however. In my case I use a lot of cartoons and I just don't get any response from students in the remote sites. I get it only from the live group. None of the microphones are on in the remote sites. I don't hear the laughter or the repartee that goes on. I may see smiles or the odd "thumbs-up" signal. I need the instant feedback from the studio group.

Kathleen: It took me the whole of my first year to learn not to just call on one person at a time. Telegraph who the next couple of speakers will be so that they all know that you saw there were other people at other sites needing or wanting to get into the conversation. This helps get away from that problem of "I was the only person in our site with my hand up and you ignored me. What are you, stupid or something?" And actually saying what is happening like, "There appears to be a lot of excitement with our western friends over this" or "It appears we've hit a hot button in the east," so that people know what happened at another site. Sometimes it's site exclusive — nobody knows so don't forget that they can't see what you can see. Keep reminding the students that you see them all the time. Watching these people on video is almost like the game kids play, "Because I can't see you, you can't see me." If I have someone talking at one site and all other screens go to that site, they forget that I can still see them. They are on all the time as I am all the time. You have to tell them what you're responding to because they can't see it.

I look for opportunities in the video environment where people in different sites have opposing views. Then I'll open up the sites and they go back and forth and the rest of the class hears and sees these two sites live. So you open up the microphones, open up the visuals and they have a debate.

I find it very difficult to keep track of participation when teaching via video conferencing. Although you have a few people who participate all the time but, because the image is much smaller, people don't stand out as much as they do in the live class. In the live class the view is much more holistic. We also have fewer classes by video. Most of the courses are only delivering 4 or 5 classes by video and the rest are live.

Chris: For me, conducting the class is mostly the same, except that I do try to think ahead to have several short, less than 10 minute, questions that I would assign to the sites. In fact, I give a different question to each site and then have them come back and talk about their responses. This technique is especially helpful when you've got a site on where there are several issues that don't seem to be clearly understood. I never do this before class. Everybody gets the same assignment for class preparation; the big assignment is always the same for everybody. But in class it is helpful to get some more detailed calculations. The other way of doing it is, if you've got six sites and there happen to be six examples of basically the same set of calculations, each site can do one.

Terry: Interactive video is naturally suited to role plays; people in different sites can put terrific energy into them. I know of one example where different sites represented the big oil side, the environmental side and the government side. Students brought in props, they had access to data and information that suited their perspective. Environmentalists had straw hat and jeans. The big oil people were slick with cigars. Video lends itself quite well to this. You get more role separation versus the regular classroom. Role plays also help to do some of the energy transfer that is sometimes hard to get.

CONCLUSION

Variation within any routine can provide a welcome change of pace. Even with the excitement that cases can create, a steady diet of routine case discussions can be tiresome. As outlined in this chapter, there are many variations available to choose from. Some focus on what students may be asked to do differently. Some focus on what instructors can do differently. Others involve technical, multimedia, and video conferencing variations.

case use in a non-case environment

Teaching with cases in an environment where the use of cases is the exception presents some special challenges. This chapter documents how patient and persistent case instructors have overcome obstacles related to facilities, student identification, material logistics and attitudes to cases. It is clear that these individuals also believed the rewards were worth the effort.

PHYSICAL FACILITIES

The first differentiating element in a non-case environment is likely to be the lack of adequate facilities. Available space tends to be characterized by row seating with benches or individual seats with folding or permanent tops all bolted to the floor. Even in new or renovated educational facilities such row seating remains the norm. Chapter 2, on prerequisites, has already presented a discussion of facility requirements and opportunities for modification necessary for case discussion. The following remarks by several teachers indicate the problems they faced and how they overcame them.

Arthur: When I came to the university, the first obstacle to using the case method I encountered was the classrooms. They were set up for the traditional lecture method of teaching. It is very difficult to carry out a case discussion in a classroom where students talk to the backs of the heads of rows of students in front of them. It literally took me two years to find out where the better classrooms were. Then I had to find out the procedures to get access to these. I found it to be just a tremendous impediment to being able to use the case method. I had to get out of the business school and into other faculties of the university to find the classrooms I could really work with.

Kim: Mine was the only course to use any cases at all, and all classrooms were set up lecture style with chairs only. All students had pads, or three ring binders, or clipboards which they balanced on their knees while writing. When I asked them to arrange their chairs in broad semicircles, most of them must have thought I was nuts. Moreover, the professor who used the room after me made it very clear that he preferred to have the room set up the old way. So we were always moving chairs at the beginning and end of class, and I had to give up class time for just that activity but it was well worth it.

Kim probably says it best,"We were always moving chairs at the beginning and end of class." It is up to the instructor to attempt certain modifications. It is naive to suppose that institutional support for such changes will be great.

The insistence that the right kind of facility is needed for participatory teaching does not get lost on students, administrators or other faculty. Few messages send a clearer intent, "To me, good case teaching is sufficiently important that I am willing to make a nuisance of myself by fighting for what I believe to be right."

The fortunate by-product of such efforts is that classrooms appropriate for case teaching are also superior for lectures compared to the old style lecture rooms. Therefore, everybody benefits from efforts to improve the physical facilities to become conducive to case teaching.

PARTICIPANT IDENTIFICATION

In many non-case environments, there is little incentive for the instructor to get to know the students in the class. Often students do not need to attend class. Since all of the grade is based on written term work and/or on the final exam, and students just have an assigned number, the need for individual identification may be seen as low. Since using cases requires a more personal approach, the instructor must develop his or her own means for student identification. A large number of potential tools and tactics have already been discussed in Chapter 2. The institutional support in providing student identification is also likely to be minimal in the non-case environment. Again, the initiative rests with the instructor

Arthur: I found I had to make all of the place cards for my students myself. Even then I ran into further difficulties, such as the name card holders. I actually ended up sawing my own blocks to hold name cards because the only university option offered me was solid walnut holders with a minimum quantity of 100 which would have cost me $10.00 a piece.

Ray: I like to work very close to my students. At this institution, that is very difficult. The interactions or the contacts are not there. There are no devices like a résumé, class photograph or a fixed seating plan to get to know your students.

It is possible to get a class photograph. I did not know that when I first arrived, but now I know where to go and get my hands on them. The difficulty is that it comes out of my hide. It does not come out of thin air. It is unexpected to have that kind of thing done, and you have to work to get it.

Learning students' names by having participants introduce themselves, fill out personal data sheets, make up name cards for class, fill out class lay-out sheets and pose for in-class photographs, becomes a routine task for case method instructors working in a non-case environment. That students appreciate being treated as human beings instead of as numbers is abundantly evident. These seemingly relatively innocuous activities allow the instructor to show that he or she cares and, in turn, that it is only fair that participants care to work appropriately on this course.

MATERIAL LOGISTICS

Even in the relatively simple area of being able to order and distribute case materials, problems crop up in the non-case environment. Cases that are included as part of textbooks may not be appropriate; too many, too few, wrong context. Cases from standard sources may not be readily available or too expensive. Reproduction and distribution facilities may not be adequate. Some typical situations encountered were as follows:

Tony: When I first arrived here there was no system set up for the ordering and distribution of cases. The Dean's assistant suggested that I pay for them myself, order them myself, and collect back from the students. That's exactly what I did my first year here. Then I talked with the manager of the bookstore who, rather reluctantly I might add, made the necessary arrangements.

Kim: A friend invited me to come and teach a case class at a non-case school. But he warned me, you had better bring your own cases, because we do not have any way here we can reproduce them. So, I went with a suitcase full of cases.

Thomas: My problem is finding the right cases for my environment and it takes a lot of effort to write my own. Developing these materials comes right out of my hide and there are very few rewards for doing it.

Even though these days access to cases from sources like ECCH, Harvard and Ivey is considerably simpler than it used to be, it is not necessarily easy to get cases to the students in a particular institution. Import restrictions, language and cost may be additional problems beyond the institutional obstacles already mentioned. The ideal solution of writing one's own cases in the language, location, culture, and economic and political environment of choice is seen by many instructors as difficult. We will say more about this solution later in this chapter.

These three fundamental prerequisites: physical facilities, getting to know students, and finding and distributing the case material are not the only challenges in teaching with cases in a non-case environment. Class sizes, student, faculty, and institutional attitudes must be addressed as well.

CLASS SIZE

It is logical that in non-case environments participants find the use of cases different, if not difficult, and may lack an appreciation of what the instructor is trying to do. Sometimes, also, the number of students is so large that case discussion does not seem to be a reasonable option.

In many institutions, particularly at the introductory levels, classes may be very large. An instructor may well feel that the numbers prohibit the use of cases. For example:

Anne: I teach a freshman class of a required course with about 250-300 students. I would like to use cases, but don't see anyway that I can. I recognize that one option would be to split the group into smaller classes. That will do nothing but increase my teaching hours, since my institution is not going to be providing me with any extra teaching assistance. So, it all comes out of my own hide. It is much simpler to just give my lectures and get my course commitments over with that way. I recognize that many of my students are not particularly excited about this way of teaching. A lot of them skip lectures which is alright by me as long as they do well on their final exam. It is just that they seem like such a big, dull bunch. I can't even get any questions out of them. I suppose they cannot even hear each other in that huge room. I have my microphone, and have thought of passing it around. That would be such a laborious process, that I have not really given it any serious thought. So, it looks like I'm stuck with what I've always been doing.

Anne's situation is a common one for many instructors. More than about 100 students per class makes it difficult to use cases effectively. Even though a number of instructors have had success with breaking very large groups into lots of small groups and appointing spokespersons in each small group, these solutions still fall far short of having each individual in class feel part of the large group discussion. Anne has already recognized the proper solution, smaller classes. At the Ivey Business School, new graduates are hired on a two-year, limited contract to teach an introductory business course to about 1800 students in class sections of about 80 to 90 students each. Another alternative is to lecture to the very large group and break it down into smaller class sizes for case discussion only.

STUDENT/FACULTY/INSTITUTIONAL ATTITUDES TO CASES

Perhaps more serious than the obstacles so far identified are the student, faculty and the institution's attitude towards the use of cases.

Student Attitudes to Cases

If only one instructor uses cases in an institution or program while other instructors use other teaching methods, participants will have to adjust significantly to the norms of case work. The habit of preparing for class rather than for exams is not an easy one to acquire. Learning to learn from each other (instead of the instructor) and learning to teach one another are often new skills for most participants. Finding time and motivation for individual preparation and small group discussion outside of class may not be easy either. The instructor needs to be very clear, therefore, in explaining why cases are an integral part of the course, what benefits can be expected from using cases in the course and how participants should do their part in each stage of the Three Stage Learning Process to maximize their learning.

Arthur and Derek have additional views on student reactions to cases.

> **Arthur:**   I find I have to be terribly explicit in class with my students to explain to them how they are supposed to use the cases, what the learning process is all about, and what the steps in analysis are.

> **Derek:** It seems to me to be quite difficult to get a very high level of student involvement and participation using cases part-time. There appears to be a tremendous amount of learning that is necessary just so the students know what they are expected to do using cases. And if we are using cases sporadically, that skill in solving cases, and suspending reality, or suspending disbelief, isn't really there. So, it's much more difficult for the students to get into a case and to do a very active case analysis job. My students are inclined to be passive. This, in itself, is of course a good reason for using cases.

Faculty and Institutional Attitudes to Cases

Faculty members may make disparaging remarks about the use of cases to case teachers, but also to students taught by the case teacher and to other faculty. These comments create an unpleasant atmosphere at best and, at worst, work counter to the case teacher's purposes.

Faculty attitudes are often also reflected in institutional attitudes, values, rules, norms and processes. These may be roadblocks to effective case teaching and learning and may also affect promotion and tenure decisions.

In some schools and some programs there is no requirement and little encouragement for students even to attend class. In some locations it is simply not allowed to evaluate participation in classroom discussions for performance assessment purposes. Incentives to encourage instructors to devote time and energy to teaching with cases are often nonexistent. Several people expressed views on what appear to be common institutional norms and constraints.

Kevin: One of the big challenges in using cases in a non-case environment is first of all ourselves. We have no, or very little, training in teaching with cases. We have no real mentors in our system to help us. Second, most of the time the physical facilities/the classrooms really stink. Thirdly, we have no tradition at our school. Not only do we have to convince ourselves but we have to convince our colleagues and, more especially, our department chairs.

Ben: I haven't used participation to assess performance here because it's not allowed. But I have done it in France where approximately a third of the grade was on participation and it seemed to work quite well. It made a difference to the class discussions.

Hendrick: Even if I had a choice to evaluate student contribution to class, which I don't, the students would not like it because they believe it to be so subjective, even though I might feel I'm being objective.

Norm: Quite often we get channeled in terms of the reward system at a particular university. Rewards are probably proportional to measurability. For example, we have three basic functions: teaching, research and service. We've got a reasonable measure of publication research. It is easy to count articles published in recognized journals. In teaching, we have some instruments, but they are just abominable. In service to the university and the community, we have probably a minimal measure.

Really, in terms of the relative level of the scales of the reward system itself, whether the university sets itself up as a teaching institution, a research institution or a balanced institution, teaching in and of itself usually ranks on a low priority. Why be a masochist? I have seen a new faculty member teach a core course in the business area. He taught it by the case method, he's just a young person. The students loved it. They said it was tough, but they really learned their material. This person was an assistant professor. Then an associate professor came in. They were both teaching different sections of the same course. The associate professor chose the lecture method and covered only theoretical models, risk analysis, investment analysis, etc. The younger faculty member, although he had a very successful experience with using cases, came back to the use of lectures. Now, it was not by any type of mandating, but almost a sense of perceived legitimacy.

Arthur: As a newcomer in this faculty, I found the case method had a reputation as an excuse for non-teaching. With the course I had, it was very important to me to use the case method. I was a risk taker; I was willing to leave the university if I could not make it pay off. The course I took over had a very poor reputation in the university and was a problem course. Fortunately, the students really took to my approach. They saw it as a breath of fresh air.

Since I was able to accomplish such a turnaround on this course, my fellow faculty left me relatively alone. I solved a problem for them and they were more concerned about having the problem solved than the way I did it.

Since that time, some others with a case background have joined the faculty. Some of our faculty members never use cases, others use one sometimes, and people have different ideas about how they should be used. We never talk to one another about these different viewpoints.

I am also sure that I am going to have to meet the promotion criteria set for everyone else, and that my quality case teaching job will not count for much. So I publish in the respected journals and fight for my respectability by their standards.

Derek: If somebody else is willing to publish your case in a case book, or use this particular material in their classes, that is an indication that somebody else is willing to say, "I think this is good material." The real issue is whether the development of new case material is a contribution to something more than teaching. And I think if I can't get any sort of academic credits for developing cases, I certainly cannot afford to write them.

CONCLUSION

When one ponders a list of obstacles to effective case teaching in a non-case environment, it is easy to become discouraged and ask oneself, "Why should I bother?" Avoiding the use of cases may well represent the way of least resistance. There are some good reasons for not giving up so easily, however.

First and foremost, all educators must be able to justify their choice of teaching methodology, not only to their students, peers and superiors, but also to themselves. The educator who is convinced that the use of cases makes sense for the educational purposes intended and who then is willing to settle for less is not living up to his or her calling. Knowing that you are not doing as good a job as you can do is not much of a life motivator or self-satisfaction generator.

There is more, however, although this first reason should be sufficient in itself. A well taught case session can generate a degree of participant satisfaction and immediate positive feedback that is very satisfying. Many case teachers have experienced this and comments like, "I saw the lights go on inside their heads," or "When they saw they could solve this problem collectively they really felt good," or "Even thirty years later they remembered that class."

Case teaching skills are part of the instructor's capability to teach and work in a participative way. Therefore, they contribute to non-case activities such as class discussions of readings, videos, presentations, team leadership and coaching and, yes, even committee work and chairing meetings. Understanding of the decision making process also has obvious professional and personal life pay-offs.

Case teaching skills are particularly appreciated in adult education. Therefore, good case teachers often are invited to participate in special training programs in or outside their own institution where significant financial rewards may be attached to the work. Such opportunities for travel and pay allow the individual to broaden his or her horizons while also earning respect in the home institution.

Unfortunately, many educators see their choice as black and white: concentrate on teaching or research. It does not have to be the trade-off. Consider, for example, the following scenario.

1. Educator X wishes to become more proficient in the use of cases, but still wants to pursue certain research interests vigorously.

2. Therefore, Educator X in the course that most closely fits these special research interests inserts a few short cases obtained from an established case clearing house.

3. Educator X goes to an academic conference where other academics share their insights and research initiatives in Educator X's specialization. Educator X asks some of these researchers whether they have any appropriate case material and where they see the biggest shortfall in decent cases.

4. Educator X goes to a mixed academic-practitioner conference and talks to some practitioners about their research needs and challenging decisions.

5. Educator X formulates a research initiative that involves some cases, but not necessarily exclusively so, and obtains funding.

6. While Educator X is engaged in field research, Educator X also writes a few small teaching cases about key issues in the field of inquiry.

7. Educator X prepares several papers and sponsors a research symposium inviting academics and practitioners to come and discuss their and Educator X's findings.

8. Educator X edits the proceedings from this conference.

9. Educator X uses the cases produced during the research in the regular course with degree students.

10. Educator X gets invited to put on a two-day in-house workshop in one of the big organizations in the field and the cases produced earlier are used for discussion in several sessions.

11. As Educator X deposits the substantial proceeds from this endeavor in the bank account, Educator X is starting to think about how many other organizations might be interested in the same or a similar workshop. Educator X is also considering how many new research contacts might be provided.

The point is that synergy is possible and desirable with case teaching and research. It does not have to be one or the other. Properly intertwined, they are preferable as a combination. Both the case teaching and the research provide contacts, feedback, credibility and insights difficult to get in any other way. Teaching and research become better as a result of engaging in both.

Such a perspective with cases in a non-case environment takes the martyr's role out of teaching with case in a non-case environment. It does not have to be a time consuming and risky allocation of resources with no pay-off other than student and self-satisfaction. It should be a well thought-out plan for personal and professional success in both teaching and research.

special considerations

It is almost inevitable that a number of interesting topics related to teaching with cases would receive insufficient coverage as a result of the topic outline chosen. It is, therefore, useful to have a chapter which can pay attention to these points. They will be addressed under three main headings: (1) Teacher training will cover such topics as recruiting, difficulties faced by new instructors, orientation methods and advice to new teachers; (2) Diversity will survey situations where students, instructors or materials are not homogeneous; (3) Student shortcuts and cheating, although an unsavory subject, will provide some insights as to how instructors might deal with such behavior.

TEACHER TRAINING

It may appear somewhat strange to treat the topic of teacher training as a special consideration, since the key purpose of this book is to help in the development of case teachers. Nevertheless, it is useful to address in a separate section the difficulties faced by instructors new to the use of cases.

Difficulties Faced by Instructors New to Cases

Don and Fred give a clear indication of the complexity of the situation for new instructors.

Don: A new instructor comes to us usually out of a doctoral dissertation with a narrow exposure. Often, this person has a strong theoretical but weak application background. All of a sudden, we throw this person into an environment which is application oriented and requiring a comprehensive knowledge and overview. He or she must master 20-30 complex cases and begin to develop a teaching style. The instructor must develop a relationship with students, make a living, and continue to produce on a research and publications front. This is a very full plate.

Fred: It is difficult for faculty who have not taught with cases before. It is an anxiety inducing teaching process because they are not in control. A lecture is a lot easier. With cases, you have to pull out concepts, modules, as things unfold. You can't just rely on abstract concepts. You have to be able to integrate practice and theory and it takes a lot of experience in both. It also takes a certain amount of tolerance for ambiguity. It takes a process awareness of the audience: how to call on and use people appropriately; an awareness of your body and where you are in the classroom; how that relates to what you are trying to do and to the tone and content of the case.

Orientation Efforts

None of the people interviewed had ever experienced a formal training program or standard procedure for integrating new instructors. There are some disagreements as to what can be done effectively, if anything, to help new instructors. Some believe only in the cold bath theory, others appear unconcerned, and yet a number seem to be looking for answers.

Walt: I think that teachers are born, not taught. Of course, a lot depends on how much they try, how much they care. Two kinds of people don't teach well: people who don't care or try and people who don't have the ability to think on their feet and react on the spur of the moment.

Scott: We're interested in results, not in approaches. We make suggestions to new faculty. For example, we suggest that they sit in on other people's classes and have other people sit in their classes. But you see, some of them won't do it and so we don't make them do it. We try to support what they want to do. But we are not interested in telling anybody how to do it.

Linda: I don't think we really understand methods for socializing new faculty into the use of cases. This may be partly because when you start, you don't know what your style is going to be. And people could tell you things that just wouldn't make sense for you.

However, a large number of case teachers are strongly in favor of some form of training in a supportive environment.

Bob: New instructors really need coaching. There is too much secret to a casual observer; it looks like the instructor is doing nothing, especially if he or she is skillful.

Ed: One of the things you do need as a new instructor is a feedback session, a bull session on how your style is effective, ineffective, and what might be useful to modify. I really do think this is teachable and you can improve upon your style, especially for young instructors before they get set in their ways.

In terms of orientation, a basic minimum is to inform new instructors about the norms and processes of their institution. Most of the time this is done informally, although we know of at least one business school which organizes, in the beginning of each academic year, an orientation session for new faculty. Spouses are included in this orientation session where presentations are made on the background of the school, how it relates to the overall university, and also on its various programs and research activities. Some documentation about the use of cases is also distributed in advance of this session.

Taking a Case Course

Another mechanism used for new faculty, who have never been exposed to the use of cases, is to have them sit in on a case course before their teaching duties begin.

Linda: I got trained by sitting in one of the executive training programs, half as a participant, half as an observer, for almost twelve weeks of classes. I got the chance to see the case method in action and I learned a lot. I learned about how students respond. . . but mostly I learned about myself.

Ron: One thing that has been helpful and that I have seen us do here is bring in a new person who hasn't been involved in cases to a short program, not only as a participant, but to join the faculty team, and ask questions, and stay around after classes. This is valuable, but it is not enough.

Teaching Groups and Teaching Notes

For many instructors, the teaching group is perceived as the most helpful training mechanism.

Don: The most important thing we have, in addition to the teaching notes, is the weekly meeting of the instructors. In the multi-section course there are different levels of seniority and experience represented and, hopefully, different personalities and approaches to individual cases.

These meetings include a general discussion of where we are in the course, what we want to try and emphasize in the next several class sessions. Then we dig in on the individual cases. Ideally, everyone would have read and prepared beforehand and the discussion would concentrate first on the unresolved analytical issues — like a simulated mini-class discussion. Secondly, it would emphasize the educational objectives and strategies. We take 30 to 60 minutes per case, depending on the case.

Dan: We rely very heavily on first year teaching groups. We have extensive teaching notes for all the cases. We meet for three or four hours a week. We first look back over what happened the previous week, if there were any problems. But the major part of the meeting goes into what's going to happen next week. Some of the more experienced members of the teaching group indicate the kinds of things that they plan to do. They augment what's already in the teaching notes. They tell about the kinds of things that could happen that might give you trouble and suggest possible ways of handling certain situations. It's not unlikely that a first time or second time teacher will go and talk to one of the more experienced people after the teaching group meeting.

Visiting Classes

Visiting classes can take two forms: the new instructor visits the class of another teacher or invites another teacher to sit in his or her class. Scott received initial training mostly through the first form.

Scott: In my first semester, I taught one doctoral seminar in finance. The rest of the time I sat in some classes of every member of this faculty. I just systematically visited every faculty member's classes no matter what the subject. Before any class, I would read and partially prepare the assigned case. I just wanted to see what they were doing with cases. The faculty were very happy to help me. At the time, there were 15-16 faculty members.

By the time I had sat in on a number of classes of each faculty, I decided there was no such thing as the case method. I saw that the students were presented with a bewildering array of different styles and approaches. I decided, based on my experience in business, that this was very useful to the students because they would have to acclimate to different styles and to learn in spite of whether the faculty was overly obtuse, devious, or excessively caustic. In my own mind, I felt that I could do anything I wanted to and not be aberrant. I felt free to choose my own style and not be perceived as too far out by the students.

Dan and Mike discuss both forms of class visiting and comment on some of the potential difficulties involved.

Dan: I think my view on class visiting is probably backward from what most people think. I believe the greatest benefits come from the new teacher visiting the class of the experienced teacher. We encourage a lot of that and we also do the more traditional type of visiting where the more experienced teacher visits the new teacher. But I find that harder to do. If it's a mechanical problem, you can say, "Don't always talk to the left hand side of the classroom; don't hold your hand over your mouth and mumble." But most of the problems that you see are not that kind and they're a lot more subtle. You know, things didn't go well, the timing wasn't good. What do you say about timing? "When you're preparing for a class, you ought to think about where you hope to be at various points along the way and not wait until there's only ten minutes to go before you move beyond the mechanics of it and move into the real managerial issues that are involved." I don't think that kind of comment is terribly helpful. But what I think new instructors do find helpful is to go and sit and watch an experienced teacher teach a case before they have to teach it. They can then get to understand what they can do with that case.

Mike: There is also the issue as to whom it is hard on. It seems to me, if the new teacher comes in and sits in on the old teacher's class, it is a non-threatening situation. Whatever you take out of the class is your own decision. You can watch what's going on, and take it or leave it. When the other one sits in on your class, both may feel a little embarrassed. There's a question as to sample, "Is this a typical sample of what usually happens? Is my presence upsetting the routine?" On the other side, the young instructor may think, "If this is a bad class, will it affect my future in this institution?" The new teacher needs to be reasonably confident and extend the invitation if the visitation is going to work.

Advice for New Instructors

Many case teachers commented on what key advice they would give to a new instructor. Collectively, these comments provide interesting insights.

Earl: You have to know your material inside and out. If you do that and if you feel comfortable with the relevance of that material to what the class will face in the future, then that really gives you an aura of confidence. Then you telegraph the usefulness of the class to the students. If you do that, you've got their attention. And you can spend 90% of the time in the class listening to what the people have to say.

Greg: My advice to new case instructors is to be thoroughly prepared. Read the case, do the analysis, get hold of a teaching note and really reconcile the note with the case and your own analysis. When I looked at new cases in my first year, I always read the teaching note first and then looked at the case. I don't do that anymore. It tends to channel your thinking. The case writer never puts down in the teaching note what the good moves are, what can come up in class. So, if you try to teach the case like a teaching note, you'll sell yourself short. Now I work through the analysis and if I can't come up with something meaningful, I can't expect the students to. That's where the rub comes. Then you really have to start asking, "Where am I going to take this case?"

Rick: I think the best thing to do is to videotape yourself. It is a terrific experience. All those little personal mannerisms that are so dysfunctional, that you are not aware of, jump out at you. For example, I discovered that I'm right-headed, or right-handed, or something like that. I really do acknowledge people and get involved with the right-hand side of the class to a greater degree than the left side. I wasn't aware of that until I saw a couple of tapes of myself. Now I work at pushing myself around the room.

Brad: My suggestions to new people are: Spend no less than a quarter of your preparation time on how you're going to stage the class. Make notes after the class on how the class went and why. Recognize the value of the case as a cycle. Don't fire all your guns the first day, students are not going to understand them anyway. Also spend as much time as you can with the students informally. If you socialize a bit with your students here and there, you're going to hear some things coming back that may help you. I think it breaks down official barriers and students are likely to say, "Gee, I really didn't like the attack you took. Why didn't you approach it this way?" My last advice is see your colleagues, ask questions and borrow notes. I really think this buddy system that your area group develops can be super. There's no sense going out and attempting to re-invent the wheel because a lot of people have been planning those wheels a lot longer than you have. And there's an incredible amount of experience on that kind of thing in this school.

Dan: We've had a number of people, who, their first year here, I'm not going to say were disasters, but were the type about which groups of students were talking to the assistant dean and wanted them removed. I suspect that about two or three things happened after their first year. The first thing was that they got a feeling through the first year of where the whole course went, rather than taking each class out of context. And so, they were better able to convey to the students the thrust of where the whole course was going. They got to recognize, by the time that first year was over, they had been through a lot of discussions and they didn't make the same mistakes the second time. I think part of the problem with student evaluations is that they form a reaction based on the early part of the process, And it's often difficult to get students to change their mind. These teachers were better by the end of that first year, but the student reaction lagged behind it. Now, in the beginning of the second year, they started off on the right foot and obtained much better results.

Jack, a renowned case teacher who does a lot of coaching, illustrates his view on case teaching with an anecdote involving a young professor he was trying to help.

Jack: The one thing that I have found that helps certain younger professors is to talk about what they're trying to do. I really feel critical of my own faculty in that we don't sit down and talk as much as we should. We're not good in talking about educational objectives. People will say, "How can you use cases so much in this day and age when there's so much theoretical and substantive material to get across?" And you see, once you use the words "get across" or "impart", you're really talking about knowledge. The job of a good case teacher I don't think is to impart anything. It's not a transfer process. The educational objectives are developing judgement and wisdom and I can't do it for you. But I can get excited and talk about it.

Let me illustrate it with a young professor I was working with a few years ago. It was towards the end of the first year course and I visited two classes in a row. His students liked him and he was trying hard. The first class had something to do with the application of the economic order quantity and the case was full of administrative and situational difficulties. He was technically very well trained, but he'd never had a day as a manager. The class got away from him completely. They were shouting back and forth across the room, and arguing, and challenging, and he was practically just looking from person to person. As I watched that class, it was great. There was breakthrough after breakthrough, getting into fundamentals, and really learning about the technique. It was fantastic. At the end as I was leaving the room, he rushed over and said, "I'm sorry about that, the class got away from me. But I'm glad you're coming tomorrow." I said, "Well, I thought it was a very good class." So I came the next day. This time, he had it beautifully under control. He had his own outline. Had about a 17 point trail he was taking them through. They'd get off that trail and he'd say, "Now wait a minute, let's talk about this. The question you really ought to be asking is this." He led them right through. At the end of the class, I turned to some of the people sitting around me, "Well, how'd you like that today?" They said, "He's back to the same old thing. He never lets us do anything." I said, "What did you think about yesterday?" They said, "Yesterday was the best class we've had the whole year." So I sat down with the young man afterwards. I said, "Which class was the better?" He said, "I really felt good about the one today. I really got a lot across there today." Then I bombed him with, "Your students felt exactly the opposite." There was silence, his face blushed, and he said, "That just can't be."

So I learned what to say to someone like this fellow. What is your job as good case instructor? The answer that I suggest, relating the very spirit of the cases to the job, is to lead a stimulating discussion. Now, you see, he thought his job was to impart knowledge. He thought his job was to make sure people understood certain theoretical things or was to lead the students to those breakthroughs in the case analysis. If you have led a stimulating discussion, everything else will take care of itself. The great teachers are those who lead stimulating discussions and let the chips fall where they may.

Having taught case teaching workshops for more than 30 years all over the world to more than 5000 participants, the author team would be uncomfortable leaving this section without at least some promotion of our position. We believe that the basics of good case teaching can be taught in a workshop setting. We also believe that experience is a great task master. Every teacher has to decide on his or her own which case teaching approach is most effective for his or her students, course, and own personality. Knowledge and understanding of the prerequisites, the preparation task, the case teaching process, evaluation and variations permit the new instructor to build on the insights and experience of others. By avoiding the most obvious mistakes and speeding up his or her learning curve, the new instructor can be effective and enjoy the case teaching experience faster.

DIVERSITY

Managing diversity is important for those trying to teach with cases. Three aspects specifically addressed here include: (1) students with a different cultural background; (2) instructors with a diverse background; (3) cases with diverse backgrounds. In addition, some general comments on teaching in a different culture will be offered.

Students with a Different Cultural Background

Many educational programs often attract substantial numbers of students from other countries. These students come from all kinds of backgrounds and bring diverse values. Ron, an organizational behavior teacher specializing in cross cultural management, gets actively involved with such students coming to his school.

Ron: We are in an environment where participation, arguments, individual effort, and respect for knowledge, not for position and authority, are all part of the dominant culture. Most of the people in the class belong to this environment. But we have an increasing number of students from other cultures with different values. With these students I talk about the advantage of adding to their behavior flexibility. If they choose to work in an international setting, they will be twice as good as anybody else because they will be able to shift back and forth culturally. I talk about how difficult it is for them to do that. By the way, I spend as much time with faculty as I do with students on these issues. There are a lot of faculty members that don't understand. I try to make sure these students understand our culture, that they understand it is not outrageous to challenge someone older than they are, even the professor. I try to interpret our culture and the demands of our culture in their terms.

In so far as different cultures also mean different educational values and norms, for example, stressing rote learning, memory work and the ability to recall large numbers of facts, cultural diversity may mean an extra challenge for the case teacher. It may be difficult to persuade minority group students to engage fully in the Three Stage Learning Process, including all of its team work and participative norms. It may also be difficult to dissuade them from trying to memorize cases instead of analyzing them and to learn from fellow students instead of the instructor.

Special training and case method familiarization workshops with minority groups have a high pay-off if they are well done. Since all participants share the minority role for the duration of such workshops, they become the majority and can collectively reflect on the implications of the case method for themselves individually and collectively. Full understanding of the challenges presented by the case method has to be an integral part of such familiarization efforts. Many "domestic" students have difficulty grasping the full implications of case study on their norms, values and behavior. The teacher, by his or her own behavior, must be a living example of what he or she is asking the minority group to accomplish.

Afsaneh Nahavandi says:

Along with courtesy and respect comes an implicit and often explicit requirement to be tolerant of views. Our students have to learn to value diversity (maybe a cliche, but true). Watching the training videos, reading the seminal articles and books, performing the various exercises, and discussing the insightful cases are all useless if students do not see diversity valued and encouraged in the classroom. For those of us who do not have culturally or ethnically diverse classrooms, the message can still be conveyed by valuing intellectual diversity. The modeling of those values through the treatment of students is key to internalization of the message (204).

Instructors with a Diverse Background

Case instructors are often invited to give seminars, to teach in executive programs or to assist in developing management programs elsewhere. Also, students go back to their respective countries and start teaching there with cases. Both types of instructors share the problem of adjusting themselves and their teaching to different cultural environments. In this section, mostly the viewpoint of the visiting teachers will be taken, assuming that the second type of instructor will find it easier to deal with the cultural issues involved.

Kim: I believe that for any teacher moving to a different culture the onus is on him or her to adapt to the new environment as much as possible. When students from different countries come to our institution, we have to say, "You're going to have to learn our ways." It is only fair that the reverse takes place on the other side. You cannot ask 30 to 100 people in a class to change completely because one teacher has a different cultural background. The ideal would be for the teacher to be not only completely culturally attuned, but also to be able to speak the local language. This is very difficult in some instances. Simultaneous interpretation, however, is expensive and adds a significant barrier to spontaneity in case discussions, as well as lengthens the time required.

Ron: When you are teaching in another country where the majority is from a different culture, it seems to me you have to do at least three things: First, you have to be honest with these students about your own cultural biases and how they come out in the materials you use. It's particularly true in organizational behavior. But it is also true in operations management, sales management, etc. Second, you better be really prepared to listen to what you think are really far out approaches, interpretations of the cases, or solutions that you think are impossible. The third deals with the choice of materials appropriate to that country.

The following quotes from the case experiences of two European instructors in China show instructor personalities and perceptions also play a significant role in dealing with their own diversity. Peter Newman, a British professor, talks about his experiences in using case studies in the People's Republic of China.

Compared with equivalent Western students, Chinese students are markedly better at identifying and analysing problems — in part, because they are happy to devote time to this aspect of case study work (in the author's experience, students new to the case method rush the identification of the problem in order to get to the "fun" of finding solutions).

Chinese students are loath to offer any solution publicly, but it is acceptable to ask students to work in groups on solutions (it appears to be necessary to first teach a method of problem solving), and for one person to act as spokesperson for the group...

... In the author's opinion, the behaviours so deeply ingrained at school and reinforced by society at large make it virtually impossible for the case method to work with Chinese professors and Chinese students in the same room. Meaningful case discussion does, however, appear to be feasible in the classroom via the use of "discussion leaders," suitably prepared with a checklist of questions, provided they are fellow students (2).

Verner has a different experience.

Verner: In some ways, I find it easier to engage Chinese students in case discussion than I do my European students. The Chinese students have a tremendous need and motivation. They are hungry for learning. In my country everybody who wants can get into the business school and in a short time they think they know the whole world. The Chinese people who have been out struggling with concrete problems are really motivated to learn some concepts, some theories, and to discuss how to solve concrete problems.

Normally, what I do with a case is assign very specific questions and the students get some time to prepare. In a way it is very old fashioned. My experience is that I have never had to conscript people to talk. Always there are people who want to participate. For example, in my very first class with Chinese students, I had this person who came to me before class started who said, "I want to sit just in front of the teacher because I like to ask a lot of questions." Just like that.

Even when the Chinese students say something that is more or less nonsense they don't feel they lose face. I know that the Chinese are very face conscious. They are very open in the class because they feel it is a safe environment. Whatever you do in class, it does not have serious consequences. They are very good with each other, very good colleagues. Whenever I ask a question, a lot of people raise their hand and then all the others start talking with each other and I have to call for quiet. I just use old fashioned discussion concepts and they work.

Afsaneh Nahavandi contributes:

I also see the cultural background that I bring to class as one of my major contributions. I am Iranian by birth. I spent my childhood in Iran while going to a French school, where I interacted with the children of diplomats from many countries. I came to the United States for my undergraduate and graduate studies. I have never fully felt a part of the Iranian, the French or the U.S. culture. I am, by definition, what sociologists call a "marginal" person. This marginality, however, has allowed me insight into all three cultures and into many others. By being closely involved with, but not fully part of any culture, and growing up never seeing them as truly separate, I have learned to see them as a whole rather than as separate parts.

This integration of cultures and learning to live with their differences, while still remaining whole, is a recurring theme in my courses. I provide students with many personal examples. I challenge their views of culture differences and force them to rethink many of their assumptions about culture. For example, as soon as they think that a concept we covered (e.g., goal setting) is well defined, I introduce the issue of culture, sometimes in very simple ways: "If you were Iranian and expected your boss to know all the answers, how would you react if your boss sat down with you and asked you for your goals and negotiated them with you? How do we need to reconsider our theories and practices of goal setting when we cross cultural borders?" Because of my background, such cultural discourse is an integral part of class and a very personal contribution to my students' learning (200).

Cases with a Different Cultural Background

A large amount of information is frequently not included in a case although many case teachers may not be overly sensitive to this fact. The missing information is assumed to be standard cultural, historical and societal knowledge that any student should know through normal upbringing. Thus, when we say an organization is located in Los Angeles, at a specific time, it is assumed that no further explanation is required regarding the city, or the economic or other conditions prevailing at that time and place. How startling a difference time and location can make is obvious when the same case is transferred to London, Moscow or Hong Kong. The simple point is that a lot of the case information is actually not included in the case. It is presumed to exist in the reader's mind. When an instructor goes to a different country, it is not safe to assume that these non-explicit case data will be recognized in the new environment.

Ron, Kim, and Roberto address the material selection issue:

Ron: You must try to get materials that reflect different ways of dealing with problems and different settings. That is, try to get international materials, preferably local, or anything out of North America. It will not only add face and credibility, but it will also automatically loosen people up to talk about their own interpretations, and label them as such. Because if you use North American material and you're North American and you're supposed to be the expert, they may be trying very hard to give you what you want to hear — and not in a manipulative way, but thinking that's the way they ought to run their businesses. I have been on some programs where I have had to undo some of what other American people had done and really screwed things up.

Kim adds a few thoughts:

Kim: All cases are culture bound. For this reason, it is frequently difficult for someone with a different cultural background to feel comfortable with a foreign case. There are no easy solutions to this. It is best for the teachers to recognize cultural and other data not explicit in the case, because what the teacher may presume to be general common knowledge may not be obvious to the students.

Sometimes, non-local cases can be used to increase student interest and to broaden their horizons. The percentage of non-local cases has to be considered carefully, though. Excessive dependence on such cases may well turn students off because they feel the material is not relevant to their own environment.

Roberto, a Spaniard trained in the U.S., affirms:

Roberto: My best cases are my own. From time to time, I use Harvard cases. The problem with these cases is that students say, "Yes, but..... here it is different..."

Some General Remarks about Teaching in a Different Culture

The following comments refer to teaching experiences in different cultures.

Frank: I was teaching in Europe. Students were mature business people. Most of them had quite traditional educational training. The use of cases was new to them. They took to it with great enthusiasm as they always do in executive programs. Where good cases are used, there's good case discussion. But one of the unique things about Europe is that theirs is a more managed economy and it's hard to talk exclusively about the corporate entity, as if decisions are made only in the corporate entity. They keep bringing you back to the environment and the system and what it's like to function in a managed economy.

Juan, who graduated from a leading American business school a few years ago, describes some cultural differences.

Juan: On the whole, my Spanish students react very positively to the use of cases. They have been exposed to lectures mostly and are happy to get the opportunity to speak up in class. The most striking contrast with the U.S.A. is that here students tend to be less competitive. They try to avoid open confrontation in class discussions. Latin people are afraid of being shown they are in a weak position in public. They are very proud. They will protect their own pride and the pride of others as well. They will make an informal agreement, something like, "Let's manage this discussion without anybody getting hurt in the process." They tend to rely more on a "smoothing" of issues.

Ron: Among some very simple operating things I do when I teach in another country is to slow down, repeat myself, but instead of twice or three times like I do in a normal class, five times. I try to alter my behavior in the class physically to fit with their culture. For example, in Brazil, I'm more animated than I am here. It's more acceptable; it's more valued; it's more expected. At the same time, I lecture more there than I do here. That's partly because of their hierarchical society. There is much more respect placed on positions in Brazil. They are more concerned with face than North Americans are. They have more of a group orientation and their places in the group are more important. For example, if you use a predictive case, you have to be delicate the way you handle it so that nobody looks bad. If you are using experiential exercises of any sort, whether it is an inventory problem or a group decision thing, you have to be careful about the vulnerability that people have.

Generally, if I am going to deal with a group that is largely from a different culture, I will, either early in the course or at the very end, give a lecture about culture and its influences on management, using references from the classroom, references to the underlining assumptions with the cases, as well as my culture and theirs.

SHORTCUTS BY STUDENTS

Students may try to avoid all or some of the responsibilities associated with their learning with cases and seek "shortcuts." It is useful for the instructor to recognize the nature of possible shortcuts and to find ways and means of dealing with them. The range of severity in terms of ethical considerations may be substantial and will have actual cheating on one extreme. Most issues deal with the preparation of a case for class and, since this may be perceived as overly time consuming by students, ways and means of avoiding the necessary time investment are the most popular form of shortcut.

Three ethical issues are: (1) giving, receiving or solicitating notes on cases before or after class; (2) contacting the case organization to find out what decision was taken; (3) avoiding preparation and depending on the small or large group discussion to reveal the salient learning points of the case.

Since the philosophy of learning with cases is based on the principle of growth through experience, the individual who is trying to bypass the system loses the most.

Moreover, if an instructor's manual gets in the wrong hands, or if extensive student note files are kept in a fraternity, sorority, student residence, or passed on from year to year by students, the net effect will be that the cases themselves become useless. Having to give up a good case because of potentially widespread distribution of the "answers" is a painful and costly decision. All instructors know good cases are difficult to find and "burned" or "blown" cases are sad victims of unfortunate circumstances.

Shortcuts to Preparation

The most obvious shortcut of all, clearly, is not to prepare for a class at all; no reading and no preparation. Some teachers tell students that they wish to be told of such a situation before class. Clearly, in case of emergency, lack of preparation is not a problem. Most students do not believe it is in their best interest to tell the instructor, for fear of creating a bad impression. Most students prefer to take their chances in class, where the random probability the instructor will find out appears to be low. Even when the instructor does ask such an unprepared student for a contribution, two options exist. One, the student may admit to not having read the case. Now it is up to the instructor to have a response ready. If the instructor has told the class, "Prior notice is required," he or she can say, "My norm is that I wish to be told before class." Some prefer to add, "Please see me after class." Others will say, "Don't let it happen again!" Barney argues it is not very likely for students to take this route.

> **Barney:** One way for a student to play it is to say, "I don't know. I didn't do it. I did not prepare. I can't say anything." That's ridiculous. The way we as faculty deal with that is normally to be very negative. We've got to recognize that someday some students won't even read the case. It would be bad if it were everyday. It would be bad if everyone did it. Students have to learn how to manage that.

The other option is for the student to try to bluff. On the basis of what discussion has already taken place, the student may be able to "grab a little piece and try to run with it "creating an awkward situation for both sides, if it is subsequently uncovered that the student does not know what he or she is talking about.

A step removed from total lack of case knowledge is the situation where the student reads the case, but does no analysis. Comments like: "I had trouble getting a handle on this case," "I did not understand the technology," "I did not understand how the system worked," are some typical warning signals in class. If the instructor takes such comments seriously, class time and effort may well be wasted chasing windmills. If situations such as these happen rarely, there is no great cause for instructor concern; although, if they are concentrated with certain individuals in class, action is clearly required.

Barney comments on the consequences of instructors accepting mediocre preparation.

Barney: The danger is when the class believes that you have been hoodwinked. If the class believes that the student got away with no preparation and fooled you into thinking that it was good preparation, you are in trouble. When the class hears students participating and saying nothing, just making sure they say something everyday, that's a bad habit to develop in the class. And it is the faculty member who encourages those habits. That is a bad outcome of "working the system" when students think they can work the system consistently and get away with it. So, you should not accept when a student participates and fumbles through and asks questions and says a whole lot of things without any content. At the very least you should joke about it or say something like, "That's good, but if you read the case, you might even do better next time." Do this not in any angry way, or a penalizing one, but in one that says, "I see what you are doing, but it didn't work."

Some students come to class with a minimum amount of preparation, but are clever enough to pick up the drift of the discussion, and come on strong near the end of the class with summarization or extraction of basic principles type of comments.

When a large segment of the class comes unprepared, it is a more serious situation.

Barney: When the whole class has not prepared, I want to know why. It depends on the why. Sometimes, I'll just stop and say, "What's going on? How come? I don't understand your problems, I guess, because no one has prepared for this. What is it? Are you fed up? Is it a party? Am I conducting a lousy course? Did you just have no interest in doing it?"

I want to know because there is some reason for these students not doing their task. I know they are not lazy as a group. They are not stupid; they are not deliberately trying to avoid learning. It isn't a game in that sense. They really want to get the most out of it. We have fairly mature students and I just assume they are here to learn as much as they can in the most effective way they can. If they are not learning, there has to be some reason for it.

Sometimes students will prepare a certain percentage of cases well and others lightly. A special type of this shortcut is where study groups assign cases for preparation to certain individuals on the understanding that others may just read them. For example, in a group of six students working on three cases, each group of two students would do a "serious preparation" of one case and read over the other two cases. Then, in the small group discussion, every participant "gets clued in" to two cases, and "presents" one case. If certain group members have special skills or backgrounds, such as accounting, computer, marketing, finance, operations, or others, this kind of arrangement is particularly appealing from a time efficiency standpoint. Letting the "experts" prepare the cases they are best equipped to handle may be tempting. Such practices may be difficult to uncover for an instructor who has no knowledge of what transpires in study groups. It is obvious that the learning of the non-experts will be shortcut by such arrangements. We do not consider this preparation sharing a desirable practice.

Occasionally, students may plan their contributions in class, preparing well near the beginning or end of the course, or doing especially careful preparation every fourth case, or some similar strategy.

Seat Visibility

Even the question of seat selection in a room may indicate a student's preference for visibility or participation avoidance. The typical case classroom may be divided into areas of high visibility to both instructor and other participants and ones of lower impact. In tiered rooms with a semi-circular arrangement, the highest visibility area is in the centre rows directly in front of the instructor. (See Exhibit 10-1.)

Exhibit 10-1
SEAT SELECTION

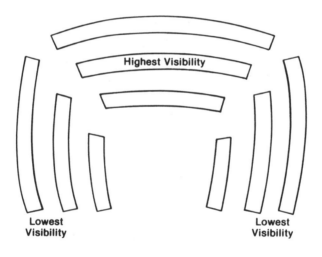

How Instructors View Shortcuts

Several interviewees argued that almost all of the student strategies or moves are to be expected by instructors, that they are part of the system, and not necessarily all bad.

Robin: First of all, the use of cases invites some people to look for shortcuts. Simply, because it is a group process and, therefore, if an individual decides to elect him or herself out of the group, and lay the responsibility for the process on the rest of the group, he or she can probably get away with it. The smaller the group, the more difficult that becomes. I think an instructor's responsibility, whether it be a regular degree session or an executive development program, is to watch the total group to see what is happening, and who is really not playing his or her role. The instructor has to listen to small groups. On an executive or night program, I think it's very useful to walk around and listen to the small group discussions. It's not only just to learn something from the groups, to put them on the track, but also to see who's not active. One can find out if people are leaning on the rest of the group. Nevertheless, any group process must allow itself to help people who are not going to perform their roles. One thing is to remind groups that they have the responsibility for their own membership. Also, each member must have a teaching and learning responsibility with respect to the others in that group. Secondly, I think you have to do more interviewing and counseling with those people who are not contributing in class.

Barney: I do not think cheating is the right term, because none of these things break any rules. They break norms, but not rules. The norm being that everyone contributes actively, participates, and is wholeheartedly a contributor to everyone else, that is not a rule; that's a norm. I think "working the system" is better than the words "cheating" or "playing the system." I don't know how bad it is that students learn about working the system, unless it is widespread and consistent. On occasion, I think it's smart to figure those things out, because we demand more than they can manage. And we don't acknowledge that they cannot meet those demands. So they have to figure out how to play it.

Group Projects

When groups work on projects together, which may or may not involve presentations in class, the work load may not be shared equally among students. Some instructors prefer to ignore this aspect and choose to give a common grade to all group members. Others ask group members to grade each other, possibly anonymously.

Exams

It is logical to use case exams on a course where a significant amount of the course is devoted to cases. Communication between students on exams, where such communication is not allowed, does constitute cheating, as on any other exam. Barney discussed this aspect along with the role the teacher might play in class to show integrity.

Barney: I have never had a specific instance where I had absolute proof that case exam cheating took place. The kind of cheating that takes place on occasion is where students leave the room for a smoke or a coffee, or something like that. They talk a bit about the case, or drop a line here or there, and somebody would say something like, "Boy, I can't figure that one out at all." It's not quite asking for an answer, but in the process, it can happen. However, I think it will happen probably less in a class where the right spirit is generated. Again, if exam grades are all important, it is the students against the faculty, or us against the one faculty member. Then we create conditions that lead to cheating.

However, the instructor can give the sense of wanting the students to do well, and hoping they do well, and encouraging them and understanding their difficulties and pressures, and not taking their grades totally seriously. The instructor must also, by a variety of individual acts during the course, establish a high sense of integrity for him or herself and for every one else in class. There are many opportunities where you can be right or half wrong just in the way you deal with some issue as a matter of integrity.

Then, I think you engender that sense in a class and they would not cheat no matter what. On my exams, I always write, "This is an open book exam but please do not discuss any aspect of the exam, or the course, with anyone during the exam." So this avoids some danger where some students say, "We have group studies for class preparation, we study as a group for our report, why don't we study as a group for our exams?" And they can make that kind of excuse as to why they were talking about an exam. So I make it explicit that the expectation is that they will not talk about it. I really cannot say that I've had any problems of this kind. And I have no fear that it might happen.

CONCLUSION

This chapter's three main topics, training of case teachers, managing diversity and shortcuts by students, all represent challenges in teaching with cases. Teachers new to the use of cases can learn the basics of effective case teaching reasonably quickly, provided they go about it the right way. Case teaching workshops, augmented by readings and the assistance of experienced case teachers, focus on the positive ways to improve teaching performance.

Diversity in students and instructors, discussed in a cultural sense in this chapter, also exists in gender, experience, age, education, and skill sets. The ability to recognize, understand and use diversity as a positive force in teaching with cases permits the instructor to impart to students skills which will allow them to manage globally. The diversity of cases presents an opportunity in course planning and classroom execution to reinforce almost all aspects of diversity management. The case instructor leads by example, a challenge that is easily forgotten and bears repeating.

Shortcuts by students may easily slip into unethical behavior. The successful case teacher manages to convey to his or her students the worth of self-discovery, of proper preparation and participation, and the pride of accomplishment, so that shortcuts are not particularly appealing.

CHAPTER ELEVEN

conclusion

Two obvious conclusions stand out. One, the world in which relatively few people teach with cases no longer exists. Teaching with cases is widespread across programs, disciplines and cultures, and case use varies from one case per course to a large number of cases per course plus the full range in between. Two, there is no one best way to teach with cases. Not only do objectives for using cases vary, but so do, for example, students, instructors, class times, facilities, and environments. In one way this lack of standardization is unfortunate. It makes the process messy. In another, it increases the challenge to perform the task well and gives the individual instructor an opportunity to custom build an approach suitable to his or her unique situation.

The following comments may apply to educational challenges other than those emanating directly from the use of cases. It is difficult to separate teaching with cases completely from teaching in general.

AN OPERATIONS OVERVIEW

It is possible to apply an operations overview to the teaching with cases. Since two of the authors have specialized in this area, it makes particular sense to take such an approach. Our overview has three main parts. The first concerns itself with the objectives of the system. Here, the relationship between course objectives and case use frequency is identified along with potential implications. The second is a detailed look at the system components and their interaction. The case learning process is viewed as an input-transformation-output system and examined accordingly. The third part concerns itself with the environment within which the system takes place and also raises some technology related issues.

Objectives and Case Use Frequency

An operations viewpoint begins with the examination of an operating system and the objectives of what the system is supposed to accomplish. The key managerial question is: "How can the operations manager contribute effectively to organizational objectives and strategies?"

In the context of teaching with cases the parallel question is: "How can the teacher using cases contribute effectively to institutional objectives and strategies?"

As is true in many non-educational institutions, the assumption that organizational objectives and strategies are clearly enumerated and clearly communicated and understood by all "managers" is a tall one. Often, in the absence of strong institutional guidance, the individual instructor is called upon to provide his or her own perception of what the institution is trying to achieve. Attribution of institutional aims is probably seldom accomplished without some personal preference coloration creeping in. Since our interest is in the use of cases, a clear indication of personal preference seems to be the frequency of case use by the instructor.

It is our opinion that the variation in case use frequency observed in the interviews stems largely from a fundamental difference in the perceived objectives held by each instructor.

Case use frequency can be expressed as the percentage of total class or course time devoted to cases. It can vary from very low to very high with a full range in between. An attempt has been made in Exhibit 11-1 to examine how perceived objectives, the role of cases, underlying assumptions, and implications might be different with varying amounts of case use. It is probably best to focus at the low and high use extremes for this purpose, without being explicit about specific amounts of case use frequency.

That cases can be used at either end of the frequency scale attests to their potential flexibility. Whether the same cases should be used on both ends or not may be a matter of dispute.

The middle area between the two extremes is the tough one. Is it possible to achieve the best of both worlds? The lack of data on results makes this a particularly difficult education design challenge. How many cases should an educator use to achieve a minimum level of competency in analytical skills, problem solving, decision making, communication? How many cases does it take before a student is considered adequate in the application of a certain technique to real life problems? Certain institutions have been able to establish a reputation which solves this problem neatly for the outside world. The institution's "brand name" on the diploma or degree guarantees the participant has successfully completed the program of instruction and the "consumers of the product" are willing to buy without worrying about detailed specifications or because they have found previous "products" to their liking.

Since, to the operations manager, the final output is a specific result designed into the total process, the process itself, its components, and their interrelationships need to be examined more closely.

Exhibit 11–1
TEACHING WITH CASES AND THE FREQUENCY OF CASE USE

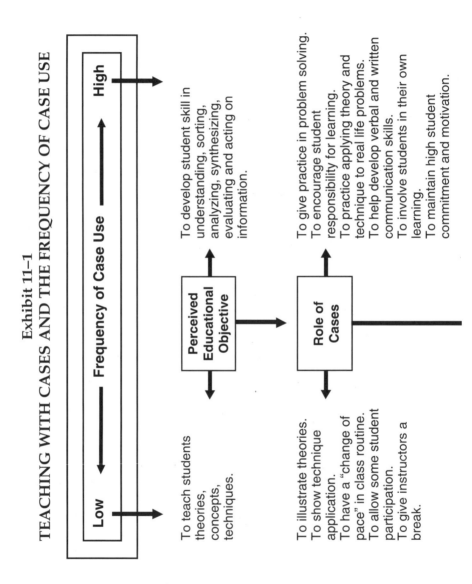

Low ——— Frequency of Case Use ——— High

Perceived Educational Objective

To teach students theories, concepts, techniques.

To develop student skill in understanding, sorting, analyzing, synthesizing, evaluating and acting on information.

Role of Cases

To illustrate theories.
To show technique application.
To have a "change of pace" in class routine.
To allow some student participation.
To give instructors a break.

To give practice in problem solving.
To encourage student responsibility for learning.
To practice applying theory and technique to real life problems.
To help develop verbal and written communication skills.
To involve students in their own learning.
To maintain high student commitment and motivation.

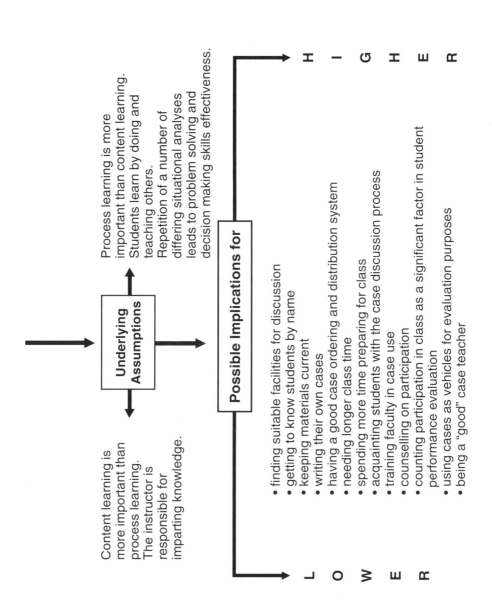

Content learning is more important than process learning. The instructor is responsible for imparting knowledge.

Process learning is more important than content learning. Students learn by doing and teaching others. Repetition of a number of differing situational analyses leads to problem solving and decision making skills effectiveness.

Underlying Assumptions

Possible Implications for

L O W E R

H I G H E R

- finding suitable facilities for discussion
- getting to know students by name
- keeping materials current
- writing their own cases
- having a good case ordering and distribution system
- needing longer class time
- spending more time preparing for class
- acquainting students with the case discussion process
- training faculty in case use
- counselling on participation
- counting participation in class as a significant factor in student performance evaluation
- using cases as vehicles for evaluation purposes
- being a "good" case teacher

The Case Teaching Process as an Input-Output System

Teaching with cases can be diagrammed as a simple input-transformation-output system. (See Exhibit 11-2.) This representation can be applied to a single class, as well as a course, a program, or an institution. Since the interest of most readers is likely to focus on the individual class and the course, discussion will be primarily at these two levels, with only an occasional reference to the program or the institutional focus.

Exhibit 11–2
THE CASE TEACHING PROCESS AS AN INPUT-TRANSFORMATION-OUTPUT SYSTEM

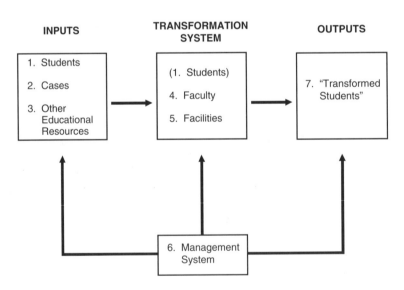

Given a first glance at what actually constitutes this system and what is happening as people teach with cases is enough to give it the appearance of a horror show for the serious operations manager. Here is a system without easily measurable output, variable inputs, high variability in the transformation process, ill-defined capacity, and a management system in which responsibilities and authority are diffused. About the only component which can be specified in reasonable form and with acceptable justification is the facility.

A more detailed look at each of the seven components may reveal issues and concerns perhaps not immediately obvious.

1. Students.   Students are supposed to be the transformable entities. As distinct from a factory input, one vital role the student with cases is supposed to play is to assist in the transformation process. The product transforms itself. It is impossible to achieve a homogeneous student input. Therefore, there is a question of desirable attributes, or prerequisites, not only as to formal education, but also as to personal characteristics, like cultural background, values, leadership, independence, social and communication skills, work experience, entrepreneurial spirit, gender, age, and health.

One of the accusations faced by the "best case schools" is that they only admit the "best students" and, therefore, their output is likely to be fairly good. It is not clear what constitutes the "best" mix of students as input or what attributes are best for the use of teaching/learning with cases. Nor is it clear what is a desirable minimum or maximum number of students that can be put into a course in which cases will be used. It is very clear that certain instructors have preferences and opinions on this subject. General practice seems to limit total class size to a maximum of about one hundred students. What the trade-off in educational quality would be between two classes of 50 students each, versus one of 100, both taught with the same instructor and identical course outline, is not clear.

The suitable age of students to consider the use of cases apparently lies between 12 and 100 years. Some experiments have been tried with even younger groups. What mix of ages in a course is desirable is not clear, although in management programs, a 30 year differential between youngest and oldest class members is not unusual.

Motivation of the student to learn is probably the single most dominant factor in education. It is argued that with cases students can be more motivated, since they can appreciate the relevance of what they are doing and become actively involved in the process. Instructors can do many things to add to this motivation as is evident throughout this book. Some relatively simple but basic actions include getting to know one's students well; grading case exams personally and handing them back quickly; showing concern in and out of class for student progress and problems with participation. Coupled with cases, these basics establish the conditions within which students can be highly motivated.

2. Cases. Cases are supposed to be the distinguishing characteristic between case teaching and other forms of instruction. As to what constitutes a case and what does not, and where the boundary line lies between a case and an exercise, or a simulation, is not commonly agreed to and understood. Confusion on this subject is logical in view of the wide range of potential teaching objectives writers may have had in mind at the time of creating the case. Confusion is unfortunate if students are misled to believe that certain materials are real life when, in fact, they are fictitious.

How long a case should be, how it should be organized, how much information should be provided of the relevant and non-relevant kind, how old or new, what kind of managerial position in what type of organization, and where in the world, are only some of the questions the instructor faces in the course design task. Despite the existence of ECCH and other case distribution centers, access to cases still faces many hurdles. "Academics are not good marketers of their own cases," one interviewee remarked. There is a huge challenge in keeping a continuous flow of new cases going, truly reflecting the reality of the changing managerial tasks. And how does one tell whether a case is any good at all? Best sellers lists identify those used more frequently. Are these necessarily the best? Various attempts to set up a case refereeing process exist in different parts of the world. What the consequences of these actions will be is not entirely clear. Will it encourage more academics to turn to case development? Will it produce more good cases? Will it create two classes of cases: refereed or good ones and others? Will it raise the overall quality level of cases?

How many cases it takes to accomplish a specific educational objective is a question already raised above. Some research has at least begun to compare cases to games, simulations, and exercises on the assumption that relatively few cases would be used. Obviously, an individual case can address a multiplicity of objectives simultaneously. Our Case Difficulty Cube, with the analytical, conceptual and presentation dimensions, gives a way of organizing key learning objectives with cases. This multiplicity makes the case selection task difficult for the instructor. A case is not just simply a good linear programming application, or a good break-even analysis case. It has other dimensions that may make it more or less desirable for the course under consideration.

The assumption that the right case will necessarily "click" with students is naive. So many factors impinge on the transformation process, that the case itself may not be dominant. It is possible for an instructor to have a good class with a "bad" case, and a bad class with a "good" case. The tenacity with which some instructors cling to their favorite cases may be partially explained by a belief that the case itself is the dominant factor. The case needs to be seen in context, not only in terms of topic or theoretical coverage, but also in its other dimensions. Envisaging a process whereby the case may be taught is a skill not born into every teacher. The trend towards greater concentration on and sharing of teaching notes, as integral with the case writing and distribution process, is a healthy recognition of this fact.

It is our belief that the participatory aspect of case teaching gives the case its greatest powers. Thus, the case needs to be sufficiently interesting for a student to prepare it properly. The assurance and expectation that the student's insights and analyses will be seriously considered and appreciated in class will be the valuable motivators for the student to do the necessary preparation.

3. Other Educational Inputs. On a course basis, other educational inputs will vary in quantity inversely with the frequency of case use. What constitutes a proper mix of lectures, simulations and exercises, readings, discussions, films, videos, computerized learning programs, problems, etc. with cases and how each interacts with the other is something each instructor must face in course design, despite a scarcity of supporting data. Interestingly enough, "what the instructor is good at" is itself an important consideration. A good case teacher is probably wise to use cases more than an instructor less comfortable with this method.

Even in the early days of using cases for management education, the dichotomy between imparting knowledge and developing people to make decisions and take action was clearly recognized. With the knowledge explosion and the increasing pressure for academic respectability, this dichotomy appears to grow larger. Fortunately, the computer has made available some new options, such as electronic cases, interactive learning, business games, and a variety of exercises which help bridge the gap. There have been, therefore, strong pressures for "case method" schools to give up class time formerly reserved for cases to other educational inputs. This process has already gone on for a considerable time and has resulted in a significant change not always appreciated by others. The increasing number of options in educational inputs available to every teacher makes proper choice more difficult.

The accompanying blurring of objectives and boundaries between inputs means the choice is no longer simply lecture or use a case.

4. Faculty. The instructor is not just a worker on the educational assembly line. Normally, he or she has a significant managerial and leadership role at the same time. On an individual course basis, the instructor may be seen as an individual craftsperson. In the use of cases, a student role may also be expected of the instructor. The teacher may become transformed along with the student. What kind of person is best suited to the case discussion leader's role has been amply speculated on. How one becomes good at it is another matter.

Despite the valiant efforts of many, it is probably true that the training of case teaching has not received sufficient attention yet. There is a considerable group of case teachers who honestly do not believe such skills are teachable. Since they themselves prove they managed to achieve their excellence without formal training, they represent ample evidence of that point. Even in their experiences, how much they may have subconsciously picked up as students in case courses themselves is something which might be looked at.

It is abundantly clear that, despite this impressive group of self-taught and self-sufficient persons, others would appreciate guidance and information, beyond being told, "Go out and try it."

What constitutes an acceptable instructor load in terms of case teaching and how much time should be allocated for preparation for a case class, the teaching of the class, and additional student contact? Institutional norms on this question have been developed, but variations between institutions may be substantial. How does an instructor get evaluated on a results basis? Is student reaction the proper way to go? Research has shown that, for non-case courses, teacher popularity and student learning do not always correlate positively. Does the same hold for case courses?

Is a serious, well intentioned young instructor new to cases likely to receive better results than a bored, experienced senior? Do older professors really "give up" on cases and "lecture in disguise," as some contributors put it?

What turns the instructor "on" when using cases? Is it the excitement of participants, fun of dealing with the real life problem, the hunt for truth, self-fulfillment? Certainly, in many institutions the reward-punishment system does not favor case teaching, or anything else associated with cases. The low esteem given to the use of cases may have been partially fostered by past incompetence of others. Nevertheless, for the younger instructor in particular, it may represent a horrendous hurdle in the immediate peer environment. Ways need to be found to increase the legitimacy of teaching with cases on bases other than faith alone. Variability in process, inputs, and other system components increase, rather than decrease, the need for guidance and support.

5. Facilities. Facilities can do so much to support the effective use of cases and so much to block results, on the other hand, that they are a significant component in the process. Since facilities well suited to case teaching can easily be used for other methodologies, including lectures, the argument for building in the case option is extremely strong. The argument gains even more validity when one recognizes the institutional obstacles to facility change, once in place. Even though the classroom is the key unit under consideration, support facilities such as small group discussion areas easily accessible to students, reproduction and distribution facilities for cases, and easy library and Internet access can lend valuable support.

6. Management System. The management system provides the design, operation and control of the transformation process. It gives commands and receives feedback. In the teaching with cases context, the responsibilities and authority within the managerial system are diffused. The instructor bears certain ones individually: identification of course objectives, case selection in course design, execution of the course plan on a regular basis and responsibility for measuring student performance are typical examples. Responsibility for facilities usually lies somewhere outside the academic stream in teaching institutions. Student admission may be handled by a registrar's office and case ordering, reproduction and distribution by two or three separate bodies. Timetabling may fall anywhere and supervision of faculty takes a variety of interesting forms. The point need not be belabored; considerable coordination is required to make sure that the whole makes sense.

The management system is also supposed to provide suitable motivation for the student to learn and the instructor to teach (both to the best of their respective capabilities), take measures of actual results and initiate corrective action. To a large extent these aspects are often left to the individual teacher.

When a process analysis is carried out, two major concerns from an operations viewpoint deal with capacity and bottlenecks. Ideally, a system should be run close to capacity and be well balanced, with few, if any, bottlenecks. As has already been mentioned, capacity in case teaching is a flexible concept. The number of students in a class, the number of cases teachable in a working day, the number of case preparations or classes by students per day are all basic measures necessary to arrive at some form of capacity consensus. Combining such simple quantity considerations with quality or functional objectives increases the measurement problem. "How many students out of the total class learned well from this experience?" is more relevant than, "How many students were present?"

The concept of a bottleneck is related to a capacity constraint, limiting the systems output. Potential bottlenecks may be: (1) the students — some or all not prepared properly, or without the necessary skills to handle the case; (2) the facilities — blocking effective learning; (3) the faculty — unskilled in its tasks and lacking in motivation; or (4) the management system — poorly designed and/or operated. The lack of congruence among system components creates an out-of-balance and out-of-focus condition.

7. The Output - The "Transformed" Students. Normally, if a system output meets quality, cost, quantity and delivery requirements, the system is a long way on the right track. The assumption is made that the process which produced the output must be, generally, in acceptable order. Measuring the output of a case class, or a course using a significant number of cases, is no easy task. Therefore, the management job of relating output to system component performance is difficult to execute. At what point should a case be changed, an instructor change the approach to a case, a class be lengthened or shortened? These are some relatively simple questions, but illustrative of the point.

One way to respond is to let the market forces have free play. "As long as our students are being hired, we must be doing alright." That may give too strong a credit to market sensitivity. Moreover, much of the discussion to this point has assumed that the purpose of the educational process has been to respond to relatively nearby foreseeable market requirements.

What will our current students be required to do twenty or thirty years from now? What skills will they be required to have? What role will additional training on and off the job have to play? What should our contribution be now so that the base for that future career will be appropriate? Is it even realistic to think in today's educational world that current education might still have an impact two or three decades later? Or should we just be teaching our students to be able to learn from their future experiences?

The Environment

The academic environment for degree programs in management is currently unsettled in many institutions. High student demand coupled with tightening purse strings, and tougher promotion and tenure rules put pressures on the academic to get the product out without much institutional support in the form of additional resources. Since it is probably easier to process large numbers of students using non-case courses, changing the status quo from non or low case use to higher case use is undoubtedly difficult. In fact, pressures will favor conversion in the other direction. Also, the current environment is not ideal for some sound academic thinking on the soft issues that have plagued the use of cases over the last ninety years.

The Technology

The technology in education is changing and must, of necessity, have an impact on the process chosen for the transformation system. Do the computer and the new telecommunications options spell a fundamentally new approach to case teaching? Is an electronic or video case still a case? Have the processes of production and the requirements of the medium altered the original data to such an extent that a similarity exists, but no more? If actors are used to portray the roles of people in the same situation, does this make it a play? When all of the financial statements of an organization are stored in a computer and students are asked to analyze them, does this constitute a case or an exercise? And, does it necessarily matter what it is called?

Opportunities for teaching with cases abound using computer and telecommunications technology. Research into the effects of new technology should be strongly encouraged. "If someone could only provide a case exam that could be computer graded . . ."

CONCLUSION

It is certainly easier to identify challenges and problems than to solve them. And it is to be expected that new times will bring new opportunities and new challenges. Teaching with cases is not stagnant. It is on the move, and the directions in which it appears to be going have exciting promises.

The case teacher is a manager of a process. To manage this process well in the educational environment is no easy task. The process is complex, with many factors requiring consideration. Shortcuts do exist, but are likely to have their own penalties attached. The astounding aspect is the number of variations around the main theme in teaching with cases. The contribution of this text was to identify these options, so that teachers could deliberate their choices and experiment to find a way suitable for their own situations. There is a difference between teaching with cases a particular way out of ignorance versus out of choice.

As is true with most research, the greatest benefits tend to accrue to the researcher. It has been an immensely valuable experience for us to receive from the contributors their insights as to what makes a person successful when teaching with cases. Their genuine concern for what happens in the classroom on a day-to-day basis, their concern for students and their concern for the learning process is the foundation of the joy of teaching.

Over the years we have experimented with a large variety of tools, concepts and techniques that might help simplify and increase the effectiveness of case writing, learning and teaching. Of these the survivors are the Case Difficulty Cube, the Three Stage Learning Process, the Case Preparation Chart and the Case Teaching Plan. We have become convinced that these four ideas can make a significant difference for those who are willing to give them a serious try. Our concern has always been with improving the effectiveness of case writing, learning and teaching while minimizing the time required. We have also tried to convey the innate joy of knowing one is doing as good a job as possible. The teaching task is such an intensely personal and yet public one. There is immediate response and appreciation from the participants for a job well done. What more can anyone ask for in life?

Appendix 1
DIMENSIONAL LAYOUTS OF CLASSROOMS
DESIGNED FOR CASE DISCUSSION

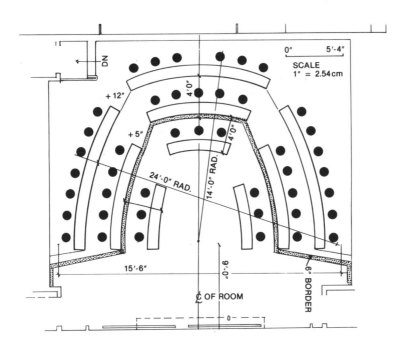

a) A 44 seat classroom layout*

---

* Courtesy Ron Murphy, architect, London, Ontario

Appendix 1 (continued)

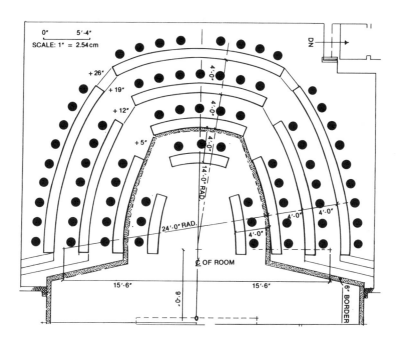

a) A 71 seat classroom layout*

---

* Courtesy Ron Murphy, architect, London, Ontario

Appendix 2

MAJOR CASE DISTRIBUTION
CENTRES OF THE WORLD

The European Case Clearing House
at Cranfield University   Tel: +44 (0)1234 750903
Wharley End, Bedford   Fax: +44 (0)1234 751125
MK43 0JR England
E-mail: **ECCH@cranfield.ac.uk**
Web site: **http://www.ecch.cranfield.ac.uk/**

at Babson College   Tel: +1 781 239 5884
Babson Park,   Fax: +1 781 239 5885
Wellesly, MA 02157
USA
E-mail: **ECCH@babson.edu**

ECCH distributes cases from the following major case
producing management schools of the world:

Darden School of Business at University of Virginia
Harvard Business School*
John F Kennedy School of
   Government at Harvard University*
IESE, Barcelona
IMD, Lausanne
INSEAD, Fontainebleau
London Business School
Richard Ivey School of Business at
   The University of Western Ontario*
School of Management at Cranfield University
Stanford University*

* ECCH does not distribute this material in the United States
  or Canada

Appendix 2 (continued)

Harvard Business School
Harvard Business School Publishing
Customer Service Department   Tel: +1 800 545 7685
60 Harvard Way   + 1 617 495 6117
Boston, MA 02163, USA   Fax: +1 617 495 6985
E-mail: **custserv@hbsp.harvard.edu**
Web site: **http://www.hbsp.harvard.edu/**

(Harvard Business School Publishing also distributes Ivey
cases in the US.)

Richard Ivey School of Business
Ivey Publishing   Tel: +1 519 661 3208
Richard Ivey School of Business   +1 800 649 6355
The University of Western Ontario   Fax: +1 519 661 3882
London, Ontario,
Canada, N6A 3K7
E-mail: **cases@ivey.uwo.ca**
Web site: **http://www.ivey.uwo.ca/cases**

(Ivey also distributes Harvard cases and Harvard Business
Review reprints in Canada.)

Darden Graduate School of Business Administration
Darden Educational Materials
  Services   Tel: +1 800 246 3367
Darden Graduate School of   +1 804 924 3009
  Business Administration   Fax: +1 804 924 4859
University of Virginia
P.O. Box 6550
Charlottesville, VA   22906-6550, USA
E-mail: **dardencases@virginia.edu**
Web site: **http://www.darden.virginia.edu/**

works cited

Bloom, J. S., *The Process of Learning*, Harvard University Press, Cambridge, Mass., 1965.

Christensen, C. Roland, Garvin, David A., and Sweet, Ann, *Education for Judgment*, Harvard Business School Press, Boston, Mass., 1991.

Dooley, A.R., Skinner, C. W., "Casing Casemethod Methods," *Academy of Management Review*, April 1977.

ECCHO, Issue No. 17, Autumn/Fall 1997.

Freeland, Alexandra, "Multimedia Copyright - An Analysis of Information Sources," *Reflections*, No. 37, Educational Development Office, The University of Western Ontario, London, Canada, October 1997.

Gallagher, Jim, "Creating Multimedia Cases," *ECCHO*, Issue No. 15, Winter 1996/97.

Hambrick, Donald C., "Teaching as Leading," in R. André & P. J. Frost (Ed.), *Researchers Hooked on Teaching*, Sage Publications, California, 1997.

Mauffette-Leenders, Louise A., Erskine, James A., and Leenders, Michiel R., *Learning with Cases*, Richard Ivey School of Business, The University of Western Ontario, London, Canada. 1997.

Nahavandi, Afsaneh, "Teaching from the Heart," in R. André & P. J. Frost (Ed.), *Researchers Hooked on Teaching*, Sage Publications, California, 1997.

Newman, Peter, "The Use of Case Studies in the People's Republic of China," *ECCHO*, Issue No. 16, Summer 1997.

Turgeon, A. J. Barbieri, K. E., and Clarke, B. B., "Case-based Instruction at a Distance Using a Mix of Technologies," *ECCHO*, Issue No. 16, Summer 1997.

index